feast

feast

GENEROUS VEGETARIAN MEALS FOR
ANY EATER AND EVERY APPETITE

Sarah Copeland

Photographs by Yunhee Kim

CHRONICLE BOOKS
SAN FRANCISCO

For my family, for teaching me how to feed body and soul.
For the eaters, let's feast.

Library of Congress Cataloging-in-Publication Data available.
ISBN 978-1-4521-0973-2

Manufactured in China

Designed by Alice Chau
Prop styling by Rebecca Ffrench
Food styling by Sarah Copeland
Typesetting by Helen Lee
This book is typeset in Eplica, Univers, and National.

Tabasco is a registered trademark of McIlhenny Company.
Maldon salt is a registered trademark of Maldon Crystal Salt Co.
Bundt is a registered trademark of Nordic Ware.
Microplane is a registered trademark of Grace Manufacturing, Inc.

10 9 8 7 6 5 4 3 2 1

Chronicle Books LLC
680 Second Street
San Francisco, California 94107
www.chroniclebooks.com

contents

introduction

AN ODE TO A RADISH SALAD

There is so much good food in the world. Sometimes so much that as a constant seeker of delicious, invigorating food experiences, the pursuit can overwhelm me. That's exactly what I was feeling one Sunday at brunch among other food writers and friends at a chic new downtown New York City restaurant. Cazuelas of sausages, eggs, and beans and platters of charcuterie were flying before me in a blur, passed between eager hands. Just then, a little wooden bowl piled loosely with quartered radishes and slender chunks of young carrots floated by. My eyes locked on the sheen of fruity olive oil and I could almost taste the careless, broken bits of aged Parmesan that nuzzled up against the blush of the radishes. *Stop. Right there,* I thought. *Please. Put that one in front of me.*

I can't say exactly what it was the radish salad had over the others. It could have been the color—our eyes love beauty—or the snap of the peppery root. It could have been the way I felt after I ate it—alive, inspired. At some point in life, you just know when something is right for you.

This sounds like a love story. And in a sense, it is. This book is a love story between you and your food. It's about food so delicious you find yourself thinking about it the next morning. Food you want to see again tomorrow. It is the kind of food that supports life—your life and the life of the planet around you. It's food that's electric with flavor and loaded with nutrients. They are platefuls of vegetables and grains, sometimes dairy, and (for those who eat it) the occasional addition of fish. These are tremendous, mostly vegetarian feasts.

THE UNLIKELY VEGETARIANS

I am an unlikely vegetarian. My parents were raised on small farms in the Midwest where their families raised cattle, chickens, and pork and rendered lard in the backyard for the flakiest cobbler crusts around. Growing up, Sunday mornings smelled like bacon. Panfried pork chops and bratwurst were favorites in my mom's repertoire.

It's not that we didn't eat vegetables. We ate loads of fresh vegetables and dozens of fruits, too. And I loved them, every one. But I grew up in a time and place where the template for family dinner was a meat-based protein, a starch, and a vegetable, something not unique to my family.

Across a big ocean, a twelve-year-old Hungarian boy refused his own family favorite, calf's liver, telling his mother that he had become a vegetarian. When I met that boy two decades later in New York City, he hadn't eaten meat in more than twenty years. By then I had come a long way from bacon and brats. I had spent almost a decade cooking—in three-star restaurants, a private villa in Saint-Tropez, and in the test kitchens of the Food Network, among others. The meat I ate was usually raised sustainably and cooked well, but it was certainly present. I felt neither devotion nor need for it, but I still held bragging rights for my ability to cook a full rack of côte de boeuf to a perfect medium-rare in a brick oven, and I enjoyed getting a crusty sear on a steak when styling food for magazines and TV.

But, though I didn't think much about it, I had all but become a vegetarian at home. Meals for myself, my favorite meals, were salads and a slab of artisan cheese, shaved vegetables tossed with good olive oil, plates of roasted green beans with shallots and almonds. And the more time I spent with the vegetarian (who is now my husband), the less interesting the other foods became.

For me, perhaps as for some of you, becoming mostly vegetarian was a very natural, gradual shift. It started long before I married one, perhaps when I luxuriated over the incredibly memorable vegetarian tasting menu at Gramercy Tavern in New York City, not long after I had graduated from culinary school. It was likely deepened by my research about the state of our food system and the tax meat consumption pays on our bodies and our land—and deepened further when each time, in heralded restaurants, I found everything around the meat to be the most exciting parts on the plate.

That didn't mean I actually knew how to cook vegetarian. To sustain 365 days of enticing meatless eating, or even 350-odd days (since I knew on occasion I'd choose culture, courtesy, or a raw craving over conviction), was going to be a challenge. And cooking vegetarian for two, and three as we soon became, had its own challenges. I couldn't just eat salad every night. I took immediately to the responsibility of making sure that our meals were well-rounded and full of protein and vital nutrients, not to mention exciting and satisfying to us and our guests, as we often have them.

So how did I learn to cook vegetarian? By paying attention to the meat-free dishes everywhere I ate: high-end white-tablecloth restaurants, mom-and-pop food shops, and, most important, ethnic restaurants and the kitchens of our friends from around the world. Japanese, Chinese, Indonesian, Mexican, and many other world cuisines have scores of mainstays and meals that are entirely plant-based or, if not (as in the case of Hungarian cuisine, for example), are very easy to make that way.

At the same time, I was digging deeper and deeper into nutrition as I became a holistic health-care coach and educator. I studied macrobiotics, raw food, vegan, vegetarian, and Ayurveda diets, along with some opposing nutritional theories like the Atkins diet. I tried on a few of these philosophies, month by month, as my husband had on his own journey to the middle path, where we both ended up. Ours is a mostly vegetarian diet—one that includes hundreds of dynamic fruits and vegetables, a fair amount of addictively good whole grains, handfuls of nuts and seeds, plenty of organic eggs, some dairy, small amounts of sustainable fish and seafood, and occasional wholesome and homemade sweets.

It turns out none of this is as far from my heritage as it would seem. Those farms where my parents grew up also boasted fruit trees, berry brambles, and impressive gardens, where most of the family meals came from. My grandparents grew, cooked, pickled, and canned every vegetable and fruit you can imagine and collected eggs for their daily protein. The meats they raised and sold were an occasional indulgence on their tables, as they were on the tables of most of the world until recently. And thankfully, that's what many thoughtful eaters in the Western world are getting back to once again.

THE MIDDLE PATH

Whether you're already a vegetarian or are just hoping to adopt a more meatless diet, this book is for you. Vegetarian diets have earned all sorts of unwarranted critiques: Vegetables are boring, hard to cook, and don't fill you up. These recipes aim to challenge every one of those judgements.

What I utterly love about mostly vegetarian eaters is that we are a choosy bunch. We believe in good, healthful food, and for all the different reasons that brought us here (ethics, ecology, economy, health), we won't accept food that is anything less that the best. I have only one rule—no judging. This book is here to exalt vegetarianism in pursuit of the delicious, not the dogmatic.

And what I love about vegetarian cooking is that it is so versatile, healthful, and truly joyful to create. It really can, and should, adapt to the seasons. It stars some of the most colorful, vibrant ingredients on the planet—the same plant-based foods that most experts now agree should make up the biggest portion of our daily plate.

Not that vegetables are the only thing we get to eat. Far from it. A mostly plant-based diet is loaded with delicious foods in every shade and shape, flavors that will rock your world. With a little dairy and seafood now and then, as used in this book, the options are infinite.

There are, of course, the pitfalls of vegetarianism—overdosing on cheese and carbs. In these recipes, pasta and bread are blank canvases for some über-satisfying meals, but more often bread is a toasted crouton in a vegetable soup, like Yellow Tomato Gazpacho (page 91). Similarly, cheese is rarely the main event. Ricotta is a luscious layer in the Radish, Ricotta, and Black Pepper Tartine (page 136), and ricotta salata, served in thoughtful amounts, turns a springtime White Pizza with Arugula and Ricotta Salata (page 214) into a memorable main event.

What really makes vegetarian food shine are the layers of texture and flavor. It's the secret of all great chefs, vegetarian or otherwise. It's that drizzle of finishing oil, the toasted nuts, the chopped fresh herbs. Together they make food that stops time, if only for seconds, as you savor and enjoy every bite. Grilled zucchini is splendid on its own but sensational with toasted hazelnuts and a tiny spoonful of rich mascarpone.

Texture and flavor are what make the meals in this book worth staying home for. Visit the Meals in a Bowl chapter, which builds on ethnic flavors, like those in bibimbap (see page 175). Sweet carrots, spicy chile-sesame paste, and oozy egg yolk get folded into soft rice, along with spicy, sour kimchi. In the somen noodle bowl (see page 166), your chopsticks go swimming for the crunch of bok choy, floating in an earthy mushroom dashi. In Sweet Potato and Kale Tortilla Soup (page 181), the tender give of sweet potato softens a fiery tomato broth, and every bite comes alive when topped with buttery avocado and fresh radish.

These are words—*buttery, fiery, fresh, alive, oozy, crispy, toasted*—you want to feel and taste in your mouth. These are foods grown, procured, and prepared with thought and care.

That doesn't mean these meals are time-consuming, difficult, or expensive. With proper planning and a well-curated larder or pantry, these are dishes that can come together on the fly—and should. Because there is no reason, really, to eat lousy take-out fried rice when you can make your own Indonesian Rice Bowl (page 178) at home. There's no reason for prepared pasta sauces when it takes no more than twenty minutes to throw together a plate of Mushroom Agnolotti with Sweet Corn, Heirloom Tomatoes, and Arugula (page 190).

THE SOURCE OF GOOD FOOD

The kind of cooking in this book is ingredient cooking—finding or growing the best ingredients and cooking them in a way that helps them shine. This kind of ingredient sourcing should take a lot of pressure off you as a cook. It matters little how skilled you think you are in the kitchen, but more that you are a discriminating gatherer, grower, or shopper. And, by getting closer to your sources of food, you build a sense of place around your plate, a story that you become a part of.

My first real glimpse of this kind of cooking was at Savoy restaurant, on Prince Street, one of the first sustainably focused restaurants in New York City. I'd read about Peter Hoffman in *The New Yorker*'s food issue. He was the guy. He'd been cooking and sourcing his restaurant this way for a decade. He wasn't trying to be a trendsetter. He was just trying to be good to his customers and good to his farmers. And he was.

I worked there just long enough to have a favorite staff meal, which was scrambled eggs and greens, generous amounts of thick-crusted European-style bread, and fresh butter. This meal featured the most simple ingredients—eggs, greens, bread, butter—but the best possible versions of them. Fresh greens that burst with life and texture. Scrambled eggs so flavorful they barely needed salt. Artisan bread crafted with a respect for centuries of bakers' wisdom and technique. The family meal for the staff was theoretically the most humble meal the restaurant served each day, and I couldn't get enough of it.

It wasn't just the quality of those ingredients that stuck with me. There I was, eating textures and types of foods together that didn't seem to belong. Warm eggs and cold greens? Bizarre. But it worked. Hot and cold. Creamy and clean. Soft and bitter. I started paying close attention to texture, and layering foods in my bowl that I'd never seen together but tasted like simple, remarkable revelations. Warm, milky polenta finished with just a touch of butter and cheese, topped with crunchy raw snap peas (Polenta and Sugar Snaps, page 155). Quinoa with toasted walnuts and crunchy red cabbage (see page 161). Winter and spring. Filling and refreshing. Like a morning on a cushy couch (a fried egg–topped yam and black bean tostada, see page 195) followed by a refreshing dip in a lake (the tostada's watercress garnish), I was learning I needed both—and sometimes all on the same plate.

This principle became increasingly important the more vegetarian my own kitchen became. The less meat and fat I consumed, the more I craved these texture contrasts. And the fresher and closer to homegrown the food I started with was, the more it delivered. And the more it delivered, the less I ever thought about the meat I mostly left behind.

THE ETHOS OF MOSTLY VEGETARIANISM

Adam Gopnik, staff writer for *The New Yorker* and the author of *The Table Comes First*, said that at any moment in the history of eating, we will be faced with ethical dilemmas. Vegetarianism looks several of them right in the face with a strong, sound answer. He also said, wisely, that change comes out of the daily table more than out of a new ecological consciousness.

There's no doubt that a vegetarian diet is almost certainly better for the health of our planet and the human race. It is convenient then—since I believe in helping to create a stronger, more viable farming and food system—that I am a mostly vegetarian. But it is just as much the pursuit of delicious flavor that leads me back to the vegetarian plate, to that plate of snappy sliced radishes with chive and creamy avocado (see page 108), or farm egg–topped pizza loaded with pungent mustard greens (see page 57). Those are the foods I prefer, the ones that reward my sensibilities and my hope for long-term health. In my opinion, they are satisfying and superior more often than not.

If you have the time, the inspiration, or the means, growing as much of your own food as possible is a wonderfully rewarding way to improve your personal food system—and the bigger one around you. And when you're eating mostly fruits and vegetables, it's actually possible to grow a very good portion of what's on your plate yourself, even in a tiny space (as a city dweller, you can trust me on that). But gardening is also a flavor-based pursuit, since homegrown vegetables are almost always the most delicious as well.

EAT CAKE AND VEGETABLES

What's the bottom line? Balance. I always say, "Eat Cake and Vegetables!" Eat wonderful, delicious, healthful foods, mostly vegetables, and leave a tiny bit of room for dessert (there are plenty in this book). There's health and joy in the middle path, and I think it's one many of us can feel good about ethically, ecologically, and even selfishly. This way of eating doesn't promise to be perfect. But it does promise to reward you with the kind of satisfying, sustaining meals you crave.

vegetarian
larder

The modern larder is a storehouse—be it a pantry, fridge, or just a few shelves—full of provisions for fine eating. Your vegetarian larder should be chock-full of vegetables and fruits, but to turn them into a meal, you also need grains, spices, flavorings, and, for some of us, fish and dairy. It's a carefully sourced pantry that truly makes this way of eating a remarkable feast.

What follows is a list of ingredients I recommend for your larder, and the ones used in the recipes in this book. There are wells of information on each of these ingredients—every one of them exploding with opportunities for vibrant health and flavor—and I encourage you to dig further as you cook and explore. Here I've included just the basics of why each ingredient deserves a spot on our shelves.

THE NATURE OF THINGS

Both health and flavor are built on the nature of our ingredients. Awareness of where they come from is a nonnegotiable for anyone who values their well-being and longs to eat the most delicious and most nutrient-rich foods available. It's worth our time to understand the nuances of food sources and classifications, like organic, natural, fair trade, and free range. Though I don't go into those details at length in these pages, my hope is to inspire you to make those thoughts second nature. When you're cooking your own food most of the time, you can't help but become connected to the story behind it. You'll taste it. Aim for foods that are as close to garden-fresh as possible—vibrant, full of water, life, and color. That usually means seasonal and locally grown foods, and if for you that means it actually is homegrown, all the better.

AROMATICS

I don't often use this technical term in my recipes, but you'll be using aromatics in dozens of meals in this book. Usually a combination of celery, carrot, onion, and sometimes garlic, aromatics deserve star status in the vegetarian kitchen. See them in action in the vegetable stock (see page 270) that so many of your soups and sauces will rely on. There are different aromatic essentials for every cuisine—like ginger, garlic, and green onion in the Asian kitchen—so keep these staples well stocked.

CHOCOLATE AND COCOA

Bittersweet chocolate has a deeper, darker chocolate flavor that's a better balance for the sweets in this book than milk or semisweet. If you like chocolate, you'll enjoy tasting and finding your own favorite types and brands. You can now buy premier brands (like Valrhona and Callebaut, among others) in blocks, the way chefs buy them, at many supermarkets and gourmet grocery stores. I'm especially fond of pistoles, round disks of high-quality chocolate that are easy to melt and nibble on, an addiction that started during my days in the pastry kitchens of New York City. I use them in my Pastry Shop Almond–Chocolate Chip Cookies (page 233). You can find them at some high-end grocery stores and gourmet markets, and easily online (see page 280). Don't use chips as a melting or baking chocolate (unless specifically called for in a recipe). The flavor and texture won't give you the same, silky results as good baking chocolate, and higher-quality chocolates (those with higher cocoa proportions and less milk fats, sweeteners, and additives) are better for you, too.

Dutch-processed (or alkalized) cocoa powder produces a deep, dark cocoa color and flavor. Natural cocoa is less processed and lends a more old-fashioned chocolate flavor. They react differently with every leavening agent (such as baking powder or baking soda), so watch for cues in the recipes when one or the other is required.

FLOURS

I love to bake, so my pantry is loaded with flours, but my mainstays are whole-wheat white flour and whole-wheat flour. Both of these flours are easy to use and have a slightly nutty flavor from the wheat and the germ, which deliver maximum protein and fiber. Whole-wheat white flour is milled to keep flour's nutritional integrity but reacts more like white flour in baking. White flour, or all-purpose flour, has its place, for things like delicate cakes and light, fluffy High-Rising Buttermilk Biscuits (page 49) that you want to almost melt in your mouth.

Semolina flour is a coarsely ground durum wheat that's light yellow, sweet, and versatile. It adds texture and great flavor to breads, pastas, pizzas, and, in this book, Whole-Wheat Semolina Pancakes with Peaches (page 45) and Toasted Semolina Raisin Scones (page 50).

It's incredibly fun to play with alternative flours. The most versatile flours I keep on hand are millet, oat, barley, and rye flour, the latter of which can debut in your kitchen in Apple-Rye Pancakes (page 47) and Strawberry-Rye Squares (page 241). Depending on what brand you buy, rye flour may contain all the health-giving benefits of rye berries, including fiber, oil, and the germ that adds iron, proteins, thiamine, niacin, riboflavin, and vitamins B and E to your baked goods.

New go-tos, like amaranth flour, make some of my favorite sweets, like Peanut Butter and Amaranth Cookies (page 232), a bit more sustaining, with the added fiber and protein they bring to the batch. Amaranth is a nutty-flavored grain packed with calcium and iron. The flour is finely ground and the color of sand, with a strong, grassy, and sometimes almost hay-like aroma—good or bad, depending on where you stand—that pairs well with strong flavors like peanut butter. It's also a great gluten-free flour.

You can buy almost any of these flours in health food stores or online (see page 280).

If you need a go-to whole-grain flour that's easy to keep stocked, make your own oat flour, a healthful and mildly flavorful flour, by grinding rolled oats to a fine powder in your food processor. These more nutrient-rich flours spoil faster, so preserve them by storing them in big plastic bags or bins in the fridge or freezer.

On very rare occasions, I call for and use cake flour. In this book, cake flour makes the batter for Vegetable Tempura (page 75) light, thin, and crackly. Wondra flour, a very fine flour usually found in the supermarket, can be useful for lightly coating vegetable tempura or tofu but is not essential.

GRAINS

When it comes to grains, I'm almost singularly focused on whole grains. Whole grains are full of fiber and protein, rich in flavor, and generally nuttier than more refined grains, a flavor I've come to prefer. One of the best ways to keep them in constant rotation in your daily diet is to cook them in advance in big batches, since flavor and texture almost always hold up during reheating. Always rinse the grains before cooking. Here are my favorites.

BARLEY You may find hulled barley (the whole-grain form that retains its bran layer and cooks longer) or pearl barley (the more hulled, polished version of this grain that is softer and cooks faster). Both are pleasingly chewy and are delicious in Barley Risotto with Radishes, Swiss Chard, and Preserved Lemon (page 174).

COUSCOUS Both white and whole-wheat couscous, staples of North African and European cuisines, are fast to cook, comforting, and so adaptable that even babies will eat it by the spoonful. Whole-wheat couscous is delicious made with vegetable stock or even water (seasoned with salt, pepper, and a pat of butter). It's the perfect bed for the Roasted Tomato–Squash Tagine Fall Feast (page 209).

FARRO AND SPELT Farro is a nutty, cheese-loving, almost buttery wheat grain that is delicious hot or cold, offering a filling option even for carnivores. It should be rinsed and can be soaked before cooking to ease digestion and cut cooking time. Farro can then be stirred into soup, tossed in cold salads, or cooked like risotto. Also look for instant farro, which is processed so that it cooks in 10 minutes instead of a half hour.

Spelt is a heartier wheat grain, full of protein, that is left whole. It requires rinsing, soaking for 1 hour or up to overnight, and longer cooking, about 40 minutes to 1 hour. Once cooked, it can be used much like farro.

OATS Oats are heart-healthy, fiber-rich whole grains that have a warming, familiar flavor. As a breakfast cereal or a baking grain, keep plenty of these in stock. Irish or steel-cut oats are a toothsome breakfast porridge. Soak the grains overnight to shorten their cooking time. Old-fashioned rolled oats are also great to keep on hand for baking and quick cooking.

QUINOA The Incas called quinoa the "mother grain" and considered it sacred, for good reason: Slightly crunchy and mild mannered, this grain delivers a huge dose of protein and is also one of the simplest grains to cook ahead. Keep extra on hand to stuff into the Artichoke Enchiladas (page 196) or make it the centerpiece, as in the Quinoa Bowl with Avocado, Red Cabbage, and Walnuts (page 161).

RICE Rice, in moderation, is a fantastic pantry staple and foundation for many filling meals. Consider keeping sushi rice, long- or short-grain brown rice, Arborio rice, and jasmine rice on rotation in your house for the recipes in this book.

LEGUMES

BEANS There are so many beans deserving of a place in your larder. In this book, I use lentils, pintos, cannellinis, and black beans because they're easily accessible. But I also love to cook the dozens of heirloom beans that are easy to grow in the garden. They are delicious simmered with aromatics and served warm, smashed, or stuffed into anything with a tortilla. See page 280 for online resources for an amazing, diverse array of dried heirloom beans.

BEANS: FRESH, DRIED, OR CANNED?

When they're in season, fresh beans are amazing. Dried beans are a very close second and are available year-round. A can of cooked beans is also a useful staple, but when you have the time, cook fresh or dried beans with aromatics for the best flavor and texture. There's evidence to suggest the health benefits of soaking or sprouting dried beans before cooking them, but some experts argue this is only valuable for shortening cooking time. In my busy kitchen, that's a sound enough argument to make soaking a habit, and I count any residual health benefits as a bonus.

CHICKPEAS Chickpeas, also called garbanzo beans, are a versatile ingredient to keep on hand for Hummus (page 60) and other quick dips and stews. Since they add so much protein to a dish, these mild-flavored beans are a staple in our home. I like to start with dried beans and cook them with onions, celery, and carrot for more flavor, but they are easily found canned as well. They can be used in some recipes as a meat substitute, with a fraction of meat's cholesterol.

EDAMAME I don't include a recipe for edamame, or soybeans in the pod, in this book because it is so easy to enjoy them steamed and seasoned with coarse sea salt. Keep on hand in the freezer for a fast snack or starter or to stir, shelled, into soups, risotto, or pasta.

LENTILS These small, round dried legumes are extremely popular in most of Europe, India, and the Middle East. Learn to integrate them into your kitchen, as they are affordable, filling, delicious, and filled with nutrients. They come in a variety of colors and textures.

Green and Brown Lentils My favorites are Puy lentils, a brownish-green French lentil, or petite brown lentils, sometimes called beluga lentils, but any Italian or French lentils work in their place. Rinse them, combing over for any pebbles (as with any dried beans), and soak them overnight for faster cooking. Use them in Lentils and Mozzarella (page 65) and Lentil-Chickpea Burgers with Harissa Yogurt (page 138), or toss lentils into soups or salads.

Red Lentils Popular in Indian cuisine, red lentils are sometimes preferred for their mild, less earthy taste. Because the husk is removed, they cook faster and purée easily, which for some people also makes them easier to digest. Try them in the Red Lentils with Yogurt (page 163).

PASTA

It's a delight to uncover the world of pasta sizes and shapes. I love ridged garganelli, tiny and tightly wound trofie, ear-shaped orecchiette, and fat bucatini, along with standard shapes such as penne, spaghetti, and angel hair. But don't stop there. Whole-wheat pasta, made from flour that contains the nutrient-rich bran, germ, and endosperm, is especially great for picky folks who have a hard time getting other whole grains into their diet. Count on more vitamins, minerals, and dietary fiber from whole-wheat pastas. Rotate them into your repertoire of favorite pasta meals.

NUTS AND SEEDS

Nuts and seeds are essentials in the vegetarian kitchen for their high doses of healthful fats and vital nutrients, as well as the satisfaction and long-lasting energy they provide. You'll find iron, calcium,

fiber, vitamin E, copper, and magnesium in many nuts, and they provide fast and healthful proteins for vegetarians. Most raw or toasted nuts and seeds are fine snacking material when eaten out of hand, and there is no shortage of ways to incorporate them into meals, such as in granola bars, as salad toppers, and sometimes as the main event.

TREE NUTS I keep pecans, walnuts, hazelnuts, almonds, pine nuts, cashews, and pistachios in my larder and tend to add a handful of one type or another to about one meal a day. Toast them in batches (see page 273) and keep them in an airtight container to add to salads, Genmaicha Granola Bars (page 54), and mainstays like Cauliflower Curry (page 162). Because of their healthful fats, they can go rancid if not used quickly. Keep small portions in the pantry and additional fresh or toasted nuts in the freezer where they'll last up to 2 months. Most nuts can quickly be turned into fresh nut flour or nut butters (with a food processor or coffee grinder). They also make rich and delicious nondairy milks and creams (see page 274).

CHESTNUTS Fresh, substantial, and mildly sweet chestnuts are a fall and winter treat that can be irresistible when roasted or puréed. They add intrigue and an element of satisfaction to the Glazed Winter Vegetable Medley with Chestnuts and Caper Berries (page 211). They can be found fresh, canned, dried, and sometimes roasted and peeled in shelf-stable packages or jars. Compared with other nuts, they are low in calories and low in fat. They are high in iron, and thanks to their subtly sweet, starchy quality, they are a delicious, satisfying snack or sweet.

SUNFLOWER SEEDS Toss together roasted carrots, shallots, avocados, and sunflower seeds for a fast fall salad. Add them to Homemade Four-Grain English Muffins (page 52) or sprinkle on top of your morning oats. Their high fat content is justified by the generous dose of iron, calcium, and protein they add to your table. They are also a good source of pantothenic acid (a B vitamin that's good for hair and skin), copper, magnesium, and phosphorus. If you like their flavor, try sunflower seed butter, too.

SESAME SEEDS Sesame flavor is most at home in Asian dishes like bibimbap (see page 175), but it mixes well with the flavors of sunflower and millet in things like Genmaicha Granola Bars (page 54). Sesame seeds are best lightly toasted, and add protein, iron, calcium, zinc, copper, manganese, thiamine, and magnesium to your diet.

OILS

Fat is flavor. That's probably the first food mantra I learned in the trenches of the restaurant world. Fat is often what makes restaurant food taste so good. The good news is we need healthful fats, in moderation, and vegetable-based fats have the essential fatty acids, omega-3 and omega-6, that our bodies need but can't make. Fats are also some of the richest sources of vitamin E. Since we're cooking at home, we have lots of control over what types of fat we use and how much of it. Different fats have different flavors and benefits. Here are the six I favor, and why.

EXTRA-VIRGIN OLIVE OIL A high-quality extra-virgin olive oil is as good as gold, adding beautiful, luscious flavor to cooked and raw foods. Good oil doesn't need to cost a mint. Find one so delicious you could drink it and affordable enough to be generous with it. Look for these five basic flavor profiles—peppery (such as a Tuscan oil); fruity; smooth and buttery (like a Provençal oil); herbal and grassy; or mild—and find the one that's the most pleasing to you. Don't get bogged down in the details. What's important, as with anything concerned with flavor, is to buy the one that tastes the best to you.

I keep an inexpensive organic extra-virgin olive oil, which can withstand a fair amount of heat, on hand for cooking. My second bottle of daily oil is a truly luscious high-quality finishing oil. These finishing oils are considerably more expensive, but they never get heated (important for preserving the nutritious properties and flavor) and are reserved for finishing pastas, pizzas, salads, and simple raw plates of vegetables and cheeses. In these recipes, finish with a drizzle of your favorite, high-quality olive oil.

COCONUT OIL Raw virgin coconut oil has earned a ready place in my pantry, though admittedly for its nourishing beauty qualities as much as for its reported health benefits. Unlike most vegetable-based oils, coconut oil contains saturated fat. It is solid at room temperature but pours like an olive oil when warmed. Its assertive coconut aroma makes it inappropriate for some forms of cooking, but it's a great substitute for shortening and sometimes for another oil in baked goods where coconut complements or improves other flavors.

COLD-PRESSED NUT OILS All nut oils, like walnut, hazelnut, or almond oil, are better used for flavoring than for cooking, since they break down quickly under high heat. Buy amber-colored oils from roasted nuts, rather than raw nuts, which have deeper flavors. How you use these or which one you choose depends entirely on how much you like the nut itself. Mix walnut oil with olive oil in a vinaigrette to deepen the flavor without overpowering the other ingredients, or drizzle hazelnut oil over a salad that stars toasted hazelnuts, like the Roasted Carrot, Hazelnut, and Radicchio Salad with Honey and Orange (page 111). Store these oils in the fridge for a longer shelf life and keep them away from light and heat. Buy from a health food store or gourmet store that is likely to have a fast turnover. These oils should smell unctuous and sweet with a pleasing nutty flavor.

PEANUT OIL For certain things, like Asian cooking and some frying, the flavor of peanut oil can be magnificent. It's affordable, has a high-smoking point, and is also considered a healthful fat. For a splurge, try toasted peanut oil for stir-fries and amplifying the flavors of vegetables in dishes like the Indonesian Rice Bowl (page 178).

SESAME OIL Most commonly used in Asian cooking, sesame oil gives a potent flavor and aroma to cooked foods and salad dressings and even deepens flavor in baked goods, such as Peanut Butter and Amaranth Cookies (page 232). Use it sparingly, particularly the toasted variety, which I prefer. Use only with medium to light heat.

OTHER VEGETABLE OILS All the preceding oils listed are derived from plants, and therefore technically vegetable oils. Besides the oils already listed, when we think of vegetable oil we are most often referring to safflower, corn, sunflower, canola, and cottonseed oils, all with disputed health claims, depending on their processing. I use high-oleic sunflower or high-oleic safflower oil, both neutral in flavor, and recommend either for the recipes in this book that call simply for vegetable oil. I also like grapeseed oil, which is high in omega-3s and mild in flavor, but it can be hard to find and expensive.

DAIRY

BUTTER Olive oil is often the preferred cooking fat for health and taste, but for some things, butter's indulgent flavor is hard to replace. Buy unsalted butter so you have control over how much salt is added to your food. For the table, serve it topped with your favorite finishing salt. I prefer organic butter, and for health and best flavor, butter from pasture-raised cows, which is higher in omega-3s.

BUTTERMILK Buttermilk originated as the milk left over after churning butter, but today it's more commonly cultured milk. It is thick and tangy and makes for wonderful biscuits (see page 49) and pancakes (see page 47). Look for full fat rather than light versions. This soured milk can also be faked on the fly (see page 260).

KEFIR This probiotic drink is protein-rich and full of calcium, with live active cultures that promote healthy digestion. It's often made from cow's milk and can be found near the yogurt in the dairy case at major supermarkets and is readily available in health food stores. Since it has both probiotics and protein, it's a great ingredient to drink or add to smoothies. Its slightly soured (think buttermilk) flavor makes it especially fitting for lightening up creamy dressings like that found in the More Greens Than Potato Salad (page 113).

YOGURT Both plain whole-milk and strained yogurt, usually labeled "Greek yogurt," have a strong standing in a vegetarian kitchen. Plain yogurt is looser and can sometimes be used like buttermilk in biscuits and pancakes and adds richness to brothy soups. Greek yogurt is a richer, creamier version and a perfect substitute for mayo, sour cream, and any number of other dolloping delights. When I call for Greek yogurt, I often leave the fat preference to you—full, low-fat or nonfat all work in these recipes, depending on which diet you subscribe to.

ORGANIC EGGS AND MILK

As a mostly vegetarian, eggs and dairy may be one of your key sources of protein, so you'll want to make sure you're getting the best. Pasture-raised, organic, or free-range eggs may seem like a splurge, but not when you consider the meals that can be made from this humble ingredient. Local pasture-raised eggs are often the best tasting eggs of all. An egg from hens that feed on pasture will likely have a rich, golden, almost marigold yolk, which translates to scrambled eggs so good you'll barely need salt. Likewise, organic, pastured, and locally raised cow's milk is tops in flavor and better for your long-term health. For the richest flavor, whole milk or reduced-fat milk (2 percent as opposed to skim or 1 percent milk) are both good choices for the recipes in this book.

CHEESES

RICOTTA In my book, ricotta and yogurt are elbow to elbow as the most versatile dairy ingredient. Ricotta is made with the whey of milk, rather than the curd, which is why it's lower in fat than many other cheeses, but it still adds luscious texture and body to more meals than I can count. It's worth sourcing a good one, locally made if you can find it, but even commercial varieties can do the trick.

MOZZARELLA AND BURRATA The mozzarella called for in this book is fresh mozzarella in the style of mozzarella di bufala (buffalo mozzarella)—the wetter kind usually found as balls in liquid, rather than pressed blocks of cheese. It is mild and pleasurable to eat and melts well on pizzas and eggplant Parmesan (see page 206). It should be white and taste fresh and reminiscent of milk. Since it's full of water, drain slices on paper towels before layering into certain baked dishes, especially those packed with vegetables, which also have a high water content. Burrata is mozzarella with an almost custard-like center that melts on the plate and in your mouth. If you can't find it locally, use the freshest buffalo mozzarella you can find. For the best flavor, serve it at room temperature. Look also for bocconcini, bite-size balls of mozzarella that are great for farro, bulgur, or other grain salads, and can be used in any version of Caprese (see page 63).

HARD AND GRATING CHEESES Hard cheeses like Parmigiano-Reggiano (cow's milk) or pecorino (sheep's milk) add depth and a touch of salt when grated over soups, stews, pastas, and salads. Parmigiano-Reggiano can be bought in large wedges and kept for a few months wrapped well in cheese paper in a cheese drawer. When recipes in this book call for freshly grated Parmigiano-Reggiano, use a Microplane or vegetable peeler (see page 277) to create shavings as a garnish fresh from the block.

MELTING CHEESES Semisoft to semifirm cheese like Gruyère, Comté, fontina, Manchego, Muenster, and cheddar are great for flavor and melting. All are versatile, filling cheeses that also keep well for several weeks, but they are far from the only ones worth exploring. While they're not completely interchangeable, with two of these on hand at any time, your repertoire could include omelets, quesadillas, enchiladas, sandwiches, and more.

FETA AND GOAT CHEESE Though in no way related, feta and goat cheese are both strongly flavored cheeses that should be used purposefully. Goat's milk cheese, or chèvre, has a sharp, tangy flavor, and can be aged or young, mild, and creamy. Feta, made from cow's, goat's, or sheep's milk, is salty and crumbly and adds punch to salads and soups. It is stored in a brine and can be kept for up to a week in the fridge.

ARTISAN CHEESE Venture out to explore the great cheese culture found all over the world and particularly what's available to you locally. You'll be hard-pressed to find a region in this locavore age that doesn't have an excellent, locally produced cheese vendor at the farmers' market. Local artisan cheeses are my preference for eating, combining with vegetables and grains in salads, serving on top of hot pastas, or even layering into sandwiches.

STORING CHEESE

Cheese is living and likes to breathe. Wrap semisoft to hard cheese in butcher or wax paper, not plastic wrap. Label and date it, and, if you use it frequently, refresh the wrapper every so often.

NONDAIRY DRINKS AND NUT MILKS

There are dozens of nondairy drinks on the market, easily found in a health food store. They can be delicious, natural, and sustaining, but the sheer number is bound to confuse. Look for simple, moderately processed versions with the fewest ingredients possible, and experiment with brands until you find the ones you like.

Whether you're vegan, lactose-intolerant, or neither, a diet rich in variety is a good reason to rotate among soy milk, almond milk, hazelnut milk, and oat milk. I find oat and nut milks' creamy, almost naturally sweet flavors preferable to soy milk. All contribute varying amounts of healthful fats to your food and add moisture to baked goods, hot cereal, and creamy-style soups. Buy unsweetened plain varieties for cooking, or vanilla, if you prefer, for drinking or baking. Most soy and nut milks contain some starch and other additives, but I enjoy their convenience. For a purer form and a richer flavor, make your own at home (see page 274).

PLANT-BASED PROTEINS

There are so many delicious, readily available natural and unprocessed plant proteins, like beans and whole grains, that I go weeks if not months without ever thinking about tempeh or tofu. But there are times when I crave that meaty texture. For those times, soy, seiten, tempeh, and tofu all offer worlds of textural possibilities. Try these out and find the proteins that best fill your plate.

SOY Soy is a plant-based protein made from the soybean. Because it is stable at high heat, it can be made into soy milk (and soy yogurts and soy ice creams), tofu, and other soy-protein products that have a ready place in the vegan and vegetarian kitchen. Soy contains isoflavones and fiber, in addition to protein, all thought to provide health benefits when included in a well-balanced diet. It can be mild to moderately flavorful or flavorless (depending on your point of view). If you find the taste offensive, it can be hard to mask the flavor (try vanilla-flavored soy milks and yogurt), but keep experimenting. Soy products, predominately tofu (see below), lend themselves well to many types of cuisines.

SEITAN Seitan is a soy sauce–flavored meat substitute, made from wheat gluten and bound with chickpea flour and soy flour. I prefer the irreplaceable taste of whole vegetables, grains, and other plant-based foods to meat substitutes, but seitan can be useful for transitioning vegetarians (for example, using seitan in your favorite cashew chicken recipe). It comes in strips, cubes, and a ground form. It is protein-dense and moderately high in iron.

TEMPEH We have Indonesians to thank for tempeh, a pressed cake of fermented soybeans that is toothy and fun to eat. It's a good transition food for meat eaters, despite its scary-sounding name, and the rice variety is the mildest in taste. It can be soaked, then stir-fried or deep-fried, and takes to most flavors well. See the Southern-Style Barbecue Spaghetti with Tempeh (page 188) for an easy introduction.

TOFU Made from soybean curd, tofu offers a world of flavor and texture possibilities, widely available in firm, extra-firm, or silken forms. Those watching their weight may want to remember that it is high in fat ("lite" versions exist), but tofu is a wonderful, protein-rich food that plays well with vegetables and grains. The recipes in this book call for firm tofu, but silken tofu is great for smoothies and dairy-free pudding and mousse, among other things.

SALTS

Most commercial table salts, iodized salts, and kosher salts are highly processed foods. You'll get better flavor and even some trace minerals from making less-refined, higher-quality sea salts your seasoning mainstays. I use fine sea salt as my table salt and for much of my cooking and baking, and for seasoning pasta water. Bigger grains of higher-quality sea salts such as fleur de sel and sel gris also bring more texture and lasting balance (rather than hard-hitting salty notes) to eggs, fish, pastas, baked goods, and, especially, vegetables. See this in the Baja Flour Tortillas (page 142), the Toasted Semolina Raisin Scones (page 50), and as a topping for the numerous vegetable dishes in this book. My four favorites are sel gris, fleur de sel, flaked sea salt such as Maldon, and flavored salts like alder or chardonnay smoked salt.

BLACK PEPPERCORNS: A TWIST OF THE WRIST

If you haven't already, buy a good peppermill and keep it filled with black peppercorns. Freshly ground pepper, called for in nearly every recipe in this book, is a flavor experience wholly unlike that of the pre-cracked flecks that come from a pepper shaker. Most recipes in this book call for seasoning with black pepper, except when a specific amount is imperative to the success of the dish. Learn your tastes and tolerance for the heat of black pepper, and play around with fine or coarse settings on your mill until you find just the right balance for you.

SPICES AND SUCH

Spices add instant flavor to numerous dishes. Some, like garam masala or curry powder, have so much flavor it makes the goal of reducing fat easier. Whether spices play heavily into your favorite foods or not, consider buying your spices whole and grinding them yourself (with a mortar and pestle, or a dedicated electric spice grinder), which will give you more potent flavor and a much longer shelf life.

Ground spices should smell fresh and potent, not musky. Buy smaller containers of ground spices and replace every six months.

BASIC SPICE SET

Spices frequently used in this book include cumin seed, whole coriander, fennel seed, curry powder (Madras), ground ginger, red pepper flakes, anise seed, garam masala, cayenne pepper, ground and stick cinnamon, paprika (see following), and turmeric. These make up my basic spice set.

PAPRIKA Paprika factors heavily into the recipes in this book. You'll often see a recipe that specifically calls for sweet, spicy, or hot paprika. Some recipes also list pimentón, Spanish (as opposed to Hungarian) paprika that is easy to find and often of high quality, which also comes in sweet, smoked, and hot varieties. Feel free to use Spanish and Hungarian paprikas interchangeably.

MUSTARD Dijon mustards (Grey Poupon, whole-grain, or country-style Dijon), whether smooth or grainy, are subtle stars in so many meals, but particularly salads, sides, and sandwiches, where their flavor waves reward with every bite.

MISO I think of miso as the mustard paste of the Japanese. A fermented rice, barley, or soybean base seasoned with salt, miso adds a deep umami flavor to sauces, soups, and, in this book, a spicy miso butter (see page 78) to accompany grilled summer vegetables. It comes in white, yellow, red, and black and can be found in most supermarkets, health food, and Asian food stores.

NORI AND BONITO FLAKES

Nori, or dried seaweed, is used in Japanese cooking to make a flavorful broth, or dashi, for many Japanese dishes, such as a somen noodle bowl (see page 166). It is packed with vitamin B12, an essential nutrient that can be hard for vegetarians and vegans to get. Its long shelf life makes it a worth-while investment even for those who only cook Japanese on occasion, especially since dashi makes a good vegetarian stock. Bonito flakes, or dried fish flakes, can be added to dashi for richer flavor by anyone who includes fish in their diet. Find them both in Asian food stores and some supermarkets in the dry goods or ethnic foods sections.

THE FLEXIBLE ASIAN LARDER

For too many years, I ate Korean, Japanese, and Indian food only in restaurants. It was the ingredients more than the techniques that kept me from cooking these delicious, healthful meals at home. Gradually the following twelve condiments and spices became staples in my kitchen, and now, I feel invincible. Mixed with ginger, garlic, green onion, and any number of hot chiles, the Asian food world is your oyster. Take-out addicts, take heed.

- sambal oelek
- Sriracha
- sesame oil
- peanut oil
- tamari
- rice wine vinegar
- ground ginger
- whole or ground coriander
- seaweed or nori
- bonito flakes
- miso paste
- fish sauce

OLIVES AND CAPERS

Meaty, briny olives like Cerignola, vivid green and buttery Sicilian Castelvetrano, fruity French picho-line, assertive Greek kalamata, juicy hondroelia, and oil-cured black olives (among a dozen others from warm climates all over the globe) add health-ful fats, salt, and satisfaction to many vegetarian meals. Whole olives make great starters and snacks if tossed with rosemary and lemon or orange peel over low heat.

Capers, usually eaten in their salty, pickled bud form, mix well with dozens of vegetables, like cauliflower and roasted root vegetables, such

as in the Glazed Winter Vegetable Medley with Chestnuts and Caper Berries (page 211), which calls for caper berries, the stemmed edible flower of the plant that's as lovely to look at as to eat.

HOT-PEPPER PASTES

Hot-pepper pastes from Europe, Asia, and North Africa deserve a permanent spot in your pantry. They are used often in this book and in the glorious plant-based cuisines of much of the world. Here are a few I keep in stock, and how to use them.

HARISSA Harissa is a rounded, soft North African hot-pepper paste made from chile peppers. It adds punch to soups as a garnish or, in spoonfuls, it gives warmth and backbone to tagines. It is mild in heat, relative to the other four pastes listed here, making it a good choice to stir into Greek yogurt for a delectable sandwich spread. Since you can't find it everywhere, I've given you a recipe to make it yourself (see page 253).

HUNGARIAN PAPRIKA PASTE When I first started making vegetarian soups, I missed the deep, satis-fying flavors of chicken stock. I quickly learned that onions cooked in oil, plus Hungarian paprika paste or red-pepper paste and water, make a fra-grant, filling broth with all the same satisfaction of the best chicken broths I'd ever had. You'll find both hot (*csípos*) and sweet (*édes*) paprika pastes in some supermarkets and specialty stores (see page 279).

SAMBAL OELEK Sambal oelek is the condiment to keep in stock if you like spicy foods, even a little. Primarily used in Asian cooking or as a condiment throughout Indonesia, Singapore, Malaysia, and the Philippines, sambal is primarily made of a blend of chiles, and a little goes a very, very long way. Like all pepper pastes, it adds great flavor and moderate to intense heat, which you can control by tasting as you add.

SRIRACHA SAUCE This smooth and spicy sauce is actually made in America but has become the ketchup of Thai cooking. It's made with chiles, garlic, vinegar, sugar, and salt and comes off as a blend of spicy and sweet. You can mix it into mayo for dipping tempura or raw crudités, and stir it into fried rice.

GOCHUJANG Gochujang is Korea's answer to hot-pepper paste. Because it is fermented, it is perhaps the most savory and pungent of pepper pastes I use. This one includes red chiles, sticky rice, fermented soybeans, and salt, and is one of the iconic flavors in bibimbap. You'll also find this in many Asian groceries and some ethnic food aisles, but I've come to prefer my homemade substitute (see page 175), which is less salted and made without any preservatives.

CANNED TOMATOES AND PASTES

Tomatoes give depth, flavor, acidity, and eye appeal to so many meals. Toast tomato paste for deeper flavor in dishes like Cauliflower Curry (page 162), or squeeze canned San Marzanos, Italy's superior sauce tomatoes, into a big pot to make marinara for eggplant Parmesan (see page 206).

SAFFRON AND OTHER SPLURGE INGREDIENTS

Years ago I splurged on a ridiculously expensive box of saffron, and I force myself to use it whenever possible. It's wonderfully fragrant and lends great color to dishes like Spring Vegetable Paella (page 204), Roasted Tomato–Squash Tagine Fall Feast (page 209), and Braised Butternut Squash with Saffron and Smoked Salt (page 124). You can buy pinches of saffron threads in supermarkets, which is usually all you need. Saffron belongs in the same category as exotic things like truffle honey, which I adore and truly use (see page 137), but don't require. Ask for these things as gifts for birthdays and holidays and I assure you, you'll put

them to good use. If you can't justify the splurge, you can live a long and satisfying life without these things, too.

VINEGARS

There are as many types of vinegar as oils. The most adaptable for cooking, pickling, and dressing are white wine, red wine, and apple cider vinegars. Many organic brands of apple cider vinegar have a superior flavor, and raw unpasteurized organic cider vinegar has been used for medicinal purposes for hundreds of years. You can fancy up your pantry with Champagne and sherry vinegars if those flavors appeal to you.

STORAGE FOR SPICES, VINEGAR, AND MORE

Potent flavor can come in the form of spices, pastes, mustards, and vinegars. These are mostly pantry ingredients, but many require refrigeration after opening to keep them fresh and full of the flavor you'll come to count on. Here are a few things I keep exclusively in the fridge after opening for longer life spans.

- sesame oil
- nut oils
- hot-pepper pastes
- tomato paste

- mustard
- raw unpasteurized apple cider vinegar
- fish sauce

NATURAL SWEETENERS

There's a good reason sweeteners are at the end of this section. When it comes to sugar, you don't need much, and you don't need it often. The best sugars for us are the natural sugars that come as a residual perk from eating lots of fresh fruits and many sweet vegetables like carrots and beets. But sometimes we need to indulge. When the texture benefits of granulated sugar aren't in question, I choose natural sweeteners. In some cases Grade B maple syrup, agave nectar or agave syrup, honey, and brown rice syrup can be used interchangeably, but not always. Pure maple syrup (never, ever use the imitation table syrup) has a roasted, caramel flavor. Maple syrup is labeled by grade, with B being more bold and potent in flavor and usually preferred. Agave nectar is the most neutral of the bunch, making it quite versatile. Too much honey can be cloying and forward, so use it sparingly, and look for local raw or creamed honey, which is always a real treat. Brown rice syrup is a rice-based sweetener that is about half as sweet as sugar and a common ingredient in vegan baking.

Molasses is another matter, sweet and malty, deep and full of robust flavor; I think of this more as a topping than a sweetener, since its flavor can't be masked. Keep it around for the iron it contains and for an occasional sweet treat smeared with butter on High-Rising Buttermilk Biscuits (page 49). Whichever sweeteners you choose, look for the ones that are minimally processed.

UNBLEACHED ORGANIC GRANULATED SUGAR

I've tried (and it's easier than one would think) to eliminate granulated sugar from my daily life, though it still has a place as the ideal tenderizer in some baked goods. Fair-trade unbleached organic sugar was used for all the baking recipes that call for sugar in this book. Organic sugar is grown without synthetic fertilizers or pesticides. Fair-trade organic sugar, commonly made from evaporated cane juice and grown without synthetic fertilizers and pesticides, is now easy to find. It's reported to be about 50 percent less processed than regular sugar. By using this sugar in the baked goods in this book, you will start to see that the small granules give the same tender texture to baked goods as granulated white sugar, but without chemicals and bleach. Brown sugar and, in some cases, powdered sugar lend a texture or flavor I find favorable for certain baked goods, so you'll find those sugars in the recipes on occasion, too.

A NOTE ON NUTRITION

A common concern and misconception about a vegetarian diet is its perceived lack of nourishment and protein. When I met my husband, he was 210 pounds of pure muscle cycling hundreds of miles a week with at least two dozen decathlons and triathlons under his belt. He hadn't (and still hasn't) touched a piece of meat since he was twelve. With a little thought, vegetarians need not be starving or slight. Protein is readily available in plant-based foods (like chickpeas, avocados, potatoes, oats, raw broccoli, and even trace amounts in a banana). I'll let you know a little more about that in the intros to some recipes. But it's smart to have a comprehensive awareness of how many nutrients you're getting in a day and week, particularly for newer vegetarians who may still be learning the ropes—and even seasoned ones stuck in a rut. In particular, note that if you opt out of eggs, dairy, or fish, you'll need to make a conscious effort to add iron and vitamin B12 to your diet. Come back to these lists often for ideas.

PLANT-BASED IRON SOURCES

- edamame and cooked soybeans
- blackstrap molasses
- cooked lentils, chickpeas, kidney beans, and lima beans
- cooked Swiss chard and spinach
- pumpkin seeds
- prune juice
- eggs
- tahini and peanut butter

B12 BOOST Pay close attention to your vitamin B12 intake, essential for red blood cell formation, nerve cell maintenance, cardiovascular health, DNA synthesis, and metabolic health. Seafood eaters will find B12 readily available in clams, oysters, mussels, octopus, herring, salmon, caviar, tuna, cod, sardines, trout, bluefish, crab, and lobster. Strict vegetarians can get B12 from cheese; chicken, goose, and duck eggs (mostly the yolk); milk; and yogurt. Vegans will find B12 in whey powder, nutritional yeast, fortified soy milk, and supplements.

If you eat fish or take a fish oil supplement, cook with olive oil and use it raw to dress salads, you might be getting enough omega-3 fatty acids, but look to other plant-based foods, too.

PLANT-BASED SOURCES FOR OMEGA-3S

- **walnuts and walnut oil**
- **flaxseed and flaxseed oil**
- **firm tofu**
- **avocado**
- **tempeh**

SEAFOOD SOURCES FOR OMEGA-3S

- **wild salmon**
- **sardines**
- **halibut**
- **scallops**
- **shrimp**

Good nutrition is like a marathon: It matters what you eat every day, but even more what you eat over the long run. Don't get caught up in the minutiae of every meal, but do make sure you're eating a wide variety of all these foods on a weekly basis.

breakfast & brunch

If you've ever felt yourself utterly torn over the menu at your favorite brunch spot, this chapter is for you. Instead of choosing, work your way through the kinds of inventive, inviting foods that have made brunching an American pastime: pancakes, eggs, and waffles with goodness written all over them.

Whether you're strictly a sweet or a savory breakfast person, I hope you'll find all your favorites here—reinvented, like nutty whole-grain waffles topped with strawberries (see PAGE 48), Apple-Rye Pancakes (PAGE 47) drizzled with pure maple syrup (and a splash of whiskey), scrambled eggs with Neufchâtel cheese and green onions (see PAGE 39), or savory oats (see PAGE 33).

For those craving a little flavor thrill first thing of the day, you will find Eggs Kimchi (PAGE 42) and Avocado-Cheese Arepas (PAGE 43) with a garlicky green sauce. And for those days when you need something sustaining and portable, plan ahead with a batch of Genmaicha Granola Bars (PAGE 54) or Homemade Four-Grain English Muffins (PAGE 52). These breakfasts are rise-and-shine foods, balanced with enough whole grains, proteins, and fruits to last you through the morning. They are smart on nutrition, but you'll barely notice. Your senses will be wholly captivated by the warmth, the smells, and the mouthfuls of flavor before you.

KALE SHAKE

There are some days that need to start with something green. It's a good reminder that fruits and vegetables should be front and center in our meals. In one glass, you'll tackle two of the most healthful of all plant foods, kale and mango, before the day has barely begun. After I drink this delicious shake, I always think harder about everything I eat for the rest of the day. It's a guaranteed renewed start. I especially love this recipe because it doesn't require a juicer to make!

SERVES 1

Heaping handful coarsely chopped kale

½ very ripe large mango, coarsely chopped

1 inner stalk celery with leaves, coarsely chopped

1 small ripe banana

½ cup/85 g crushed ice or cubes

½ cup/120 ml water

Juice of 1 lemon

Combine all the ingredients in a blender and purée until smooth and frothy, about 5 minutes. Drink immediately.

THE DIRTY DOZEN

When cooking, eating, and juicing fresh vegetables, aiming for the cleanest produce is always a good goal. Though most of us would like to always eat organic, it's not always possible. The following is a list of fruits and vegetables that have tested to have heavy traces of synthetic chemicals and fertilizers when grown conventionally. Switching to organic for just these twelve items is thought to reduce our exposure to pesticide residue by 80 percent.

- apples
- strawberries
- peaches
- spinach
- nectarines
- grapes
- bell peppers
- potatoes
- blueberries
- lettuce
- kale
- collard greens

SAVORY OATS
WITH PEAS AND AGED GOUDA

Savory oats make a superb breakfast or lunch, particularly on a rainy spring day. Top with sweet peas, aged Gouda cheese, and a drizzling of your best extra-virgin olive oil. Sprinkle with sel gris and coarsely cracked black pepper.

For a cleaner oat taste, I omit the milk that I usually use for simmering oatmeal. And because the craving might hit anytime, I use quicker-cooking rolled oats (not steel-cut) for this version. If you become a savory oats fan, you'll be happy to know your new habit (peas plus cheese) will reward you with heart-healthy fiber, vitamins C and K, and the long-lasting flavor of a good smoky cheese.

SERVES 4

2½ cups/600 ml water

Sea salt

1 cup/85 g old-fashioned rolled oats

10 oz/280 g fresh or frozen peas

2 oz/55 g aged Gouda cheese

Finishing oil for drizzling

Sel gris

Freshly ground pepper

STEP 1. Combine the water and a large pinch of sea salt in a large saucepan over medium heat. Bring to a boil, stir in the oats, and reduce the heat to medium-low. Gently simmer until the oats are just tender, stirring occasionally, 15 to 20 minutes.

STEP 2. Meanwhile, bring a small saucepan half full of salted water to a boil over high heat. Add the peas and cook until bright green and just cooked, about 2 minutes. Drain.

STEP 3. Divide the oats among bowls and top with the peas. Grate the Gouda over the top of each bowl. Drizzle with finishing oil and sprinkle with sel gris and pepper. Serve warm.

FALL

OATS WITH
GRATED PEAR, PECANS,
AND LEMON YOGURT

SPRING

OATS WITH
STRAWBERRIES
AND "CREAM"

SUMMER

OATS WITH BERRIES AND WALNUT CRUMBLE

WINTER

OATS WITH PLUMPED DRIED PLUMS AND LIME

HOT CEREAL
FOR FOUR SEASONS

For the many long, cold months of a New England winter, there's nothing that starts a morning like a bowl of hot cereal. Oats welcome dozens of toppings, sweet or savory, hot or cold, creamy or crunchy, but my four favorites follow, one for every season and mood. In the spring, when the first plump strawberries appear, lighten up the breakfast routine with strawberries and creamy yogurt, the best cream substitute. Sprinkle a blend of bursting berries and walnut crumble on top of your bowl of oats in the summer, and top with grated pear and toasted pecans on crisp fall mornings. For winter, warm up with lush stewed plums and a squeeze of lime juice.

When it comes to hot cereal, I'd be happy with anything from farina to a textured ten-grain cereal that often starts my day, but steel-cut Irish oats are a perfect middle ground for most mornings. Whether your hot cereal is polenta, old-fashioned rolled oats, barley porridge, or anything in between, the secret is to cook them in part water and part milk, stirring on occasion so the texture gets creamy, not goopy, the fatal flaw of oatmeal in any form.

COOK'S NOTE. To reduce the cooking time, soak the steel-cut oats in water overnight. Drain before cooking.

SPRING

OATS WITH STRAWBERRIES AND "CREAM"

————————————————————— SERVES 4 —————————————————————

1 cup/155 g steel-cut oats

3 cups/720 ml water

¾ cup/180 ml cow's milk, oat milk,
   or nut milk, plus more as needed

Fine sea salt

Fresh strawberries, sliced, for topping

Full-fat plain yogurt for topping

Molasses or brown sugar for drizzling

STEP 1. Combine the oats, water, milk, and a pinch of salt in a large saucepan over medium heat. Bring to a rapid simmer, then immediately reduce the heat to medium-low. Gently simmer until the oats are just tender, stirring occasionally, 25 to 30 minutes, depending on how much bite you like in your oats. Stir in additional milk, if desired, to thin to the consistency you prefer. Simmer for 5 minutes more.

STEP 2. Divide the oats among bowls and top with strawberries and a dollop of yogurt. Drizzle with molasses. Serve warm.

OATS WITH BERRIES AND WALNUT CRUMBLE

———————————————— SERVES 4 ————————————————

1 cup/155 g steel-cut oats

3 cups/720 ml water

¾ cup/180 ml cow's milk, oat milk,
or nut milk, plus more as needed

Fine sea salt

½ cup/55 g toasted walnuts (see page 273)

2 tbsp unbleached raw sugar

Fresh seasonal berries such as blueberries,
blackberries, mulberries, or currants
for topping

STEP 1. Combine the oats, water, milk, and a pinch of salt in a large saucepan over medium heat. Bring to a rapid simmer, then immediately reduce the heat to medium-low. Gently simmer until the oats are just tender, stirring occasionally, 25 to 30 minutes, depending on how much bite you like in your oats. Stir in additional milk, if desired, to thin to the consistency you prefer. Simmer for 5 minutes more.

STEP 2. Meanwhile, pulse the walnuts and sugar together in a food processor to make a coarse crumble.

STEP 3. Divide the oats among bowls and sprinkle with walnut crumble and top with berries. Serve warm.

FALL

OATS WITH GRATED PEAR, PECANS, AND LEMON YOGURT

———————————————— SERVES 4 ————————————————

1 tsp lemon zest

1 tsp fresh lemon juice

¾ cup/180 ml full-fat plain yogurt

1 cup/155 g steel-cut oats

3 cups/720 ml water

¾ cup/180 ml cow's milk, oat milk,
or nut milk, plus more as needed

1 cinnamon stick

Fine sea salt

1 or 2 firm, ripe Anjou or Bartlett pears,
unpeeled

⅔ cup/60 g toasted pecans (see page 273),
chopped

CONTINUED

STEP 1. Stir together the lemon zest, lemon juice, and yogurt in a small bowl. Set aside.

STEP 2. Combine the oats, water, milk, cinnamon stick, and a pinch of salt in a large saucepan over medium heat. Bring to a rapid simmer, then immediately reduce the heat to medium-low. Gently simmer until the oats are just tender, stirring occasionally, 25 to 30 minutes, depending on how much bite you like in your oats. Stir in additional milk, if desired, to thin to the consistency you prefer. Simmer for 5 minutes more. Remove the cinnamon stick and discard.

STEP 3. Divide the oats among bowls. Grate fresh pear over the top of your oats, peels and all. Top with the pecans and a dollop or two of lemon yogurt. Serve warm.

WINTER

OATS WITH PLUMPED DRIED PLUMS AND LIME

—————————————————— SERVES 4 ——————————————————

1 cup/155 g steel-cut oats	Fine sea salt
3 cups/720 ml water	1 cup/180 g pitted dried plums
¾ cup/180 ml cow's milk, oat milk, or nut milk, plus more as needed	½ cup/120 ml prune juice or water
	¾ cup/180 ml full-fat plain yogurt
1 cinnamon stick	1 or 2 limes, zested and quartered

STEP 1. Combine the oats, water, milk, cinnamon stick, and a pinch of salt in a large saucepan over medium heat. Bring to a rapid simmer, then immediately reduce the heat to medium-low. Gently simmer until the oats are just tender, stirring occasionally, 25 to 30 minutes, depending on how much bite you like in your oats. Stir in additional milk, if desired, to thin to the consistency you prefer. Simmer for 5 minutes more. Remove the cinnamon stick and discard.

STEP 2. Meanwhile, combine the dried plums and prune juice in a shallow pan over medium heat. Bring to a simmer, cover, and reduce the heat to low. Gently simmer until the plums are soft and plump and the juices are slightly thickened, 8 to 12 minutes. Remove from the heat and set aside, reserving the plums in their juices.

STEP 3. Divide the oats among bowls. Spoon the plumped plums over the top of your oats. Top with a dollop or two of yogurt. Sprinkle with lime zest and squeeze fresh lime juice over the top. Serve warm.

CREAMY HERBED EGGS

I learned from Rori Trovato, food stylist turned ice-cream artisan (of Rori's Artisanal Creamery in California), how to make the most decadent scrambled eggs. Many mornings on the set of a photo shoot, Rori would treat us all to a scrambled egg breakfast made with cream cheese, which created luscious little curds that were unctuous and rich. These days, I use Neufchâtel, which is slightly lower in fat and just as creamy, and cook my eggs to the edge of runny, just as Rori taught me. With almost any combination of herbs, such as dill, chervil, basil, parsley, and especially chives, and your own homemade English muffin, this is as fine a breakfast as I know.

SERVES 2

4 large eggs

1 tbsp unsalted butter or extra-virgin olive oil

3 tbsp Neufchâtel or cream cheese, at room temperature

Handful assorted fresh herbs, finely chopped

1 green onion, finely chopped (optional)

Sea salt and freshly ground pepper

Homemade Four-Grain English Muffins (page 52), toasted, for serving

STEP 1. Crack the eggs into a medium bowl and whisk vigorously until light and frothy. Melt the butter in a medium nonstick skillet over medium heat. Add the eggs and let them set a little to cook, about 1 minute. Scoot them back and forth every now and then with a heat-proof spatula until they are just cooked into large curds, about 3 minutes.

STEP 2. Remove from the heat, add 2 tbsp of the Neufchâtel, and stir with the spatula. Add the herbs, green onion (if using), the remaining 1 tbsp Neufchâtel, and season with salt (this is the rare egg dish that needs very little salt!). Stir until the cheese just melts and the eggs are just beyond runny and still pale. Season with pepper. Serve hot with English muffins.

COUNTRY EGGS AND GRAVY
WITH ARUGULA

Eggs and gravy are about as country as it gets. It's a staple of Missouri farmwives (like my grandmother) and a favorite of farm boys everywhere (like my dad). This one-dish egg bake is a quick way to feed a hungry crowd, since it's filling and delicious. Luckily for us, good country gravy is not a pleasure reserved for carnivores alone. Spicy soy sausage, should you choose to use it, imparts every bit of the addictive flavor required to make a gravy amply worth the indulgence. I like my country eggs straight up (no sausage) and topped with arugula and the heat of Spanish pimentón—not country at all but an upgrade any modern farm boy could abide. Serve warm with fresh biscuits for breakfast or brunch, or with toasted crusty bread and a big salad for supper.

SERVES 4 TO 6

---

3 tbsp unsalted butter

6 oz/160 g soy breakfast sausage patties (optional)

¼ cup/30 g all-purpose flour

3 cups/720 ml whole milk

8 to 10 large eggs

Sel gris

Freshly ground pepper

¼ tsp sweet, hot, or smoked paprika

Handful arugula

STEP 1. Preheat the oven to 325°F/165°C/gas 4. Melt 2 tbsp of the butter in an 8- to 10-in/ 20- to 25-cm skillet (preferably cast-iron) over medium-high heat. Add the sausage patties (if using) and cook until crisp on the outside and warmed through, 4 to 6 minutes. Crumble into pieces and leave in the skillet.

STEP 2. Sprinkle the flour over the fat in the pan and reduce the heat to medium. Cook, stirring occasionally with a wooden spoon, until the flour is toasted and brown, about 3 minutes. Raise the heat to medium-high and gradually add the milk, whisking constantly until it is all added. Continue to cook, without stirring, until the milk begins to bubble and thicken slightly, about 3 minutes. Turn off the heat. (The gravy will thicken further in the oven.)

STEP 3. Break the eggs into the gravy, evenly spaced around the skillet. Bake until the whites are just cooked through and the yolks are still slightly soft, 10 to 15 minutes. Sprinkle with sel gris and pepper.

STEP 4. Meanwhile, melt the remaining 1 tbsp butter in a small skillet over low heat and add the paprika. Let the paprika butter toast until fragrant and slightly toasty red, about 1 minute.

STEP 5. Sprinkle the arugula over the top of the eggs and gravy and drizzle with the spiced butter. Serve hot.

EGGS KIMCHI

I couldn't be happier that Western food culture has adopted kimchi—the national condiment of Korea—as its own. There are numerous ways to enjoy it (see bibimbap, page 175, and Kale and Kimchi Salad, page 101), but my favorite way is to fold the spicy, fermented goodness into rich scrambled eggs. This dish belongs equally in your breakfast as in your lunch files, but it's very worth starting the day with when you need a little heat. Serve it over toasted bread or warm sticky rice.

——————————————— SERVES 1 ———————————————

2 large eggs

1 tbsp unsalted butter

½ cup/85 g Kimchi (page 250) or purchased kimchi, well drained

Cooked sticky rice or toasted bread or for serving

STEP 1. Crack the eggs into a medium bowl and whisk vigorously until light and frothy. Melt the butter in a medium nonstick skillet over medium heat. Add the eggs and let them set a little to cook, 1 to 2 minutes. Scoot them back and forth every now and then with a heat-proof spatula until they are just cooked into large curds, about 2 minutes.

STEP 2. Add the kimchi and just barely stir into the eggs with the spatula. Cook until heated through, 1 to 2 minutes. Serve the eggs warm, spooned over the rice.

AVOCADO-CHEESE AREPAS

Arepas are a street food of Venezuela and Colombia—tender corn cakes often stuffed with cheese, avocado, and sometimes meat. Because it takes a bit of practice to make them sturdy enough to slice and stuff, I make them like griddle cakes and top them with sweet plantain, avocado, cheese, and a healthy dose of garlicky green sauce. This is an easy brunch food for friends who love punchy morning flavor.

MAKES 8 TO 10 AREPAS

2 cups/250 g plus 2 tbsp masarepa or masa harina (see Cook's Note)

Pinch of unbleached raw sugar

Sea salt

2 cups/480 ml warm milk

2 tbsp unsalted butter, at room temperature

1 oz/30 g queso añejo, Cotija, or Monterey Jack cheese, finely grated, plus more for topping

Extra-virgin olive oil or grapeseed oil for frying

1 very ripe plantain, very thinly sliced on the diagonal

Garlicky Green Sauce (page 255) for dolloping

1 firm, ripe avocado, peeled, pitted, and thinly sliced

STEP 1. Stir together the 2 cups/250 g masarepa, sugar, and ¼ tsp salt in a medium bowl. Add the warm milk, butter, and queso añejo and stir with a wooden spoon or fork until a thick dough forms. Feel the dough; it should be soft. Add up to 2 tbsp more masarepa and stir together until incorporated. Scoop the dough into eight or ten equal portions and put on a floured work surface. Flatten each with your hand into a small patty about ½ in/ 12 mm thick.

STEP 2. Heat a cast-iron griddle or nonstick skillet over medium-high heat until hot. To test, splash a drop of water onto the griddle; it should sizzle. Add 1 tbsp olive oil and fry the plantain slices until golden and crisp like thin potato chips, about 6 minutes, turning once. Season with salt and set aside.

STEP 3. Brush the griddle lightly with another 1 tbsp oil. Place the patties on the griddle, leaving space between them to flip. Cook until a light brown crust forms on one side, 3 to 4 minutes. Flip the arepas with a spatula and cook until the second sides are golden brown, 3 to 4 minutes more. Season lightly with salt while warm, transfer to a platter, and cover loosely to keep warm. Repeat until all of the arepas are cooked, adding more oil to the griddle as needed.

STEP 4. Dollop Garlicky Green Sauce over each arepa, and top with plantain chips, queso añejo, and avocado. Serve hot with additional sauce at the table.

COOK'S NOTE. True arepas are made with masarepa, or fine white corn flour, but masa harina, the same cornmeal used to make tortillas, is easier to find and is a good substitute (see page 280).

WHOLE-WHEAT
SEMOLINA PANCAKES
WITH PEACHES

These are a corn bread lover's pancake. They are made with a blend of whole-wheat white flour and semolina flour, which together produce a subtle, almost corn bread texture that pairs like a dream with ripe summer peaches. These are a thick, big-glass-of-milk kind of pancake, almost like a griddled corn bread. Top with a pat or two of soft butter and sweet, juicy peaches.

――――――――――――― MAKES 8 TO 10 PANCAKES ―――――――――――――

1½ cups/175 g whole-wheat white or
    whole-wheat flour

⅔ cup/105 g semolina flour

2 tbsp unbleached raw sugar

1¼ tsp baking powder

¼ tsp baking soda

Fine sea salt

1 cup/240 ml milk, plus more as needed

6 tbsp/85 g unsalted butter, melted, plus more
    for the griddle and serving

2 large eggs

2 firm, ripe peaches, thinly sliced

Grade B maple syrup or agave nectar for serving

STEP 1. Whisk together the whole-wheat white flour, semolina flour, sugar, baking powder, baking soda, and ¼ tsp salt in a large bowl. Whisk together the milk, melted butter, and eggs in another large bowl, adding a few extra splashes of milk if you prefer thin pancakes. Make a well in the center of the dry ingredients, and whisk in the wet ingredients until just incorporated into a thick batter with a few lumps. (Be careful not to overmix, which can make the pancakes tough.)

STEP 2. Heat a nonstick or cast-iron griddle or heavy skillet over medium heat until hot. To test, splash a drop of water onto the griddle; it should sizzle. Brush the griddle lightly with melted butter. Scoop about ⅓ cup/75 ml of the batter onto the griddle, leaving plenty of space between pancakes for them to spread and be flipped. Cook until the bottoms are set and a few bubbles form around the edges, about 3 minutes. Flip the pancakes with a flexible spatula and cook until the bottoms are golden brown, about 1 minute more. Transfer to a plate and cover loosely to keep warm. Repeat until all the batter is used, adding more melted butter to the griddle as needed. Serve hot with pats of butter, the peaches, and a drizzle of maple syrup.

SWEDISH PANCAKES

The city where I grew up, Rockford, Illinois, was founded by Swedes. There, Sunday morning means one thing: Swedish pancakes. This is the French crêpe's eggier cousin, which literally melts in your mouth, particularly when served with lingonberries or pure maple syrup.

MAKES 8 TO 12 PANCAKES

2 cups/480 ml whole milk

3 large eggs

5 tbsp/70 g unsalted butter, melted, plus more for the pan and serving

1 tsp pure vanilla extract

Fine sea salt

1 cup/125 g all-purpose flour

Lingonberry jam or grade B maple syrup for serving

STEP 1. Combine the milk, eggs, melted butter, vanilla, and a pinch of salt in a blender or a bowl with an immersion blender and purée until smooth, about 1 minute. Gradually add the flour, continuing to purée, until the batter is smooth and the consistency of heavy cream, about 2 minutes more.

STEP 2. Preheat a nonstick crêpe pan or well-seasoned cast-iron griddle over medium heat until hot. To test, splash a drop of water onto the pan; it should sizzle. Add a little melted butter to the pan.

STEP 3. Pour ⅓ cup/75 ml of the batter onto the hot pan, twirling the pan to coat the bottom with a thin, even layer of batter. If you're using a griddle, pour the batter and quickly smooth into a thin, even layer (it can be round or square) with an offset spatula. The batter should start cooking rather quickly. If not, raise the heat slightly. (If the batter is browning too quickly, reduce the heat slightly.)

STEP 4. Cook until the batter changes from shiny to dull and the pancake bottom is slightly bubbly and lightly brown, about 3 minutes. Roll up each pancake into a cylinder with a fork or offset spatula, and transfer to a plate to hold. Repeat until all the batter is used, adding more melted butter to the pan as needed (it's usually not necessary if using a nonstick pan), and cover the pancakes loosely as you go to keep them warm.

STEP 5. Serve warm, with butter and lingonberry jam.

COOK'S NOTE. Swedish pancakes can be round, if you have a nonstick or cast-iron crêpe pan, or square, if you're using a flat griddle. What's important is to use a well-seasoned or nonstick pan, since these pancakes are very tender and tear easily. (Unlike French crêpes, which can often be flipped without tearing, Swedish pancakes are not flipped.)

APPLE-RYE PANCAKES

I visit King Arthur Flour's Baking Education Center in Norwich, Vermont, every year to teach classes on artisan baking, and I always come home with a hearty batch of flours. Rye flour imparts wonderful texture and is often best when blended with all-purpose flour, which contributes the tenderness we all look for in our morning pancakes. Because rye flour can also soak up liquid fast and furious, measure the liquid ingredients carefully and mix with a light hand.

Adding paper-thin slices of a Pink Lady apple make these beautiful to look at and add a subtle sweetness to the rye. These are the ideal pancakes for pure maple syrup (with a shot of rye whiskey, if you please), which soak it up just as fast as can be. Eat them hot and fresh.

--- MAKES 12 TO 18 PANCAKES ---

1¼ cups/140 g all-purpose flour

1 cup/105 g rye flour

2 tsp baking powder

1 tsp baking soda

3 tbsp unbleached raw sugar

¾ tsp fine sea salt

2 large eggs, lightly beaten

3 cups/720 ml buttermilk, well shaken

5 tbsp/70 g unsalted butter, melted, plus more
    for the griddle and serving

1 sweet-tart apple such as Pink Lady or Jonagold

Grade B maple syrup for serving

Splash of rye whiskey (optional)

STEP 1. Whisk together the all-purpose flour, rye flour, baking powder, baking soda, sugar, and salt in a large bowl. Whisk together the eggs, buttermilk, and melted butter in another large bowl. Make a well in the center of the dry ingredients, and whisk in the wet ingredients until just incorporated into a thick batter with a few lumps.

STEP 2. Slice the apple as thinly as possible with a mandoline or a very sharp knife, stopping when you hit the core and starting again from the other side.

STEP 3. Warm the syrup in a small saucepan over low heat. Add the whiskey (if desired), stir to combine, and keep warm over low heat while making the pancakes.

STEP 4. Heat a nonstick or cast-iron griddle or heavy skillet over medium-high heat until hot. To test, splash a drop of water onto the griddle; it should sizzle. Brush the griddle lightly with melted butter. Scoop about ⅓ cup/75 ml of the batter onto the griddle, leaving plenty of space between pancakes for them to spread and be flipped. Cook until the bottoms are set and a few bubbles form around the edges, about 3 minutes. Lay a few apple slices on top of each pancake. Add a little more butter to the pan.

STEP 5. Flip the pancakes with a flexible spatula and cook until the second sides are golden brown and the apple a touch crisp, 1 to 2 minutes. Transfer to a plate and cover loosely to keep warm. Repeat until all the batter is used, adding more melted butter to the griddle as needed. Serve hot, apple-side up, with butter and a drizzle of warm syrup.

WHOLE-GRAIN HAZELNUT
BELGIAN WAFFLES
WITH STRAWBERRIES

Waffles are such a treat and usually much less work than they seem. Here the buttermilk does all the work for you to make these waffles light and crispy—no whipping egg whites and folding delicate batters. This batter rises to a bronzed, evenly puffed waffle in a well-seasoned iron. Though I always prefer a crunchy waffle to a soft one, the flavor comes through whether it's cooked until pale gold or dark brown. Hazelnut oil gives these waffles even more flavor and also helps to keep them crisp. Substitute your favorite neutral-flavored vegetable oil if you prefer.

MAKES 6 BELGIAN OR 12 STANDARD WAFFLES

2 cups/240 g whole-wheat flour

1 cup/125 g all-purpose flour

¼ cup/50 g unbleached raw sugar

2 tsp baking powder

1 tsp baking soda

2 tsp fine sea salt

3 cups/720 ml buttermilk, well shaken

2 large eggs, at room temperature and lightly beaten

4 tbsp/55 g unsalted butter, melted, plus more for the waffle iron and serving

2 tbsp hazelnut oil

Fresh strawberries, halved or quartered, for topping

½ cup/70 g toasted hazelnuts (see page 273), coarsely chopped

Grade B maple syrup or agave nectar for serving

STEP 1. Whisk together the whole-wheat flour, all-purpose flour, sugar, baking powder, baking soda, and salt in a large bowl. Whisk together the buttermilk, eggs, melted butter, and hazelnut oil in another large bowl. Make a well in the center of the dry ingredients and whisk in the wet ingredients until just combined into a thick batter and no lumps remain. (Be careful not to overmix, which can make the waffles tough.)

STEP 2. Preheat the waffle iron on medium heat until hot. To test, splash a drop of water onto the iron; it should sizzle. Brush the iron lightly with melted butter. Scoop about ½ cup/ 125 ml of the batter onto the iron, smoothing it with a spoon, and close the lid. Cook until the iron stops steaming and the waffles are golden brown, 3 to 4 minutes. Open up the lid and check the color, and cook another minute if needed. Repeat until all the batter is used, adding more melted butter to the waffle iron as needed. Hold the waffles on a rack (rather than stacked) in a low oven to keep them warm.

STEP 3. Serve the waffles topped with butter, strawberries, hazelnuts, and maple syrup.

HIGH-RISING
BUTTERMILK BISCUITS

Most mornings I crave whole grains and breakfast treats that deliver a little more on fiber and protein, which stick with you all day. Sometimes, though, a little white flour is in order. In this case, white flour makes buttermilk biscuits both light and fluffy on the inside, and thanks to butter, they are also crispy-golden on the outside. And speaking of butter, the very best way I know to eat a biscuit is with molasses butter slathered on top. For a savory biscuit, add in flecks of your favorite herb (I love chives) to serve with Country Eggs and Gravy with Arugula (page 40), Red Lentils with Yogurt (page 163), Pea Soup with Rye Croutons and Chive Blossoms (page 85), or Carrot Soup with Chives and Popcorn (page 86).

MAKES 10 TO 12 BISCUITS

1¾ cups/215 g all-purpose or whole-wheat white flour, plus more for dusting

2 tsp baking powder

½ tsp baking soda

¾ tsp fine sea salt

6 tbsp/85 g cold unsalted butter, cubed

¾ cup/180 ml buttermilk, well shaken

Molasses butter (blend equal parts unsalted butter and unsulfured molasses) for serving

STEP 1. Preheat a conventional oven to 425°F/220°C/gas 7 or a convection oven to 400°F/200°C/gas 6. Line a baking sheet with parchment paper or a silicone baking mat.

STEP 2. Whisk together the flour, baking powder, baking soda, and salt in a medium bowl. Using your fingers or a pastry cutter, blend the butter into the flour until it is mostly incorporated with some pea-size pieces remaining. Stir in the buttermilk with a fork until the dough just forms.

STEP 3. Turn the dough onto a lightly floured surface and turn it over on itself about eight times, until a cohesive dough forms. Pat into a round about ¹/₂ in/12 mm thick. Cut into biscuits with a 2-in/5-cm biscuit or cookie cutter or a thin-rimmed glass. Pat the dough scraps together and cut out any remaining biscuits.

STEP 4. Place the biscuits on the prepared baking sheet about 2 in/5 cm apart. Bake until golden brown and just cooked through but still moist inside, 12 to 15 minutes in a conventional oven or 12 minutes in a convection oven. Serve warm with molasses butter.

TOASTED SEMOLINA RAISIN SCONES

One of my shameless indulgences is the tender, crunchy semolina raisin bread at Amy's Bread in Manhattan, sliced and toasted with butter and crystalline sea salt. Nothing makes a better winter breakfast with a cup of hot cocoa. When I can't get to Amy's, I bake scones with the same flavor profile. Scones are always amazing hot and fresh from the oven. But these scones are still good—very good—on the second day, split lengthwise and toasted under the broiler or in the toaster oven. Smear with some locally made unsalted butter, a little dollop of orange marmalade, and sel gris.

MAKES 6 SCONES

1 cup/125 g all-purpose flour

½ cup/60 g whole-wheat flour

½ cup/90 g semolina flour

2 to 3 tbsp unbleached raw sugar, plus more for sprinkling

2 tsp baking powder

1 tsp lemon zest (preferably from a Meyer lemon)

½ tsp anise seeds

¼ tsp sel gris

6 tbsp/85 g cold unsalted butter, cut into cubes, plus more for serving

⅔ cup/115 g golden raisins

⅔ cup/165 ml whole milk or half-and-half, plus more for brushing

Orange marmalade or conserve for serving

STEP 1. Preheat a conventional oven to 375°F/190°C/gas 5 or a convection oven to 350°F/180°C/gas 4. Line a baking sheet with parchment paper.

STEP 2. Whisk together the all-purpose flour, whole-wheat flour, semolina flour, 2 to 3 tbsp sugar (depending on how sweet you like your scones), baking powder, lemon zest, anise seeds, and sel gris in a large bowl. Using your fingers or a pastry cutter, blend the butter cubes into the flour until it is mostly incorporated with some pea-size pieces of butter remaining. Stir in the raisins and milk with a fork until the dough just forms.

STEP 3. Turn the dough onto a lightly floured work surface. Gently pat (without kneading) the dough into a round about ¾ in/2 cm thick and 6 in/15 cm across. Using a sharp knife or bench scraper, cut the round into six wedges.

STEP 4. Place the scones on the prepared baking sheet, leaving a bit of space between them, and refrigerate for 15 minutes.

STEP 5. Brush the top of the scones with milk and lightly sprinkle with sugar. Bake until golden brown and just cooked through but still moist inside, 15 to 18 minutes in a conventional oven or 14 minutes in a convection oven. When fully cooked, the scones should feel firm on the outside. It's okay to cut into one to test the doneness of the inside. If the scones are a touch undercooked, turn off the oven and let them remain in the oven for 5 minutes more—my secret for the best texture, with a crispy, crunchy outside and moist, tender inside. Transfer to a wire rack to cool for 15 minutes.

STEP 6. Serve warm with butter and orange marmalade.

HOMEMADE FOUR-GRAIN
ENGLISH MUFFINS

There's a sense of pride earned from making certain things from scratch, like English muffins. Essentially small griddle breads, English muffins are a great foray into bread making and are so easy to master. Think of these as a weekend project that will make every forthcoming weekday that much more delicious. When they are freshly baked, spoil yourself with the most decadent haute breakfast sandwich imaginable made on your homemade English muffin.

—————————————————— MAKES 12 MUFFINS ——————————————————

3 cups/345 g whole-wheat flour or whole-wheat white flour

2¼ cups/290 g bread flour

2 tbsp fine cornmeal, plus more for sprinkling

2 tbsp old-fashioned rolled oats

2 tbsp millet

2 tbsp flax meal or ground flaxseed

1 cup/240 ml warm water

One ¼-oz/7-g package active dry yeast

1 cup/240 ml whole milk

2 tbsp honey

½ cup/115 g melted unsalted butter, plus more for the griddle

¼ cup/20 g raw sunflower seeds

2 tsp sel gris or fleur de sel

2 tsp extra-virgin olive oil

STEP 1. Whisk together the whole-wheat flour, bread flour, cornmeal, oats, millet, and flax meal in a large bowl.

STEP 2. Put the warm water in a small bowl and sprinkle the yeast over it. Be sure the water is between 105°F/40°C and 110°F/45°C. If it's too hot, the yeast will die; too cool, the yeast won't activate. Watch for the yeast to puff and expand, 2 to 5 minutes.

STEP 3. Meanwhile, warm the milk in a small saucepan over medium heat until just about to simmer, about 2 minutes. Transfer to a large bowl. Add the honey and stir until dissolved.

STEP 4. Add the yeast mixture, melted butter, 3 cups/380 g of the flour mixture, the sunflower seeds, and sel gris to the milk and honey.

STEP 5. If making by hand, mix with a wooden spoon until the dough is mostly smooth and slightly wet, 2 to 3 minutes. Add the remaining flour mixture, ½ cup/60 g at a time, until a soft dough forms, kneading the dough together until it is no longer sticky. Don't worry if it doesn't come together immediately; as you knead the dough, it will form a ball.

If making with a stand mixer, mix with the dough hook attachment on medium-low speed until the dough is mostly smooth and slightly wet, 1 to 2 minutes. Add the remaining flour mixture, ½ cup/60 g at a time, until a soft dough forms, increasing the speed to medium-high until the dough forms a ball with some drag slapping the sides of the bowl and pulling away as it turns, about 5 minutes. Don't worry if it doesn't come together immediately. If you need to, pull the dough away from the sides with a flexible spatula and stick it to the mass on the dough hook.

STEP 6. Lightly oil another large bowl with the olive oil. Transfer the dough to the oiled bowl and turn the dough to coat with the oil. Cover the top of the bowl tightly with plastic wrap. Let the dough rise in a warm, draft-free spot until the dough has doubled in size, about 1 hour.

STEP 7. Sprinkle the work surface with flour. Have a sheet of wax paper nearby and sprinkle with cornmeal.

STEP 8. Punch down the dough and transfer it to the floured surface. Divide the dough into 12 pieces and roll each into a ball. Lay the dough balls on the wax paper, leaving space between the balls so they have room to expand without touching. Flatten each with your hand just slightly and sprinkle the tops liberally with cornmeal. Cover loosely and let rise in a warm, draft-free spot for 30 minutes.

STEP 9. Preheat the oven to 350°F/180°C/gas 4. Heat a nonstick or cast-iron griddle or heavy skillet over medium heat until hot. To test, splash a drop of water on the griddle; it should sizzle. Brush the griddle lightly with butter. Gently brush off excess cornmeal from the dough with a dry pastry brush or your hands. Place about half of the dough rounds on the hot griddle. Cook in batches until the bottoms are golden brown, 2 to 3 minutes. Flip the muffins with a spatula and cook until the second sides are golden brown. Transfer to a baking sheet. Repeat until all the muffins are browned. Bake the muffins until the edges are firm, 22 to 25 minutes.

STEP 10. Transfer to a wire rack to cool just slightly, about 5 minutes. Just before serving, split with a fork or knife and toast until the cut sides are golden brown.

COOK'S NOTE. When making fresh dough, the best way to tell how much the dough has expanded is to draw a circle with a permanent marker on the plastic wrap around the dough and see how much the dough expands beyond the circle.

MAKE AHEAD. English muffins freeze beautifully. Let them cool completely before wrapping in plastic wrap and then aluminum foil. Freeze for up to 1 month. Defrost and warm in the toaster or toaster oven.

GENMAICHA GRANOLA BARS

Many granola bars masquerade as health food when, in fact, dozens of them are anything but, laced with sugar and chocolate chips. The granola bar of your dreams, though, can be chock-full of fast energy and lasting nutrition like this one—loaded with nuts and seeds, like almonds and sunflower, pumpkin, and sesame seeds. Millet adds incredible crunch, and naturally sweet dates and maple syrup hold it all together. Genmaicha—green tea leaves with roasted brown rice—adds depth, a malty richness, and a caffeine boost. If you can't find genmaicha or simply don't do caffeine, skip it. These granola bars will win fans far and wide either way.

—————————— MAKES 8 TO 10 BARS ——————————

2 cups/170 g old-fashioned rolled oats

½ cup/60 g millet

⅓ cup/30 g raw sunflower seeds

2 tbsp raw unseasoned pumpkin seeds (pepitas)

1 tbsp sesame seeds

1 tsp ground cinnamon

½ tsp fine sea salt

⅓ cup/50 g toasted pecans (see page 273)

⅓ cup/50 g toasted skin-on almonds (see page 273)

Packed 1 cup/170 g pitted Medjool dates

⅓ cup/75 ml Grade B maple syrup, plus more as needed

¼ cup/60 ml honey or brown rice syrup

1 tsp pure vanilla extract

1 tbsp genmaicha tea leaves

STEP 1. Preheat the oven to 325°F/165°C/gas 3. Line an 8-in/20-cm square baking pan with parchment paper so that there are overlapping flaps (see page 260).

STEP 2. Stir together the oats, millet, sunflower seeds, pumpkin seeds, sesame seeds, cinnamon, and salt in a medium bowl.

STEP 3. Pulse the pecans and almonds in a food processor until coarsely chopped (it's okay if some nuts are coarsely ground and others a little powdery). Stir into the oat mixture.

STEP 4. Pulse the dates in a food processor until a thick paste forms. Add the maple syrup, honey, and vanilla and pulse until a purée forms. Scrape out the purée with a rubber spatula and stir into the oat mixture. Add the genmaicha tea leaves and continue stirring (your clean hands work best) until the oats and nuts are sticky and coated with the purée. If the mixture doesn't clump together easily, add up to 1 tbsp of maple syrup.

STEP 5. Transfer the granola to the prepared baking pan and press into a smooth, even layer. Bake until just starting to brown around the edges, about 25 minutes. Transfer to the counter to cool slightly in the baking pan, about 15 minutes. Grab the flaps of parchment paper, lift out the whole batch, and transfer to a cutting board. Cut into eight to ten bars while still warm. Let them cool completely and serve at room temperature. Store in an airtight container for up to 1 week.

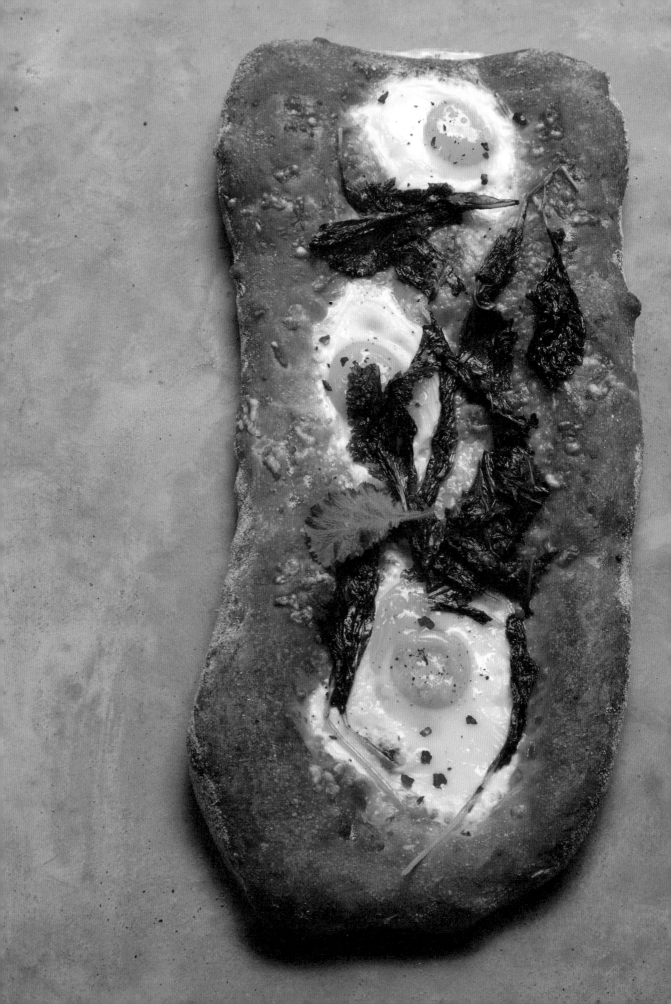

MUSTARD GREENS, CHEDDAR, AND FARM EGG BREAKFAST PIZZA

When you really want to go for it at breakfast, make pizza! Imagine it—fresh, hot, bubbling with cheese and the quivering yellow yolk of a farm-fresh egg. It's worth the effort, and it's quite a cinch if you make a habit of prepping your pizza dough ahead and keeping it in the freezer or fridge. This pizza gives glory to a good fresh egg (a duck egg also does the trick!) from your local farmers' market. I top my egg with smoked sea salt, to give it the smoky flavor some brunch-goers might crave after forgoing bacon.

SERVES 2

Fine cornmeal for dusting

Flour for dusting

One 14- to 16-oz/400- to 455-g ball homemade pizza dough (see page 260) or purchased pizza dough, at room temperature

2 oz/55 g sharp white cheddar or Comté cheese, coarsely grated

2 tbsp extra-virgin olive oil, plus more for drizzling

½ large bunch mustard greens, trimmed and chopped

Sea salt

2 or 3 very fresh chicken eggs

Smoked sea salt (such as alder smoked or smoked Maldon) and freshly ground pepper

STEP 1. Preheat the oven to 475°F/240°C/gas 9 and place a rack in the bottom third of the oven. If using a pizza stone, sprinkle a pizza peel or paddle lightly with cornmeal. If using a baking sheet, preheat it in the oven until it is very hot and then dust it with cornmeal.

STEP 2. On a well-floured work surface or the peel or paddle, sprinkle the dough and your hands with flour. Stretch the dough with your hands to make any shape of pizza you please (see Shaping Pizza Dough, page 213), roughly 12-in/30.5-cm round or oblong, stretching the edges lightly to form a circle, oval, or rectangle that is evenly thin throughout the middle. Carefully transfer the dough to the prepared pizza paddle or hot baking sheet with both hands.

STEP 3. Top the pizza with the cheddar cheese.

STEP 4. If using a pizza stone, slide the pizza onto the hot stone and place it in the oven. If using a baking sheet, place the hot baking sheet in the oven. Bake until the pizza is pale golden and starting to look crispy, about 8 minutes.

STEP 5. Meanwhile, heat the olive oil in a large skillet over medium heat. Add the mustard greens and cook until wilted, about 3 minutes. Season with sea salt.

STEP 6. Open the oven door quickly, pull out the rack, and crack the eggs over the center of the pizza. Bake until the egg whites are set and the yolks are still slightly soft, 5 to 7 minutes. Spread the mustard greens evenly over the pizza. Drizzle with more olive oil, if desired, and sprinkle with smoked sea salt and pepper. Serve warm.

little meals

This chapter is full of small meals with indulgent flavors, satisfying in their own right, but light enough to sneak in between other, larger feasts. Think of it as lunch, any time of day.

Mostly these are healthful, fast meals, some hot and some cold. These are the meals I serve my friends, vegetarian or otherwise, on a Sunday afternoon, like Stuffed Buckwheat Crêpes (PAGE 72) with spinach and Gruyère cheese. They're plates, like Romesco Vegetable Platter (PAGE 80) and Tomato, Feta, and Red Pepper Cazuela (PAGE 68), that you'd be proud to serve to someone special right from the kitchen counter, but just as likely to dish up for yourself on a quiet night after work, with a pile of warm pitas.

All these meals make absolute heroes of vegetables, grains, and beans. And the recipes include techniques, like making an omelet or perfect paper-thin crêpes, that I hope you'll learn to do in your sleep but never stop reinventing with your own favorite combinations.

Here you'll find flavor—fresh, spicy, hot, warming, deep, cooling—that bring your table to life, little plate by little plate.

HUMMUS

In some parts of the world, hummus is worthy of the word *meal*. I first experienced this kind of hummus at the many Middle Eastern restaurants in New York City, where there are whole menus made of warm platters of hummus with various enticing toppings. It opened my eyes that while the cold hummus we enjoy with pita chips or crudités is good, it's only a glimmer of what hummus can be in all its glory. This breed of hummus is creamy, unctuous, and exotic. A proper hummus should start with homemade cooked chickpeas that are puréed together while the chickpeas are still warm, which makes a world of difference. But since we all cheat now and then when pressed for time, quality canned chickpeas will do the trick, especially if it gets this sustaining dish on your table a little more often. Warm them slightly in a bit of water on the stovetop before you begin.

SERVES A CROWD

One 1-lb/455-g bag dried chickpeas, soaked overnight and cooked (see page 273), or 6 cups/985 g canned chickpeas, rinsed and warmed

1 cup/250 g tahini

3 garlic cloves, smashed

¾ cup/180 ml extra-virgin olive oil

Juice of 1 lemon

1 tsp za'atar, or ½ tsp dried marjoram and ½ tsp dried thyme

Sea salt

Plain Greek yogurt for dolloping

Finishing oil for drizzling

1 tsp sweet paprika

¼ cup/7 g finely chopped fresh parsley

Warmed or toasted pita bread for serving

STEP 1. Combine the chickpeas, tahini, garlic, olive oil, lemon juice, and za'atar in a food processor and process until smooth, about 5 minutes. (Add a bit of the cooking liquid or water as needed to reach your desired consistency.) Taste and season with salt.

STEP 2. Spoon the hummus into a shallow serving bowl while still slightly warm. Top with a dollop of Greek yogurt and drizzle with finishing oil. Sprinkle the paprika and parsley over the top. Serve with warmed pita bread.

COOK'S NOTE. When you make hummus from scratch, it's worth it to make a lot, but this recipe can be easily halved. Even if you just plan to make half the recipe, go ahead and soak and cook a whole bag of chickpeas and use any remainders in Spring Vegetable Paella (page 204) or Lentil-Chickpea Burgers with Harissa Yogurt (page 138).

ROASTED BROCCOLI, KALE, AND CHICKPEAS WITH RICOTTA

At Il Maialino in New York City, where I've spent many Sundays brunching with friends, the pastry and coffee are addictively good. But it's a plate of crispy, roasted broccoli and kale topped with a poached egg that was on special one Sunday that I can't stop thinking about. I've made a dozen versions of it since, usually with Lacinato kale (though any kale will do) and broccoli or broccolini, sometimes topped with a soft-cooked egg, other times garnished with milky fresh ricotta. I've landed on this version—amped up with chickpeas and red pepper flakes, which as a midday meal is just right.

SERVES 2 TO 4

1 bunch broccolini, or broccoli, cut into thin florets

1 bunch Tuscan or Lacinato kale, stemmed and cut into 2-in/5-cm pieces

1½ cups/240 g cooked chickpeas (see page 273) or canned chickpeas, drained and rinsed

1 clove garlic, thinly sliced

¼ cup/60 ml extra-virgin olive oil

Fleur de sel or Maldon sea salt

1 lemon, cut into wedges

8 oz/250 g fresh ricotta cheese

Freshly ground black pepper

Pinch of crushed red pepper flakes

Finishing oil for drizzling

STEP 1. Preheat the broiler to high. Toss the broccolini, kale, chickpeas, and garlic with the olive oil. Season lightly with fleur de sel and divide between two rimmed baking sheets. Broil each sheet, tossing halfway through cooking, until the kale is crispy and the broccoli just tender and charred but still bright green, about 5 minutes, rotating the trays top to bottom if two don't fit side by side in your oven. Squeeze the juice from two lemon wedges all over the top and toss together.

STEP 2. Divide between two to four small plates and top each with a dollop of ricotta. Sprinkle the ricotta with black pepper and red pepper flakes and drizzle each plate with finishing oil. Serve warm or at room temperature, with more lemon wedges for squeezing over the top.

GREEN BEANS WITH TOMATOES, ONIONS, AND GIGANTES BEANS

Everyone needs one simple but stunning one-pot dish in their repertoire. This is mine. It's easier than you could ever imagine something with so much flavor to be. It starts with crisp green beans, blanched, then cooked quickly in an oniony-tomato sauté that mingles with olive oil into a round, savory broth—perfect for sopping up with a loaf of crusty bread. Serve plenty. It's a real beauty, sprinkled with feta, and served straight from a Dutch oven.

This little meal is particularly memorable with peak-season green beans and tomatoes that are ripe with summer flavor and juice, but even in the off season, with canned butter beans and Campari tomatoes (the small, deep red and juicy gems that have become supermarket fixtures), it's a treat.

SERVES 2 TO 4

1 lb/455 g green beans, trimmed

¼ cup/60 ml extra-virgin olive oil

1 onion or shallot, thinly sliced

1 garlic clove, thinly sliced

1 lb/455 g tomatoes, chopped or quartered if small

15.5 oz/440 g Gigantes or butter beans, rinsed and drained

6 oz/170 g feta cheese

Freshly ground pepper

1 lemon, wedged

1 baguette or another crusty bread for serving

STEP 1. Bring a large pot of salted water to a boil. Set a bowl of ice water next to the sink. Add the green beans to the boiling water and cook until bright green and crisp-tender, 2 to 3 minutes. Transfer them to the ice water with a slotted spoon, drain, and pat dry.

STEP 2. Heat the olive oil in a Dutch oven or a large skillet over medium heat. Add the onion and garlic and cook to soften, 5 minutes. Add the tomatoes and cook until they release their juices, 2 minutes more. Stir in the Gigantes and blanched green beans and cook to warm through. Break the feta over the top and sprinkle with freshly ground pepper. Serve straight from the Dutch oven, or spoon into shallow bowls, with lemon wedges and crusty bread.

CAPRESE
FOR FOUR SEASONS

A Caprese salad is always a welcome addition to the table. Though the one we know best is based on sensational tomatoes and fresh mozzarella, it's not a salad to reserve for summer alone. The same principles apply to a plate of luxurious pea mash with fresh burrata and mint, topped with olive oil and a few bursting crystals of salt, or a winter plate of lentils and mozzarella dressed with a mustardy herb dressing. Serve it with beets and swap out the burrata cheese for ricotta, and you have another easy fall favorite. And, of course, relish that summer classic every moment tomatoes are in season.

SPRING

PEA MASH WITH BURRATA AND MINT

SERVES 2 TO 4

10 oz/280 g fresh or frozen peas

¼ cup/60 ml extra-virgin olive oil

2 balls burrata (see Cook's Note) or fresh mozzarella cheese, halved, at room temperature

Finishing oil for drizzling

Handful fresh mint leaves, torn

Sel gris and freshly ground pepper

Thin baguette slices for serving (optional)

STEP 1. Bring a medium saucepan three-fourths full of salted water to a boil over high heat. Add the peas and cook until bright green and just cooked, about 2 minutes. Drain, reserving about ⅓ cup/75 ml of the cooking liquid. Purée the cooked peas, the reserved cooking liquid, and the olive oil with an immersion blender or food processor to create a slightly chunky purée.

STEP 2. Spoon the warm purée onto two to four plates. Top with the burrata and a drizzle of finishing oil. Top with mint and sprinkle with sel gris and pepper. Serve warm with baguette slices.

COOK'S NOTE. Burrata is like mozzarella, but with a creamier, almost custard-like center that melts on the plate and in your mouth. If you can't find it locally, use the freshest mozzarella you can find. For the best flavor, serve burrata or mozzarella at room temperature.

HEIRLOOM TOMATOES WITH BURRATA

SERVES 2 TO 4

5 lbs/2.3 kg heirloom or beefsteak tomatoes

Sea salt and freshly ground pepper

2 balls burrata (see Cook's Note, page 63) or fresh mozzarella cheese, torn into bite-size pieces, at room temperature

¼ cup/60 ml extra-virgin olive oil

1 tsp Dijon mustard

2 tbsp red wine or apple cider vinegar

Handful fresh basil leaves, torn, or 1 to 2 tbsp finely chopped fresh chives

2 tbsp toasted pine nuts (see page 273)

STEP 1. Slice the tomatoes into thick rounds or wedges or a combination of both. Season with salt and pepper and arrange on a platter with the burrata.

STEP 2. Whisk together the olive oil and mustard in a small bowl. Gradually whisk in the vinegar until a smooth dressing forms. Drizzle the dressing generously over the tomatoes. Top with basil and the pine nuts. Serve at room temperature.

BEETS AND RICOTTA

SERVES 2 TO 4

2 large roasted beets (see page 264)

Best-quality extra-virgin olive oil for drizzling

Fleur de sel or sel gris and freshly ground pepper

2 Cara Cara or navel oranges, peeled and sliced crosswise into thick rounds or cut into segments

Handful raw shelled pistachios

½ cup/125 g fresh ricotta cheese

Handful fresh mint leaves, torn

STEP 1. Peel and quarter the beets and put in a medium bowl. Drizzle with olive oil and season with fleur de sel and pepper.

STEP 2. Arrange the beets on a plate with the oranges and pistachios. Dollop the ricotta cheese on top of the beets and oranges, drizzle with more olive oil, and top with mint. Serve warm or at room temperature.

LENTILS AND MOZZARELLA

SERVES 2 TO 4

¼ cup/60 ml plus 2 tbsp extra-virgin olive oil

1 garlic clove, minced

1 stalk celery, finely chopped

1 carrot, peeled and finely chopped

1 cup/185 g green or brown lentils, rinsed

Sea salt

½ tsp Dijon mustard

2 tbsp red wine vinegar or apple cider vinegar

Handful assorted fresh herbs such as dill, chives, basil, or mint, finely chopped

Freshly ground pepper

1 cup/510 g fresh bocconcini mozzarella, torn, or mozzarella, sliced

Coarse sea salt for sprinkling

2 tbsp toasted pine nuts (see page 273)

STEP 1. Heat the 2 tbsp olive oil in a medium saucepan. Add the garlic, celery, and carrot and cook over medium heat until fragrant, about 6 minutes. Add the lentils, ½ tsp sea salt, and just enough water to cover. Bring to a boil, reduce the heat to low, and simmer until just soft, 30 to 35 minutes. Drain the lentils.

STEP 2. Meanwhile, pulse together the mustard, vinegar, and herbs in a food processor or blender, or whisk together by hand. Drizzle in the remaining ¼ cup/60 ml olive oil and pulse or whisk to bring together. Add ¼ tsp sea salt and season with pepper. Taste and add more salt as needed.

STEP 3. Spoon the warm lentils onto plates. Top with the mozzarella and sprinkle the mozzarella with coarse sea salt. Top the lentils and mozzarella with the pine nuts and drizzle with the herb vinaigrette. Serve warm or at room temperature.

SPRING

PEA MASH
WITH BURRATA
AND MINT

WINTER
LENTILS AND
MOZZARELLA

FALL
BEETS AND RICOTTA

SUMMER
HEIRLOOM TOMATOES
WITH BURRATA

TOMATO, FETA, AND RED PEPPER CAZUELA

This is the kind of dish you should learn to make by heart. By any other name, this is baked feta. Put it in a cazuela, or a small oven-to-table casserole dish, and you have a filling lunch or first course served with toasted pita. Naturally, this is superb with summer tomatoes, but it will also improve the washed-out winter tomatoes that may have found their way onto your kitchen counter. Improvise and improve to your own liking as you go, and this dish will never let you down.

_____ SERVES 4 _____

One 1-lb/455-g block feta cheese

2 plum tomatoes, coarsely chopped

2 roasted red bell peppers (see page 269), cut into thin strips or bite-size pieces

4 thin strips lemon or orange zest

12 to 16 oil-cured black olives

Freshly ground pepper

¼ cup/60 ml extra-virgin olive oil

Whole-wheat pita or flatbread (see page 133) for serving

STEP 1. Preheat the oven to 425°F/220°C/gas 7.

STEP 2. Break the feta into large chunks and place in four 8-oz/225-g square or oval baking dishes or cazuelas or one large cazuela. Top with the tomatoes, bell peppers, lemon zest, and olives. Season with pepper and drizzle with the olive oil. Cover each baking dish with aluminum foil and place them on a rimmed baking sheet. Bake until warmed through, about 20 minutes, removing the foil after 15 minutes to let the cheese brown on the top.

STEP 3. Meanwhile, place the pita on an open flame on the stove top, turning with long metal tongs, until toasted and warmed on all sides. Cut or tear into wedges. Place each baking dish on a plate or set a larger dish in the center of the table. Serve warm with the pita.

HERBED GOAT CHEESE OMELET
WITH CHERRY TOMATO CRUSH

Herbed goat cheese is a smart shortcut for an omelet, one I would have never considered until I had my friend Megan Palmer's amazing frittata. Since an omelet is easier and faster to make for one, it's a go-to meal for breakfast or lunch. This one is easy to learn and make by heart, again and again. It's based on threes: three eggs, three minutes to cook the leeks, another three minutes to cook the eggs, and a final three minutes to burst the tomatoes. Give it a go.

--- SERVES 1 ---

3 large eggs

1 tbsp extra-virgin olive oil

Heaping handful red and yellow Sweet 100s
   or cherry tomatoes

1 tbsp unsalted butter

1 small leek, white and pale green parts,
   trimmed, cleaned, and thinly sliced
   (see page 266)

3 thin spears asparagus, trimmed and thinly
   sliced on the diagonal (optional)

Sea salt and freshly ground pepper

1 tbsp herbed goat cheese

STEP 1. Crack the eggs into a medium bowl and whisk vigorously until light and frothy.

STEP 2. Heat the olive oil in a small skillet. Add the tomatoes and cook until the skins are toasted, about 2 minutes. Add a splash or two of water, cover, and cook until most of the tomatoes burst, about 1 minute more. Remove from the heat.

STEP 3. Melt the butter in another small nonstick skillet over medium-low heat. Add the leek and asparagus to the pan and cook, stirring occasionally, until soft, about 3 minutes. Season with salt and pepper.

STEP 4. Add the eggs to the skillet with the leeks and asparagus and let them set a little to cook, about 1 minute. Gently push one edge of the eggs to the center of the pan with a heat-proof flexible spatula, tilting the pan to allow any liquid to flow underneath. Repeat two or three times around the edges of the omelet, until most of the eggs are set and the omelet looks like a bright yellow pancake.

STEP 5. Loosen the omelet from the edges of the pan with your spatula so that it will slide out of the pan easily later. Add the goat cheese to half of the omelet and cover with a lid until it melts, about 30 seconds. Lift one edge of the omelet with the spatula and fold it over the other half so that the curved edges line up in a half-moon. Gently slide the omelet into a plate and garnish with the cherry tomatoes. Serve warm.

TURKISH EGGS
WITH OLIVES

Since my first spoonfuls, I have always loved eggs. As an eater and feeder of a mostly vegetarian diet, eggs are even more revered as a source of iron, omega-3s, and protein. But I love them most of all for their versatility. There seems to always be new and even better ways to learn to enjoy them, like *menemen*, or Turkish scrambled eggs, my latest favorite. The plump olives, salty feta, and barely sweet tomatoes make a splendid meal from simple eggs.

SERVES 2 TO 4

2 tbsp extra-virgin olive oil, plus 1 tsp

3 green onions, finely chopped

2 red or green bell peppers, seeded and roughly chopped

3 firm, ripe tomatoes, coarsely chopped

1 tsp red pepper flakes

Whole-wheat pita or flatbread (see page 133) for serving

6 large eggs

½ tsp sea salt

Freshly ground black pepper

Handful fresh parsley leaves, finely chopped

4 oz/115 g sheep's milk feta cheese, broken into chunks

Green olives such as Cerignola or Castelvetrano for serving

STEP 1. Heat the 2 tbsp olive oil in a medium skillet over medium heat. Add the green onions and cook until soft, about 3 minutes. Raise the heat to medium-high, add the bell peppers, and continue cooking until soft, about 5 minutes. Add the tomatoes and red pepper flakes and continue cooking until some of the liquid from the tomatoes has evaporated, about 10 minutes.

STEP 2. Meanwhile, place the pita on an open flame on the stove top, turning with long metal tongs, until toasted and warmed on all sides. Cover loosely to keep warm.

STEP 3. Crack the eggs into a medium bowl and whisk vigorously until light and frothy. Add the remaining 1 tsp olive oil to the pan. Add the eggs and let them set a little to cook, 2 to 3 minutes. Scoot them back and forth every now and then with a heat-proof spatula until they are just cooked into large curds, but still a touch runny, about 3 minutes. Add the salt and season with black pepper. Remove from the heat, stir in the parsley, and sprinkle the feta over the top.

STEP 4. Serve hot with green olives and the pita.

STUFFED BUCKWHEAT CRÊPES

Learning to make a flawless sweet or savory crêpe is, bar none, one of the best skills I can think of for anyone who loves to cook and eat. I've listed my favorite seasonal and savory fillings for stuffed crêpes (see facing page), but first, you must master the crêpe itself. Begin with the classic combination of caramelized onions, Gruyère cheese, and spinach, and crowned it with a fried egg.

Since crêpes keep well overnight but need to be filled and heated up one at a time, it's worth making them in advance and stuffing them as the craving strikes.

MAKES 12 CRÊPES

¾ cup/90 g all-purpose flour

½ cup/70 g buckwheat flour

Heaping 1 tbsp sugar

¼ tsp sea salt

1⅔ cups/405 ml whole milk, plus 1 tbsp if needed

⅓ cup/75 ml water

4 tbsp melted unsalted butter, plus more for the pan

3 large eggs, lightly beaten, plus 12 eggs, fried over easy (see page 272)

2 cups/300 g caramelized onions (see page 266)

24 oz/720 g Gruyère or your other favorite cheese, grated

11 oz/310 g fresh baby spinach

STEP 1. Whisk together the all-purpose flour, buckwheat flour, sugar, and salt in a large bowl. Combine the milk, water, melted butter, and beaten eggs in a blender or in a bowl with an immersion blender and purée until smooth. Gradually add the flour mixture, continuing to purée, until the batter is smooth and the consistency of heavy cream, about 2 minutes more. Let rest for at least 15 minutes at room temperature or up to overnight, covered, in the fridge.

STEP 2. Preheat a nonstick crêpe pan or 8-in/20-cm skillet over medium-high heat until hot. To test, splash a drop of water onto the pan; it should sizzle. Add a little melted butter to the pan.

STEP 3. Scoop a scant ¼ cup/60 ml of the batter onto the hot pan, twirling the pan to coat the bottom with a thin, even layer of batter. (An offset spatula can help you work more quickly if you don't trust the twist of your wrist.) The batter should start cooking rather quickly. If not, raise the heat slightly. If the batter is browning too quickly, reduce the heat slightly. The first crêpe is usually a temperature test, so don't worry if it doesn't come out perfectly. My first one never does!

STEP 4. After about 1 minute, the crêpe should be bubbling along the sides. Shake the pan slightly to flip the crêpe; it should release easily. If needed, loosen the crêpe slightly with an offset or thin nonstick spatula along the edges, pick up an edge of the crêpe with your fingertips, and flip it. Toast it on the second side for about 30 seconds, then slide the crêpe onto a plate.

(Taste the first crêpe. It should be light, thin, and crisp only on the edges and in the occasionally toasty bubble that appears along the surface, not at all doughy or thick. If needed, thin the batter slightly with up to 1 tbsp milk.)

STEP 5. Repeat until all the batter is used, adding more melted butter to the pan as needed (it's usually not necessary if using a nonstick pan). Be sure to stir the batter every few minutes. Stack the crêpes on a plate as you cook them (in between parchment paper if you're making them more than a few hours in advance) and cover loosely to keep warm.

STEP 6. Wipe out the crêpe pan or skillet and heat over medium heat. Add a little melted butter to the pan and place the plain crêpe in the pan. Fill the middle with ¼ cup/25 g caramelized onions and 2 oz/60 g Gruyère. Add a handful of spinach and fold the crêpe in at four sides to make a stuffed square pouch. Flip to melt the cheese, brown and seal the folded edges, and steam the spinach.

STEP 7. Top the stuffed crêpe with a fried egg and serve warm. Repeat with the remaining crêpes, filling and cooking them one at a time, frying the eggs as you go.

COOK'S NOTE. You may need to adjust the amount of batter it takes to make a perfect crêpe depending on the size of your pan—it takes about ¼ cup/60 ml to cover the bottom surface of an 8-in/20-cm skillet, but I need closer to ⅓ cup/75 ml for my flat 11-in/28-cm nonstick crêpe pan. Adjust accordingly.

Crêpes and filling can be stored separately, refrigerated, for up to 5 days.

STUFFED CRÊPES FOR ALL SEASONS

When I asked seasoned cooks and vegetarians their favorite fillings for crêpes, I was amazed at all the delicious ideas they came up with. Here are many combinations to play with.

- roasted asparagus and robiola cheese
- grilled zucchini and onions with Jarlsberg cheese
- mashed potatoes and sautéed wild mushrooms
- radicchio, roasted cauliflower, and Gorgonzola cheese
- caramelized onions, arugula, wild mushrooms, and Brie cheese

- ratatouille
- ricotta cheese and lemon zest
- avocado, crème fraîche, and caramelized onions
- scrambled egg white, spinach, and feta cheese
- figs, Gorgonzola cheese, and caramelized onions

KIMCHI PANCAKES

There are two great reasons to make Kimchi Pancakes. First, you now have a recipe for homemade kimchi—and once your fridge is full of the addictive stuff, you'll want to put it in everything. And second, it's also a great excuse to eat pancakes more often. These savory pancakes are flavored with kimchi and green onions and get their structure from flour, egg, and seltzer water. Some Korean pancakes have seafood like shrimp or squid in them. If you eat fish, try them with easy-to-find, sustainable frozen halibut (defrosted, of course). The big chunks of fish are a tender complement to the spicy, tangy kimchi.

―――――――――――――――――― SERVES 2 TO 4 ――――――――――――――――――

½ cup/115 g Kimchi (page 250) or purchased kimchi

4 green onions, white and light green parts; trimmed, dark green parts reserved

SOY DIPPING SAUCE

¼ cup/60 ml soy sauce

¼ cup/60 ml rice vinegar

4 green onions, dark green parts, thinly sliced (reserved from green onions above)

1 cup/125 g all-purpose flour

1 large egg, lightly beaten

¾ cup/180 ml seltzer water

1 tsp toasted sesame oil

½ tsp sea salt

5 oz/140 g halibut, chopped; or shrimp, peeled and deveined, chopped (optional)

2 tbsp vegetable oil

STEP 1. Drain the kimchi in a colander, pressing with a wooden spoon to get out as much liquid as possible. Chop the kimchi.

STEP 2. Quarter the white and light green parts of the green onions lengthwise and cut into 2-in/5-cm lengths.

STEP 3. *To make the Soy Dipping Sauce:* Stir together the soy sauce and rice vinegar in a small serving bowl. Sprinkle the sliced green onions on top.

STEP 4. Whisk together the flour, egg, seltzer, sesame oil, and salt in a large bowl. Add the kimchi, halibut (if using), and the quartered green onions and stir together.

STEP 5. Heat 1 tbsp of the vegetable oil in a medium nonstick skillet over medium-high heat until shimmering. Pour half of the batter evenly into the skillet, spreading it into an even layer with a flexible spatula. Cook until the bottom is deep golden and crispy around the edges, about 4 minutes. Carefully flip the pancake and continue to cook until the second side is golden and cooked through, about 3 minutes more. Transfer to a plate lined with paper towels. Repeat with the remaining batter, adding the remaining 1 tbsp oil to the skillet.

STEP 6. Cut the pancakes into wedges. Serve hot with the dipping sauce.

VEGETABLE TEMPURA

Vegetable tempura is not vegetables posing as health food. It is vegetables, sleek and slender, donning an ethereal batter and announcing themselves as insanely delicious. Calorie counting is beside the point. You will get almost any vegetable-phobe to eat things they never dreamed of this way. Treat yourself to a meal of tempura and the Somen Noodle Bowl with Broccolini and Bok Choy (page 166), two sushi-house favorites that are easy to re-create at home.

--- SERVES 4 TO 6 ---

TENTSUYU DIPPING SAUCE
2 tsp unbleached raw sugar
2 tbsp rice vinegar
½ cup/120 ml soy sauce or tamari
½ cup/120 ml dashi (see page 166) or vegetable stock (see page 270)
Water as needed

Peanut oil for frying

TEMPURA BATTER
1 large egg
¾ cup/180 ml cold seltzer water
¾ cup/90 g cake or all-purpose flour
¼ tsp baking powder
Sea salt

2 lbs/910 g assorted vegetables such as:
- Handful okra, halved lengthwise
- ¼ butternut, delicata, or other winter squash, peeled, seeded, and sliced paper thin
- 1 small sweet potato, peeled and sliced paper thin
- 1 small zucchini, sliced on a diagonal
- 1 Japanese eggplant, sliced on a diagonal
- Handful broccoli florets
- 1 bunch asparagus, trimmed
- Handful sugar snap peas, trimmed

Sea salt

STEP 1. *To make the Tentsuyu Dipping Sauce:* Whisk together the sugar and rice vinegar until the sugar dissolves. Stir in the soy sauce and dashi. Taste and add a splash of water if the sauce needs diluting.

STEP 2. Before you begin frying, have everything you'll need handy. Set up a wire rack over a baking sheet lined with paper towels and set tongs, a slotted spoon, and a splatter guard (if you have one) near the stove.

STEP 3. In a large, deep frying pan, heat 4 in/10 cm of peanut oil over medium heat until it reaches 350°F/180°C on a deep-fry thermometer.

STEP 4. *To make the Tempura Batter:* While the oil heats, crack the egg into a medium bowl and whisk vigorously until light and frothy. Gradually whisk in the seltzer. Whisk together the flour, baking powder, and a generous pinch of salt in a large bowl. Make a well in the center of the flour mixture and whisk in the seltzer-egg mixture until it forms a thin, runny batter, like a crêpe batter.

CONTINUED

STEP 5. Check the oil temperature: It should be just under 350°F/180°C; it will drop slightly as you add the vegetable pieces. To test, spoon a drop or two of the batter into the pan; the oil should sizzle, and the batter brown slowly and evenly.

STEP 6. Working in batches, dip the vegetable pieces in the batter and turn to coat. The thin batter will just coat the vegetables. Carefully lower the coated vegetables with tongs into the hot oil. Fry until the batter puffs and is crisp and golden, 40 seconds to 2 minutes, depending on the vegetable. Flip the vegetables in the oil with a slotted spoon and continue cooking until they are evenly golden, about 1 minute more. Be sure to cover the pan with a splatter guard to protect yourself from hot oil as it pops and sizzles. Transfer the tempura to the rack over the baking sheet with a slotted spoon. Season with salt while the tempura is still warm so the salt sticks. Taste and season with more salt as desired. Repeat, whisking the batter from time to time, until all the vegetables are fried, coating the vegetables in batter as you go. Serve hot with the dipping sauce as you finish frying each batch.

GRILLED SUMMER VEGETABLES
WITH SPICY MISO BUTTER

If you've ever had the pleasure of eating grilled vegetables in a fine Japanese restaurant, you'll know what a thrill they can be—each piece the perfect size for savoring with chopsticks, a glorified version of itself, slightly charred by the hibachi or grill. The best version I've ever had were dressed with a combination of miso and green onion, as I have here, which gives a salty, umami flavor that makes vegetables taste like something you shouldn't be allowed to eat a whole plateful of—only you *can*.

This dish uses the same dipping sauce as the Kimchi Pancakes. For a feast among friends, divide the vegetables between four, or even six, small plates and pair with Kimchi Pancakes. Or serve these veggies with steamed sushi rice as a meal for two.

SERVES 2

SPICY MISO BUTTER

2 tbsp unsalted butter, at room temperature

1 tbsp yellow miso

½ tsp grated peeled fresh ginger

½ tsp toasted sesame oil

½ to ¾ tsp sambal oelek

2 green onions, trimmed and white and light green parts finely chopped

Peanut or vegetable oil for the grill and the vegetables

1 bunch thick asparagus, trimmed and cut into thirds

Sea salt and freshly ground pepper

1 eggplant, halved lengthwise and cut into bite-size pieces

2 green onions, trimmed and cut into thirds

2 portobello mushrooms, cleaned, trimmed, and cut into bite-size pieces

10 large shiitake mushrooms, cleaned, trimmed, and halved

1 zucchini, halved lengthwise and cut into bite-size pieces

Soy Dipping Sauce (page 74)

STEP 1. *To make the Spicy Miso Butter:* Beat the butter and miso together with a wooden spoon in a small bowl. Stir in the ginger, sesame oil, and ½ tsp of the sambal oelek. Stir the chopped green onions into the miso butter. Taste the miso butter; if you like more heat, add the remaining ¼ tsp sambal oelek.

STEP 2. Prepare a gas or charcoal grill to cook over medium heat, or preheat a grill pan on the stove top over medium heat until hot. Rub the grill grates (see page 259) or the grill pan with peanut oil.

STEP 3. Toss the asparagus with a little peanut oil in a large bowl, season with salt and pepper, and set aside. Continue tossing the remaining vegetables, one at a time, with the peanut oil and seasoning them with salt and pepper. Working in batches, grill the vegetables, starting with the eggplant (which takes longer to cook), then the green onions, mushrooms, zucchini, and the asparagus. Arrange the vegetables on the grill so they don't touch, ensuring that they cook evenly and get a nice char. Grill the vegetables until tender-crisp and lightly charred, turning once or twice, 6 to 8 minutes (a few more minutes for eggplant). Brush the vegetables generously with miso butter on both sides during the last 2 minutes of cooking. Or, if you're going casual, transfer the grilled vegetables to a bowl and toss them in the miso butter.

STEP 4. Stack the vegetables in groupings on a platter to share, or divide the vegetables between two plates. Serve warm or at room temperature with the dipping sauce.

COOK'S NOTE. There's enough miso butter for extra vegetables, so if you buy your vegetables in bigger batches, cook them all. Toss leftovers with the miso butter and serve over rice with chopped peanuts on top.

ROMESCO VEGETABLE PLATTER

Technically, romesco is more of a sauce than a meal, but made from scratch and served with a combination of roasted and raw vegetables, it is more often a main event in my kitchen. Here's the bad news: A true Catalan romesco sauce, based on roasted red peppers and garlic with a touch of tomato, bread crumbs, and olive oil, requires a few steps. The good news is that it's remarkable in flavor, color, and aroma. Make a big batch, which can keep for a day or two and also be served as an accoutrement for sandwiches, seafood, and every vegetable you love.

_____ SERVES 4 _____

2 to 3 sweet-hot dried peppers such as ancho or nyora

2 cups/480 ml boiling water

4 roasted red bell peppers (see page 269)

1 cup/240 ml extra-virgin olive oil

½ cup/70 g almonds

2 tbsp whole-wheat or white bread crumbs, preferably fresh

2 garlic cloves, coarsely chopped

1 firm, ripe plum tomato, coarsely chopped

2 tbsp sherry vinegar

Fine sea salt and freshly ground black pepper

2 lb/910 g assorted raw and roasted vegetables such as raw radicchio or Treviso leaves, roasted cauliflower, roasted carrots (see page 111), and roasted asparagus

STEP 1. Snap off the stems of the dried peppers, shake out the seeds, and put the peppers in a large bowl. Pour the boiling water over the dried peppers. Cover the bowl and let the dried peppers soften, about 20 minutes.

STEP 2. Drain the softened peppers and discard the liquid. Combine the softened peppers, roasted red peppers, olive oil, almonds, bread crumbs, garlic, tomato, and sherry vinegar in a food processor and process until mostly smooth, about 2 minutes. Add ½ tsp salt, season with black pepper, and pulse to blend. Taste and add additional salt as needed.

STEP 3. Keep the romesco at room temperature until ready to use, or store in an airtight container in the fridge for up to two days. Serve the romesco slightly warm or at room temperature (never cold or straight from the fridge) with assorted raw and roasted vegetables for dipping, or toss together and serve on a plate as lightly composed salad.

LECSÓ

Being married to a Hungarian, I have the joyful responsibility of uncovering Hungary's national dishes on each and every trip to the homeland. There are so many notable tastes there that I've learned to love, but none more than lecsó—a satisfying stew of onion, peppers, and tomatoes that's loaded with the heady aroma of rich paprika. If there is one meal we always eat when we're in Hungary, it is lecsó. And when we miss Hungary, it is lecsó I cook, serving it over thick slabs of rustic brown bread—if it is bread with flecks of caraway, all the better. It is great served warm or cold (though I prefer it warm), and because it keeps well for days in the fridge or freezer, I always make a big batch.

Lecsó couldn't be simpler to prepare. The trick is finding the right peppers. Hungarian long green peppers are most like banana peppers or Italian frying peppers, thin and crunchy, and melt into the stew. I always use Hungarian paprika for this dish because of the round, rich flavor and depth it lends.

SERVES 2 TO 4

3 tbsp extra-virgin olive oil

1 large yellow onion, thinly sliced

4 long banana, or Italian frying peppers, seeded and thinly sliced

1 small, hot Hungarian pepper, seeded and thinly sliced

Sea salt

5 large firm, ripe tomatoes, chopped

2 tbsp Hungarian sweet paprika

½ tsp Hungarian hot paprika

Freshly ground pepper

Buttered whole-grain bread for serving

Heat the olive oil in a large skillet over medium heat. Add the onion and cook, stirring occasionally, until soft and just golden brown, about 6 minutes. Add all the peppers, stir to coat with the oil, and season with salt. Cook the onion and peppers, stirring often, until they soften and seem to melt together, about 10 minutes. Stir together the tomatoes and both paprikas in a medium bowl and add them to the vegetables in the skillet. Continue cooking, seasoning with salt and black pepper and stirring often, until everything is soft, a roasted red color, and deeply flavored, about 10 minutes more. Serve warm over buttered bread.

GREEK LEMON AND PASTA SOUP

In the Greek neighborhood of Astoria, Queens, *trahanas* soup is a staple on nearly every menu. Whether sweet (*glykos*) or sour (*ksinos*), *trahanas* is thought to be an ancient pasta, made from durum wheat and milk, which is then soured and dried; it gives a toothsome tang to many Greek soups and stews. It sounds exotic, but I assure you it's as adoptable as the little pastina or star pastas you loved in your soup as a kid.

Like any regional specialty, the exact recipe for Greek Lemon and Pasta Soup varies from region to region, house to house, so tweak as desired to find the right balance (to add more tang, add lemon; for a softer flavor, add milk; if you like it saltier, add cheese; to up the heat, add pepper).

SERVES 4

4 cups/960 ml vegetable stock (see page 270)
    or water

1 cup/85 g sweet trahanas pasta
    (see Cook's Note)

½ lemon

2 tbsp extra-virgin olive oil

⅔ cup/165 ml whole milk

Sea salt and freshly ground pepper

6 oz/170 g feta cheese, crumbled

Finishing oil for drizzling

Smoked paprika for seasoning

STEP 1. Bring the stock to a boil in a large soup pot over medium-high heat. Add the pasta, reduce the heat to medium-low, and simmer until tender but still al dente, about 15 minutes. The soup should still be brothy.

STEP 2. Squeeze the juice from the lemon half and reserve. Throw the squeezed lemon rind into the pot with the broth, reduce the heat to low, and keep warm. Add the olive oil, milk, and reserved lemon juice. Season with salt and pepper. Taste and add more salt and pepper as needed. Keep warm over a low flame until you are ready to serve.

STEP 3. Ladle the soup into bowls, discarding the lemon half. Sprinkle with the feta, drizzle with finishing oil, and season with a dash of smoked paprika. Serve warm.

COOK'S NOTE. You can find *trahanas* in international markets as well as online; it's worth the small fee to ship them (see Sources, page 279). If you can't find *trahanas*, stir 1 cup/85 g cooked and drained pastina into the seasoned broth just before the feta. It will soak up too much liquid if you cook it in the broth.

MUSHROOM–ALMOND MILK SOUP

Mushroom soup devotees know that cream is the secret to a luxurious soup. But here's my secret: I make mushroom soup with almond milk, which complements the round creamy mushroom flavor and has less fat than soup made with cream. So far, no one has been any the wiser.

SERVES 4 TO 6

2 tbsp extra-virgin olive oil

1 garlic clove, minced

1 large leek, white and pale green parts, trimmed, cleaned (see page 266), and coarsely chopped

1 stalk celery with leaves, coarsely chopped

8 oz/225 g shiitake and/or oyster mushrooms, cleaned, trimmed (see page 266), and thinly sliced

8 oz/225 g button or cremini mushrooms, cleaned and thinly sliced

¼ cup/50 g basmati rice

4 cups/960 ml mushroom stock (see page 270) or vegetable stock (see page 270)

2 to 2½ cups/480 to 600 ml unsweetened almond milk

1 tsp sea salt

STEP 1. Heat the olive oil in a large soup pot over medium heat. Add the garlic, leek, and celery and cook until soft, about 2 minutes. Add all the mushrooms and continue cooking until the mushrooms begin to brown and release their liquid, about 5 minutes.

STEP 2. Add the rice and stock to the pan and bring to a simmer. Cover and cook until the rice is tender, about 20 minutes. Reduce the heat to your stove's lowest setting and add the almond milk to heat through. Add the salt and stir to combine. Transfer to a blender in batches or use an immersion blender to process until smooth. Return to the pot and keep warm over a low flame until you are ready to serve. Ladle the soup into bowls and serve warm.

PEA SOUP WITH RYE CROUTONS
AND CHIVE BLOSSOMS

In the spring, East Coast chefs and foragers go nutty for wild ramps. Their pink bulbs are roasted, pickled, and primped over on every New York chef's spring menu. Around the same time ramps appear, last season's chives return to the garden almost before you remember they were there, growing up tall alongside your tender sweet peas. On top, chives' delicate purple blooms pack a sweet oniony punch that I sprinkle recklessly over every salad and this, the simplest of pea soups, the week they both arrive. For me, chive blossoms are the gardener's ramp, the promise of spring you can cultivate simply by putting a few seeds in the ground, and the perfect complement to this luscious, rye crouton-topped pea soup.

───────────────── SERVES 4 ─────────────────

1 tbsp extra-virgin olive oil

2 thick slices whole-grain rye bread, cut into small cubes

Sea salt and freshly ground pepper

Fresh chives with blossoms for scattering

2¾ cups/660 ml vegetable stock (see page 270) or water

10 oz/280 g fresh or frozen peas

¼ tsp wasabi powder or paste (optional)

¾ cup/180 ml full-fat plain yogurt

Finishing oil for drizzling

STEP 1. Heat the olive oil in a small skillet over medium heat. Toss the bread cubes in the oil, turning with tongs or a heat-proof spatula to toast on all sides, about 4 minutes. Season with salt and pepper. Transfer to a plate to cool. (You can make these up to one day in advance; just be sure to cool completely and store in an airtight container.)

STEP 2. Pull the chive blossoms from the chives and chop the green shoots.

STEP 3. Heat the stock in a large soup pot over high heat until simmering. Add the peas and cook until bright green and just cooked, 8 to 10 minutes. Remove from the heat and use an immersion blender or transfer the soup to a blender in batches to process until smooth, about 3 minutes. Add the wasabi (if using) and season with salt and pepper. Add the yogurt and process until smooth and slightly creamy, 2 to 3 minutes. Return to the pot and keep warm over a low flame until you are ready to serve.

STEP 4. Ladle the soup into bowls, top with croutons, and drizzle with finishing oil. Season with pepper and scatter the chopped chives and their blossoms generously over the top. Serve warm.

COOK'S NOTE. Rye flour packs a decent amount of iron and B6, two hard-to-come-by nutrients for vegetarians. We all know we're not going to get our daily allowance of iron and B6 from a few buttery-rye croutons, but they taste especially nice floating atop this bright bowl of soup, so don't skimp on them here.

CARROT SOUP
WITH CHIVES AND POPCORN

At the world's greatest restaurants, the soup, no matter how simple it is, is always garnished in a way that makes it seem so much greater than the sum of its parts. And usually, it is. This soup is the perfect example of how easy it can be to do that at home. A simple carrot soup, inspired by a hearty bunch of young carrots from the garden, came together one night in my kitchen right before popcorn and a movie. A few plucky kernels made their way to the top of the soup, along with chives and a drizzle of olive oil, and the memorable little combo stuck. This is now our house carrot soup.

SERVES 4 TO 6

2 tbsp olive oil

1 yellow onion, thinly sliced

1 garlic clove, smashed

One 1-in/2.5-cm piece peeled fresh ginger, chopped

2 lbs/910 g carrots, peeled and coarsely chopped

4 to 5 cups/960 ml to 1.2 L vegetable stock (see page 270) or water

1 sprig fresh thyme (optional)

Sea salt and freshly ground pepper

2 cups/480 ml fresh carrot juice

1 to 2 tbsp extra-virgin olive oil (optional)

Finishing oil for drizzling

½ cup/120 ml full-fat plain yogurt

Handful popped popcorn

3 to 4 tbsp chopped or snipped fresh chives

STEP 1. Heat the olive oil in a large soup pot over medium heat. Add the onion and cook, stirring occasionally, until soft and translucent, 6 to 8 minutes. Add the garlic and ginger and cook until fragrant, about 1 minute. Add the carrots, enough stock to cover (4 cups/960 ml if you like a thicker soup, 5 cups/1.2 L if you like yours thinner), and the thyme (if using) and bring to a boil. Season with salt and pepper. Cover loosely and reduce the heat to low.

STEP 2. Simmer until the vegetables are completely tender, 20 to 30 minutes. Remove the thyme and discard. Transfer the soup to a blender in batches or use an immersion blender to process until smooth, about 3 minutes. Return to the pot and stir in the carrot juice with a wooden spoon, reheating over a low flame if needed to warm through. Taste and season with salt and pepper. Stir in the extra-virgin olive oil, if desired. Keep warm over a low flame until you are ready to serve.

STEP 3. Ladle the soup into bowls and drizzle with finishing oil. Top with a dollop of yogurt, a couple of popped popcorn kernels, and a sprinkle of chives. Serve warm.

COOK'S NOTE. Fresh herbs make everything better, especially soup, which is the best advertisement for growing them at home. If you have thyme in your windowsill garden, throw it into this soup. If you don't, skip the expense.

KABOCHA SQUASH SOUP
WITH SPICED FENNEL BUTTER

Kabocha, a fall and winter squash whose flavor is akin to pumpkin or sweet potato, makes a mighty good soup, one that even squash-soup naysayers are bound to find inviting. You can use any of your favorite fall or winter squashes for this dish, with equal success. This vitamin A–rich purée is topped with big flavors of spiced fennel butter, which takes its cue from Indian cuisine, and harissa, which adds a note of heat when drizzled over the soup.

—————————————— SERVES 4 TO 6 ——————————————

One 2½- to 3-lb/1.2- to 1.4-kg kabocha squash, peeled, seeded, and cut into cubes

2 tbsp extra-virgin olive oil

Sea salt and freshly ground pepper

1 tbsp unsalted butter

1 yellow onion, coarsely chopped

1 bay leaf

1 to 2 tbsp Hungarian hot-pepper paste or Harissa (page 253)

4 cups/960 ml vegetable stock (see page 270) or water

SPICED FENNEL BUTTER

1 tsp fennel seeds

2 tbsp unsalted butter

2 tbsp finely chopped fresh parsley

1½ to 2 tsp fresh lemon juice

About ½ cup/120 ml Greek yogurt or crème fraîche

STEP 1. Preheat the oven to 400°F/200°C/gas 6. Toss the squash with the olive oil and 1 tsp salt in a large bowl, season with pepper, and spread out on a baking sheet. Roast until almost fork-tender, 30 to 35 minutes.

STEP 2. Heat the butter in a large soup pot over medium heat. Add the onion and bay leaf and cook, stirring occasionally, until the onion is soft and translucent, 7 to 10 minutes. Stir in 1 tbsp of the pepper paste. Add the stock and ½ tsp salt and bring to a boil. Add the roasted squash, along with any juices and oils from the baking sheet, and simmer until the squash is completely tender and the flavors have developed, about 15 minutes.

STEP 3. Remove the bay leaf and discard. Remove the soup from the heat and use an immersion blender or transfer the soup to a blender in batches to process until smooth, 2 to 3 minutes. Taste and season with salt and pepper. (Adjust to your desired consistency with a little more warm broth or water.) Keep warm over a low flame until you are ready to serve.

STEP 4. *Meanwhile, make the Spiced Fennel Butter:* Toast the fennel seeds in a small dry skillet over medium heat. Transfer the seeds to a spice grinder or mortar and pestle and crush; or transfer the seeds to your cutting board and crush with the flat side of your knife. Melt the butter in the skillet over medium heat until fragrant, light brown, and toasty, about 2 minutes. Add the fennel seeds back to the pan and swirl over the heat for 1 minute more. Remove from the heat and add the parsley. Set aside near the stove top to keep warm, reheating over low heat just before serving if needed.

STEP 5. Just before serving, stir $1\frac{1}{2}$ tsp of the lemon juice into the soup. Taste and add up to $\frac{1}{2}$ tsp more lemon juice if needed. Ladle the soup into bowls. Top with a dollop of yogurt and a touch of the remaining pepper paste and drizzle with warm spiced fennel butter.

CELERY ROOT SOUP
WITH APPLE BUTTER

Often in a puréed vegetable soup, the cream is gratuitous. I almost never use it. But celery root, either in a purée or a soup, begs a little pour of heavy cream or half-and-half, which makes it so rich and pleasurable to eat. If you don't eat dairy, make this rich and creamy with homemade cashew cream. Swap out celery root for cauliflower to keep this winter soup a staple in your repertoire.

SERVES 4

2 tbsp extra-virgin olive oil

1 yellow onion, thinly sliced

2 garlic cloves, minced

2 tsp grated peeled fresh ginger

¼ tsp turmeric

⅛ tsp roasted or toasted ground cinnamon (see Cook's Note)

2 parsnips, peeled, cored, and coarsely chopped

1 large tart apple such as pippin or Macoun, peeled, cored, quartered, and coarsely chopped

1 large celery root, peeled and coarsely chopped

4 cups/960 ml vegetable stock (see page 270) or water

Sea salt and freshly ground pepper

1 to 2 cups/240 to 480 ml heavy cream, half-and-half, or cashew cream (see page 274)

Apple butter for dolloping

Finishing oil for drizzling

Aleppo pepper for sprinkling (optional)

STEP 1. Heat the olive oil in a large soup pot over medium heat. Add the onion and cook, stirring occasionally, until soft and translucent, 5 to 8 minutes. Add the garlic, ginger, turmeric, and cinnamon and cook until fragrant, about 1 minute. Add the parsnips, apple, celery root, and stock and bring to a boil. Season with salt and pepper. Cover loosely and reduce the heat to low. Simmer until the vegetables are completely tender, 25 to 35 minutes. Remove the soup from the heat and let cool slightly.

STEP 2. Use an immersion blender or transfer the soup to a blender in batches to purée until smooth, about 4 minutes. Return the soup to the pot. Taste and season with salt and pepper. Add 1 cup/240 ml of the heavy cream and stir to combine. Taste and add up to 1 cup/240 ml more heavy cream, if desired. Keep warm over a low flame until you are ready to serve.

STEP 3. Ladle the soup into bowls and top with a dollop of apple butter. Drizzle with finishing oil and season with a pinch of Aleppo pepper, if desired. Serve warm.

COOK'S NOTE. In many cuisines, whole spices are toasted before grinding for a more robust flavor. Some spice companies now sell roasted or toasted cinnamon and ginger, both fuller in flavor, which I use when I can find it. You'll also have great results with regular ground cinnamon.

YELLOW TOMATO GAZPACHO

Yellow tomatoes are milder and less acidic than most red ones, and often so good you could eat them by the bucketful. Blend them with your best olive oil and pair with the summer's best peaches, which give a subtle sweet note to balance the peppery refreshing brilliance of a classic summer gazpacho.

SERVES 4 TO 6

CROUTONS

1 tbsp extra-virgin olive oil

3 to 4 thick slices white or sourdough bread,
    cut into small cubes

Sea salt and freshly ground pepper

4 large firm, ripe orange and yellow tomatoes,
    coarsely chopped

6 fresh basil leaves, plus handful small fresh
    basil, lemon basil, or opal basil leaves

1 or 2 garlic cloves, coarsely chopped

Sea salt

1 seedless cucumber, peeled and finely chopped

1 lb/455 g firm, ripe heirloom tomatoes,
    finely chopped

1 small purple onion or shallot, finely chopped
    (optional)

1 red or yellow bell pepper, seeded and
    finely chopped

2 firm, ripe peaches, peeled (see page 226)
    and finely chopped

Finishing oil for drizzling

Freshly ground black pepper

STEP 1. *To make the Croutons:* Heat the olive oil in a small skillet over medium heat. Toss the bread cubes in the oil, turning with tongs or a heat-proof spatula to toast on all sides, about 4 minutes. Season with salt and pepper. Transfer to a plate to cool. (You can make these up to 1 day in advance; just be sure to cool completely and store in an airtight container.)

STEP 2. Combine the orange and yellow tomatoes, basil, garlic, and salt in a large bowl. Cover and refrigerate for 30 minutes. Chill the individual serving bowls.

STEP 3. To finish the soup, remove the basil from the chilled tomato mixture and discard. Transfer the mixture to a blender or use an immersion blender to process until frothy and smooth, 2 to 3 minutes.

STEP 4. Ladle the soup into the chilled bowls and mound a bit of the cucumber, heirloom tomatoes, onion (if using), bell pepper, and peaches in the center. Top with small basil leaves and the croutons. Drizzle with finishing oil and season with salt and black pepper. Serve cold.

ROASTED TOMATO BISQUE

Sometimes, there's no improving on a classic, like tomato soup and grilled cheese sandwiches. Cooking tomatoes not only makes tomato bisque taste warming and familiar, but also boosts their nutritional value by raising the levels of lycopene—the beneficial antioxidants that make most tomatoes red. This is especially delicious with a little creamy something to thicken the soup and soften the tomatoes' acidity. Use almond milk, heavy cream, or half-and-half, all welcome additions. When grilled cheese is not in season (wink), a dense, chewy olive bread is my sidekick of choice for this soup.

SERVES 4

Extra-virgin olive oil for the baking sheets and the vegetables

5 large tomatoes or 7 plum tomatoes, quartered

Sea salt and freshly ground black pepper

½ tsp Hungarian sweet paprika, plus more for seasoning

1 red or orange bell pepper, seeded and quartered

2 large yellow onions, quartered

4 garlic cloves, smashed

2½ cups/600 ml warm vegetable stock (see page 270) or water (see Cook's Note)

½ to 1 cup/120 to 240 ml almond milk, heavy cream, or half-and-half

Finishing oil for drizzling

Parmigiano-Reggiano cheese for shaving

STEP 1. Preheat the oven to 400°F/200°C/gas 6. Brush two rimmed baking sheets with olive oil. Spread the tomatoes out on one of the baking sheets, season with salt, black pepper, and the ½ tsp paprika. Toss the bell pepper and onions with olive oil in a large bowl, season with salt and black pepper, and spread out on the second baking sheet.

STEP 2. Put the baking sheets in the oven. After about 5 minutes, add 2 garlic cloves to each baking sheet. Continue to roast the vegetables until they are soft and just starting to caramelize, 25 to 35 minutes, stirring the vegetables about halfway through cooking.

STEP 3. Transfer the vegetables to a large soup pot and add the stock. Use an immersion blender or transfer to a blender in batches to process until smooth, about 3 minutes. Add ½ cup/120 ml of the almond milk and stir to combine. Taste and add up to ½ cup/120 ml more almond milk, and season with salt and more paprika, if needed. Keep warm over a low flame until you are ready to serve.

STEP 4. Ladle the soup into bowls and drizzle with finishing oil. Shave Parmigiano-Reggiano over the top with a vegetable peeler. Serve warm.

COOK'S NOTE. Homemade vegetable stock lends richness and flavor to any soup. But sometimes even water can do the trick, especially with strong flavors like the ones in this soup. As always, start with clean, filtered water and add a pinch of sea salt.

GRILLED CHEESE

You don't really need a recipe to make grilled cheese, but here's a gentle suggestion for how to make one you'll never forget. The best grilled cheese sandwiches are made with fresh, flavorful bread, a rich melty cheese or a combination of melting cheeses (like cheddar, Muenster, fontina, or Gruyère), and plenty of butter. Use a hot cast-iron pan or griddle, and make sure it's evenly hot. Slather one side of each slice of bread with butter, making sure to spread it all the way to the edges so that the bread browns evenly. Layer the cheese on the unbuttered sides, being sure to let a little overhang the edge, which will ooze out the side. Press the cheese sides together, and lay the sandwich on the hot pan. Resist the temptation to press down on your sandwich with your spatula. Let it cook until evenly golden brown and delightfully crispy. Flip the sandwich, and cover with a pot lid until the bread is irresistibly golden and the cheese is melted from edge to edge.

salads & sides

If it's vegetables you crave, this chapter is loaded with the season's best, casually composed in combinations that weaken any reluctance to eating greens. In these pages, "salad" is a far more delicious thing than the word alone could conjure. There is so much to explore, from nutty farro studded with root vegetables (see PAGE 114) to a veggie-rich potato salad with nourishing heaps of leafy greens (see PAGE 113).

Let these recipes inspire and empower you to get footloose and fancy-free with your seasonal loot and transform any freshly plucked vegetable into a stunning meal, brimming with flavor. The whole idea here is to become enamored with vegetables (and grains), to learn to play up their strengths—the bite of a barely cooked carrot in Moroccan Carrot Slaw (PAGE 121), the give of a subtly sweet roasted rutabaga tossed in butter and herbs. It's very hard to eat just one plate of Braised Butternut Squash with Saffron and Smoked Salt (PAGE 124) or share even a bite of the reinvented wedge salad (see PAGE 112)

All of these salads and sides deserve a spot on any restaurant menu, though I promise you'll master them at home on your first try.

THE ITALIAN CAESAR
(CHICORY, DANDELION, LITTLE GEM, ANCHOVY, CROUTONS)

There is good Caesar salad, and then there is lick-the-fork-good Caesar salad. This one is built on the unexpected combination of chicory, dandelion, and Little Gem lettuces. Choose any greens you want—greens with substance, bite, and beautiful shapes or a classic and crispy head of romaine—what really matters is how fully flavored your dressing is. Then go for the gusto with the croutons, which really must be homemade. I make them with a rustic sourdough sesame loaf—my go-to bread for croutons with great flavor, but your favorite rustic breads will give homemade croutons a superior crunch to anything you'll find that's premade.

SERVES 4

CROUTONS

2 tbsp extra-virgin olive oil

½ loaf pugliese or Italian peasant bread, cut into bite-size chunks

Sea salt

DRESSING

1 garlic clove

Sea salt and freshly ground pepper

1 large egg

2 salt-packed anchovies

1 tsp Dijon mustard

Juice of ½ lemon

1 to 2 tsp Tabasco sauce

½ cup/120 ml extra-virgin olive oil

¼ cup/30 g freshly grated Parmigiano-Reggiano cheese

1 small bunch dandelion greens, trimmed and torn into bite-size pieces

½ head chicory, torn into bite-size pieces

2 heads Little Gem, 1 head Bibb, or 1 heart of romaine lettuce, torn into bite-size pieces

½ cup/60 g freshly grated Parmigiano-Reggiano cheese for sprinkling

STEP 1. Bring a small pot three-fourths full of water to a boil over high heat.

STEP 2. *To make the croutons:* Heat the olive oil in a large skillet over medium heat. Working in batches, toss the bread cubes in the oil, turning with tongs or a heat-proof spatula to toast on all sides, about 7 minutes. Season with salt.

STEP 3. *To make the dressing:* Rub the garlic clove all over the inside of a large wooden salad bowl. Smash the remainder of the garlic clove on your cutting board, add a pinch of salt, and make a paste (see page 265). Set aside.

STEP 4. Drop the egg into the boiling water to sterilize it (a little food safety measure) and quickly remove it with a slotted spoon. Crack the egg and separate the yolk from the white, reserving the white for another use.

STEP 5. Combine the anchovies, egg yolk, mustard, lemon juice, Tabasco, and garlic paste in a blender and purée until smooth, about 2 minutes. While the blender is running, gradually pour in the ½ cup/120 ml olive oil until a smooth dressing forms. Transfer the dressing to the salad bowl, stir in half of the Parmigiano-Reggiano, add ½ tsp salt, and season with pepper.

STEP 6. Add the dandelion, chicory, and lettuce to the bowl with the dressing, and toss together until the leaves are evenly coated. Divide among plates, top with croutons, and sprinkle with Parmigiano-Reggiano cheese. Serve immediately.

COOK'S NOTE. Completely drying your washed greens for every salad, particularly this one, is essential. You want every crevice to lock in the flavor of anchovy, egg, and Parmigiano-Reggiano, the magic trio that characterizes Caesar's classic, addictive flavor.

GREEK SALAD

The best Greek salads are little more than fresh and crispy chunks of cucumber and tomato, savory chunks of feta, and olives the size of your thumb. It is a different breed of Greek salad than the bowls of liberally dressed greens and crumbles of feta that bear the same name. A true Greek salad is equal parts crunch, flavor, and satisfying salty cheese—bite-size cubes mingling in luscious oil. Start with the best-quality feta, olives, and olive oil you can find and be generous with all. For the best flavor and contrast, use a bell pepper and cucumber that are crisp and cold straight from the fridge, and make sure your tomatoes and feta are at room temperature.

─────────────────────── SERVES 2 ───────────────────────

1 green bell pepper, chilled

1 cucumber, chilled

2 large firm, ripe tomatoes

1 small red onion or large shallot

6 oz/170 g Greek or Bulgarian sheep's milk feta cheese, at room temperature, broken into bite-size pieces

1 tsp dried oregano

Heaping handful unpitted kalamata or your favorite black olives

Finishing oil for drizzling

Freshly ground black pepper

Red wine vinegar for sprinkling

STEP 1. Start with cold, crisp bell pepper and cucumber straight from the fridge. Seed the bell pepper and cucumber and cut them into bite-size pieces. Cut the tomatoes into bite-size pieces and thinly slice the onion. Toss together with the feta and oregano in a medium bowl.

STEP 2. Divide the salad between plates or bowls. Top with a few kalamata olives, drizzle with finishing oil, and sprinkle with black pepper and vinegar. Serve cold and offer a little bowl to collect the olive pits.

CHOPPED CSA-BOX SALAD
WITH TORN MOZZARELLA

If you are of the belief that the best salads should require very little to no work, then this salad is for you. It makes something brilliant out of the gleanings of your CSA (Community Supported Agriculture) box (see page 279), whatever the season. In late summer, for example, enjoy the snap of tiny, fresh green beans, juicy bell peppers, and lush knobs of mozzarella with a bracing bite of tender spring onions. No fancy dressing or whisking necessary here, just olive oil, sea salt, and freshly ground pepper.

—————————————————— SERVES 1 TO 2 ——————————————————

Contents of your CSA box

4 hard-boiled large eggs

1 ball fresh mozzarella cheese

Finishing oil for drizzling

½ lemon

Coarse sea salt and freshly ground pepper

Pick up your CSA box and put out everything on the counter. Pick out three or four of the freshest fun-to-eat raw vegetables (say haricots verts, spring onions, and bell peppers), and chop them all up into bite-size pieces (trim and chop the green beans, slice the onions, chop the peppers, for example). Add some halved or quartered hard-boiled eggs and tear the mozzarella over the top. Drizzle with finishing oil, add a squeeze of fresh lemon juice, and toss it all together in your favorite salad bowl. Season with salt and pepper. Pull out a fork or two, and share with a friend or devour the whole vibrant bowl on your own.

RAW KALE AND STRAWBERRY SALAD

For a gardener and a health nut, I was a late adapter to the raw kale salad. I nibbled raw kale in the garden and drank it juiced with pear and lemon. But the kale salad as an easy, everyday art form didn't enter my repertoire until I started writing this book. I'm proof: It's never too late!

There are two things about kale that make it a rock star in the salad world. First, for just 20 calories per handful, kale delivers higher doses of vitamins A and C than most other vegetables, which means you can have lots of it. That's great news because it's also easy to grow. Second, kale salads get better when dressed overnight. The secret is to massage the greens in luxe olive oil and sea salt, which coats every bit in flavor and softens the otherwise overtly chewy leaves. In season, I add deep red, locally grown strawberries for even more pulsating flavor and vitality. Make the salad ahead, or keep extra (sans strawberries) in the fridge in an airtight container for up to two days. Add the strawberries just before serving.

—————————————— SERVES 2 TO 4 ——————————————

1 bunch kale, stemmed

¼ cup/60 ml extra-virgin olive oil

Juice of 1 lemon

¼ tsp sea salt

Freshly ground pepper

Handful ripe, fresh strawberries, halved

Wash and dry the kale and tear into bite-size pieces. Toss together the kale with the olive oil and lemon juice in a large bowl. Add the salt, season with pepper, and toss again. Massage the kale, squeezing and rubbing the leaves together with your hands, working the oil, lemon juice, salt, and pepper into the leaves to flavor and tenderize them. Toss with the strawberries. Serve at room temperature.

KALE AND KIMCHI SALAD

Once you've fallen in love with kale salad, you'll likely want to change it up from time to time. I came up with this version the day after I'd finished the last of my homemade kimchi (see page 250). I drizzled a little leftover kimchi liquid over oil-massaged kale and added crunchy sunflower seeds and salty ricotta salata, giving my everyday kale salad just the fire it needed to make it new again.

———————————————— SERVES 2 TO 4 ————————————————

1 bunch kale, stemmed

¼ cup/60 ml extra-virgin olive oil

¼ tsp sea salt

1 to 2 tbsp kimchi liquid (see headnote)

¼ cup/20 g sunflower seeds

Ricotta salata or pecorino cheese for grating

Wash and dry the kale and tear into bite-size pieces. Toss together with the olive oil in a large bowl. Add the salt and toss again. Massage the kale, squeezing and rubbing the leaves together with your hands, working the oil and salt into the leaves to flavor and tenderize them. Transfer to a large serving bowl and toss with about 1 tbsp of the kimchi liquid and sunflower seeds. Taste and add more kimchi liquid for extra heat and flavor if desired. Grate ricotta salata generously over the top with a vegetable peeler and toss together. Serve at room temperature.

BUTTERMILK FRIED TOFU SALAD WITH GREENS AND ASPARAGUS

This salad is an intriguing celebration of spring, with arugula, pan-roasted asparagus, and fried tofu tossed in classic buttermilk dressing (think ranch). The tofu takes its cues from all-American buttermilk fried chicken, featuring a crispy cornmeal crust with the heat and flavor from cayenne and za'atar, a Middle Eastern spice blend made from marjoram, oregano, thyme, and sesame seeds. The tofu takes on an almost crouton-like role but yields to the tooth beautifully. Tofu-phobes, this salad is for you.

SERVES 4

Extra-virgin olive oil for the pan

1 bunch asparagus, trimmed

Sea salt

3 to 4 tbsp fine cornmeal

1 tbsp all-purpose flour

1 tsp za'atar

Pinch of cayenne pepper

Freshly ground black pepper

One 14-oz/400-g package firm tofu, drained and patted dry, cut into 1¼-in/3.25-cm cubes

5 oz/140 g arugula

1 head Belgian endive, leaves separated

2 inner stalks celery with leaves, thinly sliced

2 green onions, finely chopped

¾ cup/180 ml Buttermilk Chive Dressing (page 251), plus more for serving

STEP 1. Heat a thin layer of olive oil in your largest frying pan or cast-iron skillet over medium heat. Add the asparagus with half the stalks pointing one way, half the other way, so that they aren't touching and are in an even layer. Season with salt. Fill up the pan with water so that it goes halfway up the asparagus. Cook over medium-high heat until the asparagus is bright green and tender-crisp, about 5 minutes. Transfer to a plate and let cool completely while you prepare the rest of the salad.

STEP 2. Discard the water and wipe the frying pan dry. Whisk together the cornmeal, flour, za'atar, cayenne, a pinch of salt, and a pinch of black pepper in a shallow bowl.

STEP 3. Line a plate with paper towels and set near the stove. Heat another thin layer of olive oil in the frying pan over medium heat. To test the oil, spoon a drop or two of cornmeal mixture into the pan; the oil should sizzle.

STEP 4. Working in batches, lightly dust the tofu cubes in the cornmeal mixture, tossing to coat and shaking off any excess. Add the tofu to the hot oil with a slotted spoon, making sure that none of the pieces touch. Fry until the tofu cubes are golden with a thin crust on most sides, turning as needed, about 8 minutes. Lift the fried tofu out of the oil with the slotted spoon, letting the oil drip back into the pan, and transfer to the paper towel–lined plate. Taste and season with salt and pepper, if needed, while the tofu is still warm so the salt and pepper stick. Repeat until all the tofu cubes are fried, coating the tofu in the cornmeal mixture as you go and adding more oil to the pan as needed.

STEP 5. Toss together the asparagus, arugula, endive, celery, green onions, and about ¹/₂ cup/ 120 ml of the buttermilk dressing in a large bowl. Taste and add up to ¹/₄ cup/60 ml more dressing if desired. Divide the salad among plates or bowls and top with the fried tofu cubes. Serve with extra dressing on the side.

COOK'S NOTE. Pan-roasting, as done in this recipe, is a fast way to roast asparagus, and it doesn't require turning on the oven just for a few stalks. But I also often use my toaster oven to roast, because it heats up and cools down quickly, and it's the perfect size when you need to roast just a few things.

WATERMELON, CUCUMBER, AND AVOCADO SALAD WITH RICOTTA

In the summer, I can't imagine anything better than crisp, juicy watermelon, fresh cucumber, and creamy avocado bathing together in a bowl of peppery finishing oil. The simplicity of this breezy salad doesn't negate the attention to detail required. The watermelon and cucumber should be cool, if not downright cold, and the avocado perfectly ripe. Be sure to play up the peppery finish with the freshly ground pepper and olive oil.

Lavish dollops of fresh ricotta or shaved ricotta salata are like gilding the lily, especially if you're lucky enough to have access to a great locally made cheese. As for presentation, you can make this salad into art by pulling out your best knife skills and cutting everything into perfect cubes. I'm more likely to chop haphazardly, in a rush to get these intoxicating ingredients straight to my plate.

SERVES 4

8 oz/225 g seedless red or yellow watermelon or sugar baby watermelon, chilled

1 large seedless cucumber, chilled

2 firm, ripe avocados, peeled and pitted

1⅓ cups/195 g ricotta salata cheese or 1⅓ cups/335 g fresh ricotta, at room temperature

Finishing oil for drizzling

Flaked sea salt such as Maldon and freshly ground pepper

Start with cold watermelon and cucumber straight from the fridge. Cut the watermelon, cucumber, and avocados into bite-size cubes and arrange artfully on a platter or toss them loosely together in your favorite salad bowl. Shave ricotta salata over the top or dollop with fresh ricotta and drizzle with finishing oil. Season with salt and pepper. Serve cold.

RADISH SALAD
WITH AGED PARMESAN

This is the radish salad that I mentioned in the introduction of this book. Like an inviting plate of raw radishes with coarse sea salt and good butter, this casual first course hardly needs a recipe. But consider this a nudge to plant radishes, buy them, and eat them in every form as they pop up row by row from April to June. When the bulbs are peppery fresh and exploding with their illustrious crunch, quarter your favorite round radishes (globe or Cherry Belles) and throw them in a bowl. Thinly slice another variety or two (black or watermelon radishes). Toss them with young heirloom carrots, your best olive oil, and chunky portions of aged Parmigiano-Reggiano, and take your time making it all disappear.

SERVES 2

1 black radish

1 large watermelon radish

Handful small globe, Cherry Belle, or French
   Breakfast radishes per person, quartered

4 small young heirloom carrots, scrubbed and
   cut into bite-size pieces

2 to 4 tbsp finishing oil

Fleur de sel or sel gris and freshly ground pepper

2 oz/55 g aged Parmigiano-Reggiano

Slice the black and watermelon radishes as thinly as possible with a mandoline or a very sharp knife. Toss together with the quartered radishes, carrots, and finishing oil in a large bowl and sprinkle with fleur de sel and pepper. Break the Parmigiano-Reggiano into bite-size pieces and toss together with the vegetables. Serve at room temperature in a shallow bowl or on a small platter.

RADISH, ENOKI, TANGERINE, AND AVOCADO SALAD

Sometimes a dish needs no name, just a list of ingredients that leave to your imagination how they might all come together. This is that kind of dish. It's little more than a composed plate of ingredients—some of my favorites—that eaten together one afternoon when I was at home alone became something special. This is a first course or a salad that's crispy and bright, bitter and bold, creamy and earthy, every little bite.

SERVES 4

8 Cherry Belle, globe, or French Breakfast
   radishes

4 tangerines

3 tbsp extra-virgin olive oil

Sea salt

2 heads Belgian endive, leaves separated

2 firm, ripe avocados, peeled, pitted, and
   quartered lengthwise

6 oz/170 g enoki mushrooms, cleaned and cut
   into small bunches

Freshly ground pepper

½ bunch fresh chives, chopped

STEP 1. Slice the radishes as thinly as possible with a mandoline or a very sharp knife.

STEP 2. Place a tangerine on the cutting board and cut off a little bit from both ends to create flat surfaces. Set the tangerine on one of the flat ends. Using a large, sharp knife, shave off the skin, peel, and as much of the pith as possible along the curve of the fruit. Squeeze any juices from the skin into a small bowl and reserve.

STEP 3. Working over the bowl with the juices with a sharp paring knife, hold the tangerine in your nondominant hand and use your dominant hand to cut the segment along the membrane. Cut along the opposing membrane (in a V), releasing the segment and collecting any juices and the fruit itself in the bowl below. Repeat with all the segments, then squeeze any remaining juices from the membranes and toss. Repeat with the remaining tangerines.

STEP 4. Whisk together the tangerine juice with 2 tbsp of the olive oil and a pinch of salt.

STEP 5. Arrange the endives, radishes, tangerine segments, and avocados among plates.

STEP 6. Heat the remaining 1 tbsp olive oil in a medium skillet over medium heat. Add the enoki, season with salt, and cook until crispy and brown, 3 to 4 minutes. Sprinkle the cooked enoki over the salad. Drizzle with the dressing, season with salt and pepper, and scatter with chives. Serve immediately.

COOK'S NOTE. Make this salad with oranges or clementines if you can't find tangerines.

ROASTED CARROT, HAZELNUT, AND RADICCHIO SALAD WITH HONEY AND ORANGE

One of my favorite vegetarian restaurants in New York City is Le Verdure, the vegetables-only section of the artisanal Italian food and wine marketplace Eataly. I'm fond of taking carnivores there and blowing their minds with how satisfying vegetables can be. This salad is inspired by one such experience, a late summer day when heirloom carrots had just arrived at the market. Roasted carrots have a number of consummate companions, from olives to endive to avocado. This is one lovely place to start—paired with the bitterness of blood orange and radicchio and the subtly sweet complement of honey.

——————————————— SERVES 2 TO 4 ———————————————

1 blood orange, Cara Cara orange, or tangerine

2 lb/910 g young heirloom carrots, scrubbed

3 small or 2 large shallots, quartered

4 tbsp/60 ml extra-virgin olive oil

Fine sea salt and freshly ground pepper

1 tbsp honey

1 small head radicchio, torn into bite-size pieces

¼ cup/40 g toasted hazelnuts (see page 273), coarsely chopped

Flaked sea salt such as Maldon

STEP 1. Preheat the oven to 400°F/200°C/gas 6.

STEP 2. Take two swipes of peel off the orange with a vegetable peeler and set the orange aside. Toss together the carrots, shallots, orange zest, and 3 tbsp of the olive oil in a medium bowl. Season with fine sea salt and pepper, toss again, and spread out on a baking sheet. Roast until the carrots are fork-tender, about 20 minutes.

STEP 3. Place the orange on the cutting board and cut off a little bit from both ends to create flat surfaces. Set the orange on one of the flat ends. Using a large, sharp knife, shave off the skin, peel, and as much of the pith as possible along the curve of the fruit. Squeeze any juices from the skin into a small bowl and reserve.

STEP 4. Working over the bowl with the juices with a sharp paring knife, hold the orange in your nondominant hand and use your dominant hand to cut the segment along the membrane. Cut along the opposing membrane (in a V), releasing the segment and collecting any juices and the fruit itself in the bowl below. Repeat with all the segments, then squeeze any remaining juices from the membranes and toss.

STEP 5. Whisk together the juice with the remaining 1 tbsp olive oil and the honey. Taste with a tip of radicchio; the dressing should be subtly sweet and not too bitter.

STEP 6. Arrange the radicchio on a platter. Arrange the roasted carrots, shallots, and orange segments over the radicchio and top with the hazelnuts. Drizzle with the dressing and sprinkle with flaked sea salt. Serve immediately.

WILD MUSHROOM AND LITTLE GEM SALAD

When you can get your hands on some good mushrooms, they deserve to be the star of their own show. This salad gives mushrooms a crispy platform of halved heads of Little Gem lettuces, easy to find at the farmers' market or grow in your own garden in the cool spring and fall months. That's when you're likely to find the best mushrooms, too. Top with your own homemade Buttermilk Chive Dressing for a creamy, tangy finish that's a splendid complement to the earthy mushrooms.

——————————— SERVES 4 ———————————

8 oz/225 g assorted mushrooms such as trumpet, shiitake, oyster, and cremini, cleaned and trimmed

2 tbsp extra-virgin olive oil

Sea salt and freshly ground pepper

¼ cup/15 g toasted pine nuts (see page 273)

4 heads Little Gem or baby butter lettuce, halved

About ¾ cup/180 ml Buttermilk Chive Dressing (page 251)

STEP 1. Cut the mushrooms into bite-size pieces. Heat the olive oil in a large skillet over medium heat. To test the oil, add a mushroom piece to the pan; it should hiss. Add the remaining mushrooms and cook, stirring occasionally, until they are crispy but still juicy, 4 to 6 minutes, seasoning with salt and pepper toward the end of cooking. Stir in the pine nuts and remove from the heat.

STEP 2. Toss the lettuce with the buttermilk dressing in a large bowl. Divide the salad among plates and top with warm mushrooms and pine nuts. Serve immediately.

COOK'S NOTE. When you can't find Little Gems or butter lettuce, opt for iceberg, coring and cutting it into quarters for an update on the classic wedge salad.

MORE GREENS THAN
POTATO SALAD

Vegetarian fare has often gotten a bad rap—people say it requires that one eat too much bread or potatoes to fill up. But it turns out that potatoes, in moderation, are full of vitamin C, potassium, and vitamin B6. As good as they are in a balanced diet, potatoes are still more of a starch than a vegetable, so veggie lovers will adore a potato salad that's as much about the green and red leaves as it is about the potatoes.

This modern potato salad uses healthful fats like kefir, olive oil, and avocado rather than relying on heaps of heavy mayo. Potatoes cooked whole with the skins on deliver every bit of their flavor and nutrients. Mix in a yellow bell pepper for crunch and cider vinegar for tang, and you'll find every forkful irresistible.

──────────── SERVES 4 TO 6 ────────────

2 large russet or 4 large red bliss or 4 medium
    Yukon gold potatoes, scrubbed and unpeeled

½ head red leaf lettuce

1 small bunch arugula

DRESSING

½ cup/120 ml plain kefir or full-fat plain yogurt

2 tbsp olive-oil mayonnaise

1 tbsp cider vinegar

2 tbsp extra-virgin olive oil

½ tsp cayenne pepper

¼ tsp sea salt

¼ tsp freshly ground black pepper

1 yellow bell pepper, seeded and chopped

1 firm, ripe avocado, peeled, pitted, and cut
    into bite-size pieces

STEP 1. Add the potatoes to a medium pot with enough salted water to cover and bring to a boil over medium-high heat. Cook until the potatoes are fork-tender, about 20 minutes. Drain and let the potatoes cool.

STEP 2. Meanwhile, wash and dry the lettuce and arugula well (see page 265) and tear into bite-size pieces.

STEP 3. *To make the dressing:* Whisk together the kefir, mayonnaise, vinegar, olive oil, cayenne, salt, and black pepper in a large bowl.

STEP 4. When the potatoes are cool enough to handle, cut into bite-size chunks. Add the lettuce, arugula, potatoes, bell pepper, and avocado to the dressing in the bowl and toss together. Serve at room temperature.

WARM WINTER VEGETABLES WITH FARRO

This is one of my absolute favorite salads in this book. Warm root vegetables, nutty farro, creamy yogurt, and toasty nuts flatter each other in this filling winter meal. Farro cooked like rice tastes almost buttery; toss with warm vegetables and it will satisfy to the very last grain.

─────────────────── SERVES 2 TO 4 ───────────────────

8 red or yellow baby beets, scrubbed and
    trimmed

¼ cup plus 2 tbsp/90 ml extra-virgin olive oil

Fine sea salt and freshly ground pepper

6 young heirloom carrots or baby turnips,
    scrubbed, trimmed, and halved lengthwise

1 tbsp honey

1 sprig fresh thyme

8 oz/225 g farro

6 radishes

DRESSING

¼ cup/60 ml full-fat plain yogurt

Juice of ½ lime, plus more as needed

2 tbsp finely chopped assorted fresh herbs

1 tbsp hazelnut oil

1 tbsp extra-virgin olive oil

Fine sea salt and freshly ground pepper

2 heaping handfuls arugula or baby leaf lettuce

Small handful toasted hazelnuts (see page 273)

Flaked sea salt such as Maldon

3 oz/85 g aged Parmigiano-Reggiano or pecorino
    cheese

STEP 1. Preheat the oven to 400°F/200°C/gas 6. Drizzle the beets with the olive oil and season with salt and pepper. Wrap them tightly in aluminum foil and roast until they can easily be pierced with a fork, about 20 minutes. Remove from the oven and cool in the foil.

STEP 2. Combine the carrots, honey, thyme, and 1 cup/240 ml water in a medium skillet over medium heat. Bring to a simmer and cook until the vegetables are fork-tender and the broth has reduced to a glaze, about 25 minutes. Remove from the heat and keep warm.

STEP 3. Meanwhile, put the farro in a medium pot and add enough water to cover by about 2 in/5 cm. Bring to a boil over medium-high heat, reduce to low heat, and simmer until tender, about 20 minutes. Drain.

STEP 4. When the beets are cool enough to handle, peel the skins with a paring knife and quarter. Slice the radishes as thinly as possible with a mandoline or a very sharp knife.

STEP 5. *To make the dressing:* Whisk together the yogurt, lime juice, herbs, hazelnut oil, olive oil, ¼ tsp salt, and ¼ tsp pepper in a medium bowl. Taste with a leaf of arugula; adjust the salt, pepper, or lime juice as needed.

STEP 6. Divide the farro among shallow bowls. Drain the carrots. Combine the beets, carrots, and arugula in a large bowl; toss together; and arrange over the farro. Top with the radishes, drizzle with the dressing, and sprinkle with hazelnuts and flaky salt. Generously grate or shave Parmigiano-Reggiano over the top with a vegetable peeler. Serve warm.

SUMMER
GREEN BEANS WITH YOGURT AND CINNAMON

SPRING
ASPARAGUS WITH MISO BUTTER

WINTER
BUTTERED RUTABAGA
AND OTHER WINTER
VEGETABLES

FALL
DELICATA SQUASH
WITH POMEGRANATES

ROASTED VEGETABLES
FOR FOUR SEASONS

Roasting is a fuss-free way to indulge in each diverse vegetable at its very best, no matter what the season. High-heat roasting brings out the natural sweetness in root veggies and winter squash and also accentuates the texture of summer's crisp green beans. Roasted vegetables are brilliant spooned over Blank-Slate Baked Risotto (page 172) or stuffed into buckwheat crêpes (see page 72), but they also stand on their own as wonderful sides, fit even for a holiday table. These four recipes will get you started roasting your way through the vegetable kingdom, with a little schooling in how to dress them up for dinner.

SPRING

ASPARAGUS WITH MISO BUTTER

SERVES 2 TO 4

2 bunches asparagus, trimmed

Extra-virgin olive oil for tossing

Sea salt and freshly ground pepper

MISO BUTTER

2 tbsp unsalted butter, at room temperature

1 tbsp yellow miso

½ to ¾ tsp sambal oelek

STEP 1. Preheat the oven to 400°F/200°C/gas 6. Toss the asparagus with olive oil in a large bowl and season with salt and pepper.

STEP 2. Spread the asparagus out in a single layer on a baking sheet so that they don't touch. Roast until the asparagus is tender-crisp, 12 to 15 minutes, depending on the thickness of the asparagus, turning with tongs halfway through cooking.

STEP 3. *Meanwhile, make the Miso Butter:* Beat the butter and miso together with a wooden spoon in a small bowl. Stir in ½ tsp of the sambal oelek. Taste the miso butter; if you like more heat, add the remaining ¼ tsp sambal oelek.

STEP 4. Arrange the asparagus on a small platter and top with pats of the miso butter. Serve warm.

GREEN BEANS WITH YOGURT AND CINNAMON

SERVES 2 TO 4

1 lb/455 kg haricots verts or thin green beans, trimmed

Extra-virgin olive oil for tossing

Fine sea salt and freshly ground pepper

Generous pinch of cinnamon

Fleur de sel

Plain Greek yogurt for dolloping

STEP 1. Preheat the oven to 400°F/200°C/gas 6. Toss the haricots verts with olive oil in a large bowl and season with salt and pepper. Add the cinnamon and toss again.

STEP 2. Spread the haricots verts out in a single layer on a baking sheet so that they don't touch. Roast until the beans are tender-crisp, 15 to 20 minutes. Arrange the beans on a small platter, season with fleur de sel, and top with a dollop of yogurt. Serve warm.

FALL

DELICATA SQUASH WITH POMEGRANATES

SERVES 2 TO 4

One 2-lb/910-g delicata squash, kabocha squash, or pumpkin

3 tbsp extra-virgin olive oil, plus more as needed

Sel gris or fleur de sel and freshly ground pepper

Seeds from 1 large pomegranate (see Cook's Note, page 120)

Fresh cilantro leaves for scattering (optional)

STEP 1. Preheat the oven to 400°F/200°C/gas 6. Halve the squash and scoop out the seeds. Trim the woody stem and cut each half into five or six wedges about 1¹/₂ in/4 cm thick. Do not peel the skin. Toss the squash with the olive oil in a large bowl and season with sel gris and pepper.

STEP 2. Spread out the squash wedges in a single layer on a baking sheet so that they don't touch. Roast until the squash is lightly browned and just tender, about 45 minutes, turning with tongs halfway through cooking. Remove from the oven and toss with additional olive oil if needed.

CONTINUED

STEP 3. Arrange the squash wedges on a platter and season with more sel gris. Scatter pomegranate seeds and cilantro leaves (if using) over the top. Serve warm.

COOK'S NOTE. To remove the jewel-toned pomegranate seeds from the skin and pith, slice the pomegranate in half with a sharp knife. Holding the pomegranate cut-side down over a bowl, whack the skin side rather forcefully with a wooden spoon until the seeds and some juice fall out into the bowl. Alternatively, to avoid pomegranate juice splattering over the countertop, submerge the halved pomegranate in a bowl of water and use your fingers to dislodge the seeds from the membrane and skin.

WINTER

BUTTERED RUTABAGA AND OTHER WINTER VEGETABLES

SERVES 2 TO 4

2 lbs/910 kg assorted winter vegetables such as rutabaga, parsnips, cauliflower, and carrots

2 medium red or yellow onions or 4 shallots, quartered

Extra-virgin olive oil for tossing

Sea salt and freshly ground pepper

2 tbsp unsalted butter, at room temperature

Handful fresh parsley, coarsely chopped (optional)

STEP 1. Preheat the oven to 400°F/200°C/gas 6. Prepare the rutabaga and other winter vegetables as necessary and cut into 1-in/2.5-cm chunks. Toss the vegetables and onions with olive oil in a large bowl and season with salt and pepper.

STEP 2. Spread out the vegetables and onions in a single layer on a baking sheet so that they don't touch. Roast until the vegetables are lightly browned and just tender, 45 minutes to 1 hour, turning with tongs halfway through cooking. Remove from the oven and toss with the butter and additional olive oil if needed. Arrange the vegetables and onions on a platter, season with more salt and pepper, and top with parsley (if using). Serve warm.

MOROCCAN CARROT SLAW

I've always been an enormous fan of cooked carrots, but it took me years to learn how to enjoy them raw. This is the best of both worlds: raw, grated carrots, flash-cooked and tossed with the contrasting flavors and textures of dried currants and toasted almonds and then served over toast. This is a fast first course for a rustic party centered around cheeses, breads, salads, olives, and whatever other nibbles you dream up.

SERVES 2 TO 4

1¼ lb/570 g carrots, peeled

2 tbsp extra-virgin olive oil

1 garlic clove, thinly sliced

Sea salt and freshly ground pepper

2 tbsp fresh lemon juice

2 tbsp finely chopped flat-leaf parsley

2 tbsp torn fresh mint or fresh cilantro leaves

2 tbsp dried currants

⅓ cup/30 g toasted almonds (see page 273), coarsely chopped

4 slices peasant bread, grilled or toasted (see page 261; optional)

½ cup/120 ml nonfat or full-fat plain Greek or full-fat plain yogurt

STEP 1. Grate the carrots on the large holes of a box grater over a large bowl. Heat the olive oil in a medium skillet over medium heat. Add the carrots and garlic and cook until the carrots are wilted, about 2 minutes. Remove from the heat and season with salt and pepper.

STEP 2. Toss together the carrots, lemon juice, parsley, mint, and currants in a large bowl. Top with the almonds. Serve at room temperature as a side dish, or spoon warm over toasted bread, if desired, and top with a dollop of yogurt.

COOK'S NOTE: When in season, I use Meyer lemon juice, or sometimes a combination of lemon and orange juice.

PEAS WITH TAHINI
AND YOGURT

Fresh peas, almost sing of spring. They are so sweet and green and truly alive with a flavor all their own. But here's the real truth: Even frozen peas can be fantastic. Give them surprising, nutty finish with this savory tahini dressing.

———————————————————— SERVES 2 TO 4 ————————————————————

10 oz/280 g fresh or frozen peas

Extra-virgin olive oil for drizzling

Sea salt and freshly ground pepper

DRESSING

¼ cup/60 ml full-fat plain yogurt

2 tbsp tahini

1 tbsp fresh lemon juice

2 tbsp water

Pinch of sea salt

Smoked paprika or pimentón for sprinkling

Smoked sea salt such as alder smoked or
smoked Maldon

STEP 1. Bring a medium saucepan three-fourths full of salted water to a boil over high heat. Add the peas and cook until bright green and just cooked, about 2 minutes. Drain and rinse under cold running water. Pat them dry, transfer to a small serving bowl, drizzle with olive oil, and season with sea salt and pepper.

STEP 2. *To make the Dressing:* Whisk together the yogurt, tahini, lemon juice, 2 tbsp water, and sea salt in a medium bowl.

STEP 3. Divide the peas among bowls and drizzle with the tahini dressing. Sprinkle with smoked paprika and smoked sea salt. Serve warm or at room temperature.

GRILLED ZUCCHINI WITH HAZELNUTS AND BABY BASIL

Zucchini, freshly plucked from the plant, should be bursting with water (you'll see the droplets as soon as you cut into it). On the dry heat of the grill, the fresh summer flavor is especially good. Sear in the flavor with olive oil, salt, and pepper—which is all truly fresh zucchini needs—and serve with toasted hazelnuts and basil. Dress it up a bit for company, if you like, with ricotta or mascarpone and a drizzle of hazelnut oil.

SERVES 4

3 tbsp extra-virgin olive oil, plus more for the grill and for drizzling

2 large zucchini, thinly sliced lengthwise

Coarse sea salt and freshly ground pepper

Juice of ½ lemon

¼ cup/60 g fresh ricotta or mascarpone cheese (optional)

½ cup/70 g toasted hazelnuts (see page 273), coarsely chopped

Leaves from 2 sprigs fresh baby basil, lemon basil, or globe basil

Hazelnut oil for drizzling (optional)

STEP 1. Prepare a gas or charcoal grill to cook over medium-high heat, or preheat a grill pan on the stove top over medium-high heat until hot. Rub the grill grates or the grill pan with olive oil (see page 259).

STEP 2. Toss the zucchini with the olive oil in a large bowl and season with salt and pepper. Add the zucchini to the grill. Cook until tender-crisp and lightly charred, about 8 minutes, turning once.

STEP 3. Arrange the zucchini on a platter. Drizzle with the lemon juice, and top with a dollop of ricotta (if using), the hazelnuts, and basil. Drizzle with hazelnut oil or more olive oil, if desired. Serve warm or at room temperature.

BRAISED BUTTERNUT SQUASH
WITH SAFFRON AND SMOKED SALT

This recipe happened by accident one winter day when all that remained of my in-house stash of vegetables was a single butternut squash. The pantry supplied some rather exceptional ingredients (saffron and smoked salt) for elevating this humble squash to something new and quite pleasing. The tender, amber-colored butternut squash flecked with ruby saffron is especially lovely when served as a first course to a winter feast.

SERVES 4

One 1½-lb/680-g butternut squash, peeled, halved, and seeded

Generous 2 pinches of saffron threads

Fine sea salt

Extra-virgin olive oil for drizzling

Zest and juice of ½ lime

Smoked sea salt such as alder smoked or smoked Maldon

Freshly ground pepper

STEP 1. Cut the squash into slices about ½ in/12 mm thick. Place the squash and saffron in a shallow saucepan with just enough water to cover the squash. Season with fine sea salt, but only lightly, because the big wow will come from the smoked salt at the end.

STEP 2. Cut a round piece of parchment paper that just fits inside the circumference of the pan and set it on top of the water. Bring the water to a boil over medium-high heat, reduce the heat to medium-low, and simmer until the squash is just tender, 20 to 25 minutes.

STEP 3. Transfer the squash to a platter with a slotted spoon, reserving the broth for soup or stock. Drizzle with olive oil and top with the lime zest and juice. Season with smoked sea salt and pepper. Serve warm.

CONFIT FRENCH BEANS

Despite my utter devotion to fresh fruits and vegetables, I have a secret love affair with frozen peas and beans, especially the buffet-style Frenched green beans that all but melt when they are cooked in water, salt, and an opulent pour of olive oil. Feeling lavish one day with a new bottle of my best extra-virgin olive oil, I drenched my stash of frozen beans and let them bubble slowly on the stove, transforming them into a confit of sorts. They are *Frenched* beans, after all. This is as delicious as it is ridiculous, my foray into the art of highbrow-lowbrow vegetables.

―――――――――――――――――― SERVES 4 ――――――――――――――――――

1 lb/455 g frozen French-cut green beans

1 cup/240 ml water

¾ cup/180 ml extra-virgin olive oil

¼ tsp fine sea salt

Smoked sea salt such as alder smoked or smoked Maldon

Combine the green beans, water, olive oil, and fine sea salt in a small pan or skillet over medium heat and bring to a simmer. Cover loosely, leaving enough air for the green beans to stay bright green, and continue cooking until the beans are tender, about 15 minutes. Transfer to your most elegant platter with a slotted spoon. Sprinkle the smoked salt over the top. Serve warm.

CRISPY SMASHED CREAMER POTATOES
WITH ROSEMARY

These home fries–meet–boiled potatoes are a hybrid of beloved potato textures. Boiling the potatoes highlights their creamy insides, which take on a golden, crunchy skin when oven-fried in olive oil and salt. Serve with sofrito for an indulgent appetizer.

SERVES 4

1 lb/455 g red creamer or Ruby Crescent
fingerling potatoes

3 tbsp extra-virgin olive oil

Fine sea salt and freshly ground pepper

2 sprigs fresh rosemary

10 garlic cloves, peeled

Sofrito (page 256) for dolloping (optional)

STEP 1. Preheat the oven to 450°F/230°C/gas 8. Add the potatoes to a medium pot with enough salted water to cover and bring to a boil over medium-high heat. Cook until the potatoes are fork-tender, about 20 minutes. Drain and let the potatoes cool until easy to handle. Pat very dry with paper towels. Smash each potato on a cutting board with your fist or a small frying pan to make it flat.

STEP 2. Spread out the potatoes on a baking sheet. Drizzle with the olive oil, season with salt and pepper, and toss until evenly coated. Add the rosemary and garlic to the baking sheet. Roast until the potatoes are crispy and golden, 20 to 25 minutes, turning the potatoes with a spatula halfway through cooking. Discard the rosemary.

STEP 3. Arrange the hot potatoes and garlic on small plates or a platter and dollop with sofrito, if desired, before serving.

STEAMED SPINACH
WITH FETA AND PAPRIKA

One of the last things I cooked before I turned in my first draft of this book was steamed spinach, sprinkled with Bulgarian feta and sweet paprika. It was an off-the-cuff creation with no intention but to accompany seared artic char for a casual dinner at home. It did the trick. It tasted healthful but somehow indulgent, too—everything this book is meant to be about. So I had to include it here.

It's obvious, of course—spinach and feta—but somehow I had never served it just like this. In case you, too, had overlooked the obvious, here's a quick how-to.

———————————————— SERVES 4 ————————————————

2 tbsp extra-virgin olive oil, plus more for drizzling

10 oz/280 g Bloomsdale or thick-leafed spinach, stemmed and washed

Fleur de sel or sel gris

6 oz/170 g feta cheese

Sweet paprika for sprinkling

STEP 1. Heat the olive oil in a large skillet over medium-high heat. Add the spinach, which will likely have some residual water in its creases and folds. Cover with a splatter screen, if you have one, or partially with a lid so that the oil doesn't snap up on to you, but leave enough air for the spinach to stay bright green. Cook until the leaves start to wilt but still hold some shape, about 2 minutes. Season with fleur de sel.

STEP 2. Arrange on a small platter and break the feta over the top in large pieces. Drizzle with olive oil and sprinkle with paprika. Serve warm.

COOK'S NOTE. Don't be tempted to use baby spinach here. The crinkly folds of ruffled full-size garden or market-fresh spinach are slow to wilt, giving the dish structure and shape.

CHAPTER 4

sandwiches & tortillas

Sometimes, the most satisfying meal in your whole week can be a sandwich. I didn't always feel that way, but every sandwich lover has the sandwich that turned them on. Mine was the Veggie Stack at Mary's Market, a café in my hometown. In its parts, it wasn't much. Stacked up with a signature sauce on a nutty, whole-grain bread, it was an entire meal—filling, and full of crunch and zing. Between those slices of bread, I became a sandwich lover.

Some sandwiches are messy mouthfuls, the kind that fill up your whole hand, like the fried egg and arugula on homemade flatbread (see PAGE 133). Others are understated masterpieces, like the Knife-and-Fork Grilled Portobello Sandwich (PAGE 130), that deserve a place on your dinner plate. And others, like my version of the Veggie Stack Sandwich (PAGE 132), would be right at home wrapped in parchment, destined for a cooler, picnic, or bike basket.

I believe Mexico gave us one of the best, most versatile "sandwiches"—the soft taco. Both corn and flour tortillas can be filled to the high heavens with any imaginable vegetable or bean—from stuffed squash blossoms (see PAGE 146) to mushrooms, greens, and onions (see PAGE 145) to seared halloumi with pea guacamole (see PAGE 148).

KNIFE-AND-FORK
GRILLED PORTOBELLO SANDWICH

When you've been a vegetarian for more than twenty years, it's likely you've eaten a lot of portobello sandwiches. So the fact that my husband never orders them was inspiration enough to come up with a new one he couldn't resist. I think of the grilled portobello more as a decadent vegetable sandwich rather than a default vegetarian option in a burger joint. Layering on grilled eggplant, zucchini, and creamy avocado only makes it better.

_____ SERVES 2 TO 4 _____

WALNUT BUTTER

½ cup/70 g toasted walnuts (see page 273)

1 tbsp unsalted butter, at room temperature

Sel gris or fleur de sel

4 large portobello mushrooms, cleaned, stemmed, gills removed, and peeled (see page 266)

1 large eggplant, thinly sliced lengthwise

1 large zucchini, thinly sliced lengthwise

⅓ cup/75 ml extra-virgin olive oil, plus more for the bread

Sea salt and freshly ground pepper

2 to 4 oz/55 to 115 g good melting cheese such as Muenster or fontina, very thinly sliced

4 thin slices full-flavored rustic bread such as whole grain or sesame

1 bunch arugula, stemmed

1 firm, ripe avocado, peeled, pitted, and thinly sliced

½ lemon

STEP 1. *To make the Walnut Butter:* Grind the walnuts to a fine meal in a food processor or coffee grinder, stopping just before they turn into a paste, about 2 minutes. Pulse in the butter, or if using a coffee grinder, transfer the walnut meal to a bowl, add the butter, and stir into a chunky paste. Season with sel gris.

STEP 2. Prepare a gas or charcoal grill to cook over high heat, or preheat a cast-iron grill pan on the stove top over high heat until hot.

STEP 3. Brush the portobellos, eggplant, and zucchini generously with the olive oil. Season with salt and pepper. Working in batches, if needed, grill the portobellos until tender, turning once, about 8 minutes, and the eggplant and zucchini until tender-crisp and lightly charred, turning once, 6 to 8 minutes. Add the cheese to the tops of the mushrooms during the last 2 minutes of cooking. While the cheese melts, brush the bread with olive oil and grill until lightly charred, turning once, 2 to 4 minutes.

STEP 4. Place the bread slices on a work surface and spread with walnut butter. Layer the bread slices with arugula, eggplant, mushroom, zucchini, and avocado. Squeeze fresh lemon juice over the top and season with salt and pepper. Serve warm with a knife and fork.

THE VEGGIE STACK SANDWICH

This sandwich is all-American and an easy pleaser. The starting point, as with all good sandwiches, is very good bread. The ingredients within are subject to your own preferences—start with something crisp and crunchy (cucumber, lettuce), add something creamy and unctuous (hummus), something filling and satisfying (cheese), then stack and stuff to your heart's delight. I like pungent raw watermelon or globe radishes, arugula, and ripe avocado, and have been known to embellish the Veggie Stack with a thin smear of Buttermilk Chive Dressing (page 251) when I have extra in the fridge. This is a particularly good companion for a cup of soup and a handful of thick-cut sourdough pretzels.

SERVES 4

8 thick slices whole-grain Pullman or sandwich bread, lightly toasted

1 cup/245 g Hummus (page 60) or purchased hummus

8 crisp leaves of lettuce such as Little Gem, butterhead, Boston, or romaine

½ seedless cucumber, thinly sliced

4 to 8 slices of dill Havarti or your favorite cheese

Sliced radishes for topping

Sprouts (any kind) for topping

Sliced avocado for topping

Place the bread slices on a work surface and spread them with a thin layer of hummus. Stack half of the bread slices high with lettuce, cucumber, Havarti, radishes, sprouts, and avocado. Top with the remaining bread slices, hummus-side down. Slice in half and serve.

COOK'S NOTE. Spreading sandwich bread with hummus, butter, mayo, or any of the adventurous sauces in chapter 9 adds flavor. But even better, it also seals the bread so that any wet ingredients (like tomatoes) don't seep into the bread, giving the sandwich a longer shelf life, a particularly important detail when making sandwiches for brown-bag lunches and picnics.

A KILLER SANDWICH FORMULA

Since no two sandwiches in this book look alike, it could seem subtle, but there is a science to the sandwich that once mastered, delivers a hundredfold.

GOOD BREAD

+

SOMETHING TO SPREAD

+

CRISPY GREEN

+

FAT OR CHEESE

+

FILLING CRUNCH

ARUGULA, EGG, AND AVOCADO ON FLATBREAD

Whenever I have leftover pizza dough, I make grilled flatbread. Bread and salad is the most classic combination, but when I'm really hungry, there's nothing better than salad in a sandwich, stuffed to the gills with the lively finesse of freshly picked arugula and lush slices of avocado. Consider the fried egg both the backbone *and* the icing on the cake, or the sandwich in this case, fried over easy so every bit of oozy yolk seeps into the tender crumbs of your homemade flatbread.

———————————————— SERVES 2 ————————————————

FLATBREAD

Extra-virgin olive oil

One 14- to 16-oz/400- to 455-g ball homemade pizza dough (see page 260) or purchased pizza dough, at room temperature

Coarse sea salt and freshly ground pepper

Dijon mustard for spreading

1 large bunch arugula, stemmed

1 firm, ripe avocado, peeled, pitted, and thinly sliced

2 large eggs, fried over easy (see page 272)

STEP 1. *To make the Flatbread:* Prepare a gas or charcoal grill to cook over medium-high heat, or preheat a double-burner cast-iron grill pan on the stove top over medium-high heat until hot. Rub the grill grates or the grill pan with olive oil (see page 259).

STEP 2. Divide the pizza dough into two pieces. Stretch or roll each piece of dough into an 8-by-4-in/20-by-10-cm rectangle that's about 1/4 in/6 mm thick. Brush the top of the dough generously with olive oil and season with salt and pepper. Let rise in a warm, draft-free spot for 10 minutes.

STEP 3. Set the olive oil, salt, and pepper near the grill or stove top. Using both hands, gently lay the flatbreads on the grill or grill pan, oiled-side down. Grill the flatbreads until set and lightly charred on the bottoms, about 6 minutes. Brush the other side with oil, season with salt and pepper, and flip them carefully with tongs. Cook until lightly charred on the second sides, about 6 minutes more. Transfer the flatbreads to a cutting board and cut them in half.

STEP 4. Spread a thin layer of Dijon on two of the flatbread halves, then layer with arugula, avocado, and fried eggs. Top with the remaining flatbread halves. Serve warm.

COOK'S NOTE. Though a grill is the fastest way to quick-cook your bread, you can bake the flatbread in a 450°F/230°C/gas 8 oven as well. Cook the dough until golden brown and evenly baked through, about 12 minutes.

WINTER

APPLE, AVOCADO,
AND GRAVLAX TARTINE

SUMMER

HEIRLOOM
TOMATO TARTINE

ENDIVE, PEAR, AND
TRUFFLE HONEY TARTINE

RADISH, RICOTTA, AND
BLACK PEPPER TARTINE

TARTINE FOR
FOUR SEASONS

When you want to eat very well without cooking, make a tartine—an open-faced sandwich made of fresh bread layered with a stack of seasonal goodies. A number of topping combinations win praise, but for the sake of starting somewhere, here are my four favorites. In spring, luscious layers of ricotta and peppery radishes are quick to please. On summer days, I pile my plate with an open-faced tomato tartine that drips with crème fraîche and is topped with pungent greens. A fall tartine of endive, blue cheese, and truffle honey lingers with long-lasting flavor and satisfaction. And simple sandwich bread becomes a rich open-faced winter sandwich with avocado, apple, and a bit of gravlax, if that's your thing. These sandwiches are icons of flavor for each season of the year, inspiring starting points for a lifetime affair with sandwiches.

SPRING
RADISH, RICOTTA, AND BLACK PEPPER TARTINE

———————————————— SERVES 2 TO 4 ————————————————

2 pretzel rolls, halved, or 4 thick slices rye bread

¼ cup/60 g fresh ricotta cheese

4 globe, French Breakfast, or watermelon
   radishes, thinly sliced

Peppery extra-virgin olive oil for drizzling

Coarse sea salt and freshly ground pepper

A few sprigs of peppery microgreens

Toast the pretzel rolls until crisp. Dollop the ricotta on each toasted half and top with the radishes, dividing them evenly. Drizzle with olive oil, season with salt and pepper, and top with microgreens. Serve immediately.

SUMMER
HEIRLOOM TOMATO TARTINE

———————————————— SERVES 2 TO 4 ————————————————

4 thick slices hearty seven-grain bread

Peppery extra-virgin olive oil for drizzling

3 tbsp crème fraîche

1 or 2 large firm, ripe beefsteak tomatoes,
   thickly sliced

Sea salt and freshly ground pepper

3 oz/85 g smoked or aged Gouda cheese

Large handful microgreens, broccoli sprouts,
   or arugula shoots

Toast the bread until crisp. Place the toasted bread on a work surface and drizzle lightly with olive oil. Smear with the crème fraîche and top with the tomatoes, dividing them evenly. Season with salt and pepper. Shave the Gouda over the top with a vegetable peeler and top with microgreens. Serve immediately.

FALL

ENDIVE, PEAR, AND TRUFFLE HONEY TARTINE

SERVES 2 TO 4

4 very thin slices pumpernickel raisin bread

Extra-virgin olive oil for drizzling

Head Belgian endive, leaves separated

1 ripe pear, thinly sliced

8 oz/220 g Gorgonzola dolce or other soft blue cheese, cut into thin slivers

Truffle honey or raw honey and truffle oil for drizzling

Toasted hazelnuts (see page 273)

Toast the bread until crisp. Place the toasted bread on a work surface and drizzle lightly with olive oil. Top with an endive leaf, sliced pear, and cheese, dividing them equally. Drizzle with truffle honey and top with nuts. Serve immediately.

WINTER

APPLE, AVOCADO, AND GRAVLAX TARTINE

SERVES 2 TO 4

4 thick slices whole-wheat bread

Extra-virgin olive oil for drizzling

1 firm, ripe avocado, peeled, pitted, and thinly sliced

4 oz/115 g gravlax or smoked salmon, thinly sliced

1 Gala apple, thinly sliced

Maldon sea salt

Cracked black pepper

1 lemon, cut into wedges

Toast the bread until crisp. Place the toasted bread on a work surface and drizzle lightly with olive oil. Layer with avocado, gravlax, and apple, dividing them evenly. Sprinkle a few flakes of salt and pepper on top. Serve with lemon wedges to squeeze over the top.

LENTIL-CHICKPEA BURGERS
WITH HARISSA YOGURT

A common complaint about veggie burgers is that they either fall apart or they are flavorless. Using legumes cooked with good flavor, such as leftovers from the lentils from the winter Caprese (page 65), and seasoning them well are the first fixes to this. The flatbread makes these burgers extra special, and because you can make it from scratch (stretch it on the thin side, for this) or buy it big and flat, you can add in your burger and fold it over to eat your burger falafel- or gyro-style. As with any burger, toppings are what elevate a good burger to greatness. I like this with harissa yogurt and pickled onions.

As for keeping your homemade veggie burger all in one piece, sear it first on a cast-iron griddle or pan in a little oil, which creates a crispy outside that holds it together. If you're craving that summer grilling experience, reheat the burgers on a grill just before serving.

―――――――――――――――――――――― SERVES 6 ――――――――――――――――――――――

HARISSA YOGURT

½ cup/120 ml nonfat or full-fat plain Greek or
   full-fat plain yogurt

2 tsp Harissa (page 253), purchased harissa, or
   other hot-pepper paste (see page 26)

2 cups/200 g cooked green or brown lentils
   (see page 65)

½ cup/80 g cooked chickpeas (see page 273)

½ medium red, white, or yellow onion, coarsely
   chopped

3 garlic cloves, smashed

2 large eggs

½ cup/40 g old-fashioned rolled oats

1 tsp chili powder

1 tsp smoked paprika

1 tsp Harissa (page 253), purchased harissa, or
   other hot-pepper paste (see page 26)

1 carrot, peeled and coarsely grated

Sea salt and freshly ground pepper

All-purpose flour for dusting

Extra-virgin olive oil for the pan and the grill

6 slices fontina, aged Gouda, or Manchego
   cheese

6 large pieces flatbread (see page 133 or
   purchased), toasted

Avocado, thinly sliced for topping (optional)

2 handfuls arugula, mizuna, or other greens for
   topping

Pickled Onions (page 249) for topping

STEP 1. *To make the Harissa Yogurt:* Stir together the yogurt and harissa until smooth.

STEP 2. Pat the lentils and chickpeas dry with paper towels, especially if using canned legumes (see Cook's Note). Combine the lentils, chickpeas, onion, garlic, eggs, oats, chili powder, paprika, and harissa in a food processor and process until it's the consistency of thick, chunky hummus. Do not overprocess, which can result in flimsy, pasty burgers. Stir in the carrot. Taste and season with salt and pepper.

STEP 3. Divide the chickpea-lentil mixture into six portions and shape them into patties about 1 in/2.5 cm thick. Season generously with salt and pepper. Dust lightly with flour on both sides and gently brush off any excess.

STEP 4. Heat a thin layer of olive oil in a medium skillet over medium-high heat. Working in batches, cook the burgers until crispy on the bottoms and the chickpea-lentil mixture holds together, about 5 minutes. Flip them carefully with a spatula and continue cooking until the second sides are firm and brown, about 5 minutes more. (You can make these up to 1 month in advance; just be sure to cool completely. Store in an airtight container in the freezer with a layer of parchment paper between each burger.)

STEP 5. If you prefer a grilled flavor, prepare a gas or charcoal grill to cook over medium-high heat, or preheat a grill pan on the stove top over medium-high heat until hot. Rub the grill grates or the grill pan with olive oil (see page 259).

STEP 6. Grill the cooked burgers until the outsides are deeply brown, about 5 minutes. Do not move the burgers during cooking except to flip once halfway through cooking. Add the cheese to the tops of your burgers during the last 2 minutes of cooking. If using a gas or charcoal grill, close the lid to let the cheese melt, or, to melt on a grill pan, cover the burger with a heat-proof bowl.

STEP 7. Place the flatbread on a work surface and slather with harissa yogurt. Place the burgers on the flatbread and top with avocado, arugula and pickled onions. Fold the flatbread over the burger (like a taco) and serve immediately.

COOK'S NOTE. Home-cooked chickpeas and lentils have great flavor, but some nights you need to cut right to the chase with canned legumes. When you do, rinse, drain, pat them dry, and season them with salt and pepper before processing to give the burger a flavor boost.

CORN TORTILLAS

Even the most devoted Mexican-food enthusiast doesn't make tortillas from scratch every time they eat a taco or quesadilla, but once you learn how easy they are to create at home, you'll be tempted to do just that. I got hooked on homemade tortillas in Mexico, where my husband and I ate them by the dozens, fresh from the *tortilleria* with nothing more than salt and lime.

Masa harina, salt, and water come together into chewy, toothsome tortillas in minutes with the help of a tortilla press, and make an irresistible starting point for so many delicious dishes.

——————— MAKES TEN 6-IN/15-CM OR TWELVE 4-IN/10-CM TORTILLAS ———————

Scant 2 cups/250 g masa harina

¾ tsp fine sea salt

1¼ cups/300 ml warm water, plus cold water as needed

STEP 1. Mix the masa harina, salt, and warm water in a large bowl. Knead with your hands until just combined. Cover the bowl with plastic wrap and let rest for 15 minutes.

STEP 2. Preheat a cast-iron griddle pan or a two-burner griddle pan on the stove top with one burner set over high heat and the other burner set over medium heat (if your cast-iron pan only covers one burner, set it over medium heat). Set a bowl of water nearby for dipping your hands while you work. Set your tortilla press nearby. Line a basket with a kitchen towel and keep it near the griddle pan.

STEP 3. Gently squeeze the dough in your hands. It should feel like soft cookie dough. If it is too stiff, add 1 to 2 tbsp cold water at a time, until it is soft but not too sticky. Re-cover the bowl with the plastic wrap.

STEP 4. With scissors, separate a large sturdy resealable plastic bag (such as a freezer bag—not plastic wrap) into halves, making two squares that are slightly larger than your tortilla press. Open the press and lay down one piece of plastic. Pinch off a heaping 1 tbsp of dough and place it in the center of the plastic. Flatten it with your hand, top with the second piece of plastic, and close the tortilla press, gently flattening the dough with the lever into a disk that's about ⅛ in/3 mm thick. Open the tortilla press and peel off the top piece of plastic.

If you don't have a tortilla press, roll the tortillas on a lightly floured work surface with a rolling pin between the two halves of the plastic bag until they measure 4 to 6 in/ 10 to 15 cm wide. Press or roll the tortillas one at a time, cooking them as you go.

STEP 5. Once the griddle is hot, test the consistency of the dough by making your first tortilla. If the tortilla sticks, knead in a few more sprinkles of flour, keeping the remaining dough covered with plastic as you work so it doesn't dry out.

STEP 6. Let one edge of the tortilla touch the cooler side of the griddle, then lower your hand slightly and move it away from you, allowing the tortilla to roll onto the griddle.

STEP 7. Cook until the tortilla dries out slightly and releases from the griddle easily, about 30 seconds. Flip the tortilla onto the hotter side of the griddle with a spatula or your fingers. Cook until lightly browned, about 30 seconds. Flip and cook 30 seconds more until it puffs up all over or in places—to encourage puffing, gently tap on the tortilla lightly with your fingers or a spatula to create tiny pockets of air. Transfer to the basket lined with a kitchen towel and keep covered, stacking fresh tortillas on top of one another to steam.

STEP 8. Press and cook tortillas with the remaining dough, adjusting the heat as needed. Serve warm.

COOK'S NOTE. I've never, ever had leftover tortillas when I've made them from scratch. If you do, wrap them tightly and keep them up to overnight at room temperature, or freeze for up to 1 month. To reheat, see page 144.

BAJA FLOUR TORTILLAS

When I was about twelve, my siblings and I discovered that a stack of flour tortillas that were buttered and warmed for 10 seconds in the microwave was about as soothing a snack as it got. As an adult, I discovered you could improve upon this good thing by making tortillas from scratch. Made with your loving hands and big crystals of sel gris, these will blow any commercial variety out of the water. Toast day-old tortillas on the cast-iron griddle or open flame until just warm.

MAKES SIXTEEN 8-IN/20-CM TORTILLAS

½ cup/115 g vegetable shortening

3¼ cups/410 g all-purpose flour

Sel gris or fleur de sel

1 tsp baking powder

1 cup/240 ml warm water

STEP 1. Pulse the shortening, flour, 1 tsp sel gris, and baking powder in a food processor for about 20 seconds. Add the warm water and pulse together until just combined, about 15 seconds. Transfer the dough to a lightly floured work surface and knead until soft and smooth.

STEP 2. Cut the dough in half with a bench scraper or a knife, and cut each half into eight pieces, about 1½ oz/40 g each. Form each piece into a small ball with your hands and cover with plastic wrap. Flatten the balls, one by one, on a lightly floured work surface and roll with a rolling pin to about 8 in/20 cm wide, turning constantly to keep their round shape.

STEP 3. Preheat a large cast-iron griddle pan or a two-burner griddle pan on the stove top over high heat. Place a plate and a kitchen towel near the griddle pan.

STEP 4. Let one edge of the tortilla touch the griddle, then lower your hand slightly and move it away from you, allowing the tortilla to roll onto the griddle.

STEP 5. Cook until lightly browned with a few bubbles, 3 to 4 minutes. Flip the tortilla with tongs, a spatula, or your fingers. It should be pale golden brown. Continue cooking on the other side until the tortilla puffs and separates and then deflates, 2 to 3 minutes more. Stack on a plate as you remove them from the griddle and cover loosely with a kitchen towel to keep warm. Serve warm, or cool completely, wrap tightly, and keep on the countertop for the next day.

TORTILLA TUTORIAL

The first few months I shared a mostly vegetarian kitchen with my fully vegetarian husband, I could have written a dissertation on sixty ways to serve salad and cheese plates. I quickly learned that wouldn't cut it. We both wanted and needed a hot dinner most nights of the week to feel we'd really feasted. I soon figured out that with a stack of fresh tortillas in the fridge, I could make fast work of an exciting dinner packed with any or all of the flavors we love. I made dinner with tortillas so often we started Tortilla Tuesdays, a weekly feast of quesadillas, soft tacos, and tostadas, which, after four years and counting, never gets old.

Tortillas are such a practical staple in the vegetarian kitchen that they are always, always on hand in mine. Most of the following recipes taste brilliant on purchased tortillas, but both flour and corn tortillas are truly simple to make, addictively so. I've given you two easy-to-follow recipes for both on the preceding pages so that you can make them yourself at least once.

Whether homemade or purchased, a tortilla is often enjoyed more when it's warm, which also makes it more pliable and easy to work with.

There are a few good ways to warm a tortilla. I love the char and finish of a tortilla warmed on a cast-iron pan or griddle, especially when I'm using them for soft tacos. It requires no extra fat and imparts a just-cooked flavor. But steaming for even a few seconds in the microwave works well, too, and keeps tortillas, homemade or otherwise, soft and supple, which is important for preparations like enchiladas.

TOAST Preheat a dry cast-iron skillet or griddle pan on the stove top over medium-high heat. Toast the tortilla for 1 to 2 minutes on each side. Wrap in a kitchen towel to steam and keep warm.

ROAST Lay a tortilla over a low flame on a gas stove top. Flip with tongs and rotate until just lightly browned. Wrap in a kitchen towel to steam and keep warm.

STEAM Set up a vegetable steamer in a large saucepan filled with about 1 in/2.5 cm of water. Bring to a boil over high heat. Wrap the tortillas in a thick kitchen towel and place in the steamer. Cover with a lid; boil about 1 minute, then turn off the heat and let steam for 12 minutes. Remove the lid carefully. Bring the steaming tortillas to the table wrapped.

ZAP Wrap a stack of tortillas in barely damp paper towels and microwave for 20 to 30 seconds. Wrap in a kitchen towel to keep warm.

Once tortillas are warm, serve them immediately.

SOFT TACOS WITH MUSHROOMS, GREENS, AND ONIONS

There are a thousand ways to fill a tortilla, and none of my favorites rely on meat or even heavily on cheese. This is one simple, fast favorite that makes fine use of any greens, from chard to spinach. Top your vegetables with whatever semisoft or soft cheese you have on hand and ditto on toppings—tomatillo salsa, Pico de Gallo (page 252), or a squeeze of lime all dress these up just fine and dandy.

MAKES 8 TACOS
---

8 small Corn Tortillas (page 140) or Baja Flour Tortillas (page 142) or purchased small corn or flour tortillas

1 or 2 bunches Swiss chard or mustard greens, stemmed and thinly sliced

1 tbsp extra-virgin olive oil or grapeseed oil

1 white or yellow onion, halved and thickly sliced

8 oz/225 g wild or button mushrooms, trimmed and sliced

Sea salt and freshly ground pepper

3 garlic cloves, minced

½ cup/55 g crumbled queso añejo, queso fresco, feta, or goat cheese

Tomatillo salsa (optional) for topping

2 limes, cut into wedges

Several sprigs fresh cilantro

STEP 1. Bring a large saucepan three-fourths full of salted water to a boil over high heat. Meanwhile, warm the tortillas (see facing page) and wrap to keep warm.

STEP 2. Add the chard to the boiling water and cook until just tender, 3 to 4 minutes. Drain and set aside. Heat the olive oil in a large skillet over medium-high heat. Add the onion and cook, stirring occasionally, until soft and just golden brown, about 5 minutes. Add the mushrooms and cook, stirring occasionally, until they are crispy but still juicy, 4 to 6 minutes, seasoning with salt and pepper toward the end of cooking. Add the garlic and cook until fragrant, about 30 seconds, then add the chard, stirring to warm through. Continue cooking until the liquid from the chard has evaporated.

STEP 3. Transfer the mushrooms and chard to a serving bowl and sprinkle with queso añejo and sea salt. Serve warm with the tortillas, tomatillo salsa (if using), lime wedges, and cilantro. Assemble the tacos tableside.

STUFFED SQUASH BLOSSOM
SOFT TACOS

Growing your own zucchini can quickly turn you into a squash blossom devotee. The blossoms, which appear all over the zucchini plant before the fruit, are always tempting you to pluck them for a summer treat. Since they can be found at the farmers' market, these delicate blooms aren't for gardeners alone to enjoy. They come into season about the same time as sweet corn and cherry tomatoes. Stuffed with cheese and lightly battered, they take just a minute in a shallow frying pan to become beautiful golden crowns to top your tortillas.

—————————————————————— SERVES 4 ——————————————————————

8 squash blossoms, cleaned (see Cook's Note)

1 to 2 oz/30 to 55 g Manchego or fresh mozzarella cheese, cut into ¼-in/6-mm cubes

1 to 2 ears of corn, kernels removed and milked (see page 265)

Heaping handful Sungold, Sweet 100, or other cherry tomatoes, halved

1 garlic clove, smashed and minced

1 tbsp best-quality extra-virgin olive oil

Sea salt

½ cup/120 ml buttermilk

¼ cup/30 g all-purpose flour

2 tbsp semolina flour

Peanut or vegetable oil for frying

Freshly ground pepper

8 fresh small Corn Tortillas, (page 140) or purchased corn tortillas

Handful fresh cilantro leaves or small fresh basil leaves, torn

1 lime, cut into wedges

STEP 1. Gently open the squash blossoms at the base of the petals and tuck in a few pieces of cheese and a few corn kernels with a small spoon or your fingers. Twist the top of the petals together to close and set aside. Repeat until all the blossoms are stuffed, using all the cheese but reserving about half of the corn kernels. Meanwhile, toss together the remaining corn and corn milk, tomatoes, garlic, and olive oil in a medium bowl. Season with salt.

STEP 2. Line a plate with paper towels and set tongs and a splatter guard (if you have one) near the stove. Pour the buttermilk into a shallow bowl and set near the stove. Whisk together the all-purpose flour, semolina flour, and a generous pinch of salt in another shallow bowl and set it next to the buttermilk.

STEP 3. In a large frying pan, heat 2 in/5 cm of peanut oil over medium heat until it reaches 350°F/180°C on a deep-fry thermometer.

STEP 4. While the oil heats, dip a stuffed blossom in the buttermilk and turn to coat, then roll the wet blossom into the flour mixture. Shimmy it around a little to thoroughly coat inside all the creases; shake off any excess. Set the breaded squash blossom on a plate until it's ready to be fried. Repeat with the remaining blossoms until they're all breaded.

STEP 5. To test the temperature of the oil, drop in a few flecks of the flour mixture or a kernel of corn; the oil should sizzle. Carefully lower the breaded blossoms into the hot oil with a long-handled spoon and baste the tops of the blossoms in the oil. Leave the blossoms undisturbed to fry until pale golden brown, about 1 minute. Flip the blossoms in the oil and continue cooking just long enough to crisp the petals and melt the cheese inside, about 2 minutes. Be sure to cover the pan with a splatter guard to protect yourself from hot oil as it pops and sizzles. Transfer the fried blossoms to the paper towel–lined plate with a slotted spoon. Season with salt and pepper while the fried blossoms are still warm so the salt and pepper stick.

STEP 6. Roast the tortillas over an open flame on your stove (see page 144). Stuff the tortillas with the fried blossoms and the corn-tomato salad. Scatter the cilantro and add a squeeze of fresh lime juice over the top. Serve while the blossoms are crunchy and warm.

COOK'S NOTE. Choose the freshest blossoms you can find—big, almost bulbous blossoms are the easiest to stuff—and open them carefully. If you pull them from your own garden, you'll be short eight zucchinis this season, but you'll never miss them. Peel the blossoms back and lightly brush out any dirt.

PEA GUACAMOLE AND
SEARED HALLOUMI SOFT TACOS

Sweet peas and avocados make a dreamy guacamole combo that happens to also be lower in fat. The mild sweetness from the peas make it a perfect pairing for the toothsome chew of salty, seared halloumi, a Greek sheep's and goat's milk cheese that is sometimes labeled grilling cheese (since its high melting point helps it hold up beautifully on the grill). Paneer, a South Asian cheese with a similarly tight curd, will work just as well. Top with tomatoes marinated in garlic and your best olive oil, which adds juice, depth, and acidity to every bite and any taco. Fish eaters will love these tacos with seared Pacific halibut in place of the cheese. See Cook's Note, below.

———————————————— SERVES 2 TO 4 ————————————————

1 pt/250 g cherry tomatoes, halved

1 garlic clove, pressed or finely chopped

¼ cup/60 ml extra-virgin olive oil, plus more for frying

2 tbsp chopped parsley

Sea salt and freshly ground pepper

2 cups/285 g fresh or frozen shelled sweet peas

1 firm-ripe avocado

6¼ oz/250 g Halloumi or paneer, cut into "steaks"

8 Flour Tortillas (page 142) or purchased flour tortillas

STEP 1. Toss together the tomatoes, garlic, 2 tbsp of the olive oil, and the parsley. Season with salt and pepper. Set aside to marinate until ready to serve.

STEP 2. Cook the peas in just enough water to cover in a small pot over medium heat, about 4 minutes. Drain, reserving about ¼ cup/60 ml of the pea cooking liquid. Add the reserved cooking liquid and 2 tbsp olive oil to the peas and puree with an immersion blender or food processor until mostly smooth with some small pieces of peas remaining. Add the avocado and pulse to a slightly chunky puree. Season with a pinch of salt and set aside.

STEP 3. Heat a thin layer of olive oil in a medium nonstick or well-seasoned cast-iron skillet over medium-high heat. Season the Halloumi on both sides with pepper. Add to the hot pan and cook until crisp and brown on one side, 2 minutes. Flip and continue cooking until just browned, 1 to 2 minutes more.

STEP 4. Toast the tortillas over an open flame on your stove (see page 144). Add a spoonful of the warm pea guacamole to each, top with the Halloumi and the tomatoes and their juices. Serve warm.

COOK'S NOTE. For fish tacos, start with 10 oz/280 g boneless, skinless halibut, cut in pieces. Heat a thin layer of olive oil in a medium nonstick or well-seasoned cast-iron skillet over medium-high heat. Season the fish on both sides with salt and pepper. Add to the hot pan and cook until crisp and brown on one side, 2 minutes. When the fish pulls away easily from the pan, it's ready to flip. Flip and continue cooking until just opaque throughout, 2 to 4 minutes more, depending on the thickness of the fish. Top the tortillas with guacamole, halibut, and tomatoes, and serve.

ZUCCHINI QUESADILLAS
AND SUMMER TOMATO SALSA

Quesadillas are a vegetarian standard, but with a little creativity, their versatility might astound you. Most of the year, make them on a cast-iron griddle, but in the summer, take them outside to the grill where the char of charcoal gives them a hard-to-replicate satisfaction. This quesadilla is Mexican by way of the American farm stand, stuffed with zucchini, tomatoes, and basil. Start with firm, freshly picked zucchini and in-season tomatoes, which, when grated, become salsa to top a quick lunch or dinner.

— SERVES 2 TO 4 —

4 tbsp extra-virgin olive oil, plus more for the grill

2 medium zucchini, thinly sliced lengthwise

8 fresh small Corn Tortillas (page 140) or purchased corn tortillas

1 large firm, ripe beefsteak or 2 medium heirloom tomatoes

1 large green zebra tomato, halved

Sea salt and freshly ground pepper

1 or 2 dashes of cider vinegar (optional)

2 or 3 fresh basil leaves, thinly sliced

6 oz/170 g fresh mozzarella cheese, thinly sliced

Corn Crema (page 254; optional)

STEP 1. Prepare a gas or charcoal grill to cook over medium-high heat. Rub the grill grates with olive oil (see page 259). Brush the zucchini slices and tortillas on both sides with 2 tbsp of the olive oil.

STEP 2. Chop the beefsteak tomato into bite-size chunks. Grate the green tomato on the large holes of a box grater over a bowl all the way down to the skin. Discard the skin. Add the beefsteak tomato and the remaining 2 tbsp olive oil to the bowl. Season with salt and pepper. (If your tomatoes are a little underripe and need extra acidity, stir in cider vinegar.) Stir in the basil.

STEP 3. Grill the zucchini until it is lightly charred and it bends easily when you lift it with a fork, about 2 minutes. Flip with tongs, and cook until lightly charred on the other side. Transfer the zucchini to a platter. Add four of the tortillas to the grill. Top each tortilla with enough zucchini and mozzarella to cover. Top with the remaining tortillas. Grill the quesadillas until evenly crisp on the bottoms, about 4 minutes. Flip them carefully with a spatula, and cook until the cheese is melted and the quesadillas are evenly crisp on the second sides.

STEP 4. Transfer the quesadillas to a platter, and spoon the salsa on top. Dollop with corn crema, if desired. Serve warm.

TACO TRUCK
VEGETABLE BURRITO

I've had enough mad-hungry nights in New York City to have learned the beauty of the taco truck burrito, the food I crave when I want to fill up and fill up good. It's messy in that good way that things are when flavors mix together just right. It's thanks to the flattop griddle most food trucks use to sear onions and squash before tucking them into a soft flour tortilla with cushy yellow rice, pinto beans, and guacamole. It's just good.

SERVES 4

1½ cups/315 g long-grain white or brown rice

3 cups/720 ml vegetable stock (see page 270) or water, plus more for the beans

One 15-oz/430-g can pinto beans, rinsed and drained

2 tbsp extra-virgin olive oil

2 yellow onions, thinly sliced

1 zucchini, halved lengthwise and cut in thick half-moons

1 yellow summer squash, halved lengthwise and cut in thick half-moons

¼ tsp cayenne pepper

Sea salt and freshly ground black pepper

2 firm, ripe avocados, peeled and pitted

4 extra-large whole-wheat or white flour tortillas, homemade (see page 140) or purchased

4 oz/115 g sprouts (any kind)

Low-fat plain Greek yogurt for dolloping

1 cup/180 g Pico de Gallo (page 252) or purchased deli-fresh pico de gallo

1 or 2 limes, cut into wedges

STEP 1. Combine the rice and stock in a medium pot with a tight-fitting lid. Bring to a boil over medium-high heat, reduce to medium-low, cover, and cook until the rice is tender, about 30 minutes. Meanwhile, warm the beans with 2 to 3 tbsp water—just enough to make them saucy and enticing—in a small skillet over low heat.

STEP 2. Heat the olive oil in a large cast-iron skillet or griddle over medium-high heat. Add the onions, zucchini, summer squash, cayenne, and ³/₄ tsp salt. Season with black pepper. Cook until tender-crisp, 7 to 8 minutes, stirring occasionally. Cover to keep warm.

STEP 3. With a spoon, scoop the avocado into chunks and place in a bowl. Season with salt.

STEP 4. Place a tortilla on a work surface. Spoon one-fourth of the rice and one-fourth of the beans down the middle, leaving plenty of space on each end to tuck into a tight burrito later. Top with one-fourth of the onion-squash mixture, one-fourth of the avocado, one-fourth of the sprouts, and a dollop of yogurt.

STEP 5. Fold two sides over the filling until they meet in the middle. Roll the burrito tightly, tucking in the ends, and roll onto a plate seam-side down. Repeat with the remaining tortillas and fillings. Top each burrito with ¼ cup/45 g pico de gallo. Serve warm with lime wedges and a knife and fork.

COOK'S NOTE. Vegetable burritos are the easiest thing to spruce up with any vegetable you love (cucumbers, radishes, sautéed spinach) and a smart use for leftover grilled veggies or rice.

CHAPTER 5

meals in a bowl

At home I have a favorite bowl—handmade from clay with lots of grooves and character. That bowl drives my husband crazy. It doesn't stack well with any of the others, but if I could, I'd eat every meal in it, resting in the curve of my hand.

In much of the world, the best meals come in bowls meant to be spooned, slurped, or savored close to your mouth. Consider risotto, bibimbap (see PAGE 175), Sweet Potato and Kale Tortilla Soup (PAGE 181). These are meals that could be eaten while curled deep in the corner of the couch. These recipes, like Blank-Slate Baked Risotto (PAGE 172) or Cheese Grits with Black Beans and Avocado (PAGE 154), hail from all over the globe—the healthful comfort foods from many cultures. But don't let that intimidate you. These meals are harder to resist than they are to adapt to your liking.

CHEESE GRITS WITH BLACK BEANS AND AVOCADO

Grits are fill-your-belly food, a soothing Southern version of polenta that loves to be topped with your favorite things. Like polenta, grits can be made lean (with water) or rich (with milk, butter, and cheese). I'm always one for the middle path—a little cheese and butter go a long way—but use your judgment as to what's best for you.

This topping—creamy black beans, ripe avocado, and pico de gallo—is a trio to remember, equally at home on a cheese quesadilla or seared piece of fish as it is here. Pico de gallo is a cook's cheat for fast flavor, since the onion, jalapeños, and cilantro flavor the whole dish, making the rest quick and easy. Make your own, or if your local market or grocer makes a good fresh version, this could be the time to give yourself an easy out.

SERVES 4

1¾ cups/420 ml whole milk

1¼ cups/300 ml water

Sea salt

¾ cup/135 g quick-cooking grits

2 cups/340 g cooked black beans (see page 273) or one 15-oz/430-g can black beans, rinsed and drained

2 tbsp unsalted butter (optional)

2 oz/55 g sharp white cheddar, Manchego, Gouda, or Dubliner cheese, grated

1 firm, ripe avocado, peeled, pitted, and chopped

Pico de Gallo (page 252) for serving

Fleur de sel (optional)

STEP 1. Combine the milk with 1 cup/240 ml of the water and ¾ tsp sea salt in a large saucepan over medium-high heat. Bring to a boil and slowly whisk in the grits. Continue cooking, whisking occasionally, over medium-low heat until no lumps remain, about 10 minutes.

STEP 2. Meanwhile, warm the beans with the remaining ¼ cup/60 ml water—just enough to make them saucy and enticing—in a small skillet over low heat.

STEP 3. Remove the grits from the heat and stir in the butter, if desired, and the cheddar.

STEP 4. Spoon the grits into shallow bowls and top with the black beans, avocado, and pico de gallo. Season with fleur de sel, if desired, before serving.

POLENTA BOWL
FOR FOUR SEASONS

Polenta is a warm, savory corn porridge, a staple in Italian homes and a bed for any number of luxurious accompaniments, from poached eggs and tomato sauce to savory, garden-vegetable ragu. Here it shines through four seasons, with contrasting textures and tastes for embellishment. Served simply with sugar snaps and cheddar cheese, it's an easy lunch for spring, or with bursting grilled cherry tomatoes and ribbons of zucchini for a summer supper. In the fall, ladle lush mushroom pomodoro over polenta for a bowl you wish would never end, and give it a showstopping raddichio and poached egg crown in the winter, studded with pungent blue cheese.

SPRING

POLENTA AND SUGAR SNAPS

SERVES 4

3 cups/720 ml water

1 cup/140 g polenta

1 tsp fine sea salt

1¼ cups/300 ml whole milk

2 tbsp unsalted butter

1 oz/30 g cheddar or Dubliner cheese, grated, plus more for topping

Handful sugar snap peas, trimmed and halved on the diagonal

Fleur de sel or coarse sea salt

Freshly ground pepper

STEP 1. Bring the water to a boil in a medium saucepan over medium-high heat. Slowly add the polenta, stir with a wooden spoon, and add the sea salt. Reduce the heat to medium and cook, stirring occasionally, until the polenta is tender and fully cooked, about 20 minutes. Add the milk, butter, and cheddar to the polenta and stir together over medium-low heat until just warmed through and soft enough to drop easily from a spoon, a few minutes more.

STEP 2. Spoon into bowls and top with sugar snap peas and more cheese. Season with fleur de sel and pepper before serving.

SPRING
POLENTA AND
SUGAR SNAPS

SUMMER
POLENTA WITH
GRILLED TOMATOES
AND ZUCCHINI

FALL
POLENTA WITH
MUSHROOM POMODORO

POLENTA WITH WINTER SALAD, POACHED EGG, AND BLUE CHEESE

POLENTA WITH GRILLED TOMATOES AND ZUCCHINI

SERVES 4

¼ cup/60 ml extra-virgin olive oil, plus more for the grill

3 cups/720 ml water

1 cup/140 g polenta

Sea salt

1¼ cups/300 ml whole milk

2 tbsp unsalted butter

1 oz/30 g aged Gouda cheese, grated

2 small zucchini, thinly sliced lengthwise

Freshly ground pepper

2 handfuls yellow, red, or orange pear and cherry tomatoes

Handful small fresh oregano leaves, finely chopped (optional)

STEP 1. Preheat a gas or charcoal grill to cook over medium-high heat, or preheat a grill pan on the stove top over medium-high until hot. Rub the grill grates or the grill pan with olive oil (see page 259). Soak eight wooden skewers in water or set out eight small metal skewers.

STEP 2. Bring the water to a boil in a medium saucepan over medium-high heat. Slowly add the polenta, stir with a wooden spoon, and add 1 tsp salt. Reduce the heat to medium and cook, stirring occasionally, until the polenta is tender and fully cooked, about 20 minutes. Add the milk, butter, and Gouda to the polenta and stir together over medium-low heat until just warmed through and soft enough to drop easily from a spoon, a few minutes more. Cover to keep warm.

STEP 3. Drain the wooden skewers (if using). Brush the zucchini slices on both sides with the olive oil and season with salt and pepper. Fold and loop the zucchini and place on the skewers, alternating with the tomatoes. Grill the skewered vegetables until the zucchini is charred and beginning to soften, but the tomatoes have not completely burst, turning once, 4 to 6 minutes. Sprinkle with oregano, if desired.

STEP 4. Spoon the polenta into bowls and top with the zucchini and tomato skewers before serving.

POLENTA WITH MUSHROOM POMODORO

SERVES 4

3 cups/720 ml water

1 cup/140 g polenta

Sea salt

1¼ cups/300 ml whole milk

4 tbsp unsalted butter

1 oz/30 g Parmigiano-Reggiano cheese, plus more
for topping

¼ cup/60 ml extra-virgin olive oil

3 lb/1.4 kg assorted wild mushrooms such as
morels, chanterelles, trumpets, and oysters,
cleaned and trimmed

Freshly ground pepper

1 shallot, finely chopped

1 garlic clove, smashed

1 sprig fresh thyme

¼ cup/60 ml half-and-half

1 tbsp Cognac (optional)

Small handful fresh parsley leaves, coarsely
chopped

STEP 1. Bring the water to a boil in a medium saucepan over medium-high heat. Slowly add
the polenta, stir with a wooden spoon, and add 1 tsp salt. Reduce the heat to medium and
cook, stirring occasionally, until the polenta is tender and fully cooked, about 20 minutes.
Add the milk, 2 tbsp of the butter, and the Parmigiano-Reggiano to the polenta and stir
together over medium-low heat until just warmed through and soft enough to drop easily
from a spoon, a few minutes more. Cover to keep warm.

STEP 2. Meanwhile, heat your largest skillet over medium heat. Add the olive oil and
mushrooms and cook until they begin to brown and release their liquid, about 5 minutes.
Raise the heat to medium-high and cook, stirring occasionally, until the mushrooms are
crispy but still juicy, seasoning with salt and pepper toward the end of cooking. Add the
shallot, garlic, and thyme and cook 4 minutes more. Add the half-and-half and Cognac (if
using). Reduce the heat to medium and cook, stirring frequently, until the liquid thickens
just slightly and coats the mushrooms evenly (like a saucy mushroom gravy), a few minutes
more. Discard the thyme sprig and stir in the remaining 2 tbsp butter. Taste and season
with more salt and pepper as needed.

STEP 3. Spoon the polenta into bowls and top with the mushrooms and sprinkle with parsley
before serving.

POLENTA WITH WINTER SALAD, POACHED EGG, AND BLUE CHEESE

SERVES 4

3½ cups/840 ml water

1 cup/140 g polenta

Sea salt

1¼ cups/300 ml whole milk

3 tbsp unsalted butter

1 oz/30 g cheddar or Dubliner cheese, grated

3 tbsp extra-virgin olive oil

1 handful cherry tomatoes

Freshly ground pepper

¼ small head radicchio, chopped into bite-size pieces

½ head frisée, torn into bite-size pieces

Dash white or regular balsamic vinegar

4 large eggs, poached (see page 272)

1 to 2 oz/30 to 55 g Danish blue, Roquefort, Valdeon blue, or Gorgonzola cheese

STEP 1. Bring 3 cups/720 ml of the water to a boil in a medium saucepan over medium-high heat. Slowly add the polenta, stir with a wooden spoon, and add 1 tsp salt. Reduce the heat to medium and cook, stirring occasionally, until the polenta is tender and fully cooked, about 20 minutes. Add the milk, 2 tbsp of the butter, and the cheddar to the polenta and stir together over medium-low heat until just warmed through and soft enough to drop easily from a spoon, a few minutes more. Cover to keep warm.

STEP 2. Heat the olive oil in your largest skillet over medium-high heat. Add the tomatoes and cook, stirring occasionally, until they are charred and have burst, about 4 minutes. Season with salt and pepper. Add the radicchio and frisée and cook until wilted, about 3 minutes. Stir in the vinegar, the remaining ½ cup/120 ml water, and the remaining 1 tbsp butter. Reduce the heat to medium-low and toss together.

STEP 3. Spoon the polenta into bowls and top with the salad and poached eggs. Crumble the blue cheese over the top before serving.

QUINOA BOWL WITH AVOCADO, RED CABBAGE, AND WALNUTS

I've decided there are two kinds of quinoa eaters: Those who eat it because it's so darned good for you, and those who eat it because it can be, when treated right, truly delicious. I'm firmly in the second camp, and this is the dish that did it for me. It happened one chilly day when all the seasonal staples of my fridge and pantry (avocado, citrus, quinoa, and walnuts) came together, warm and cool, crisp and soft, in my favorite bowl. It's a nurturing, filling, invigorating, and dependable bowl of health and flavor.

SERVES 4

2 cups/240 g quinoa

4 cups/960 ml water

Handful haricots verts or thin green beans, trimmed and chopped

Sea salt

⅓ cup/30 g walnuts

3 tbsp unsalted butter

1 tbsp extra-virgin olive oil, plus more for drizzling

1 firm, ripe avocado, peeled, pitted, and thinly sliced

2 grapefruit, navel oranges, or clementines, peeled, halved, and cut into half-moons

½ head red cabbage, thinly sliced

Smoked or coarse sea salt

Freshly ground pepper

STEP 1. Rinse the quinoa in a strainer under cold running water until the water runs clear, about 45 seconds. Bring the 4 cups/960 ml water, quinoa, haricots verts, and 1 tsp salt to a boil in a medium pot over high heat. Boil, uncovered, 10 to 15 minutes.

STEP 2. Meanwhile, toast the walnuts in 1 tbsp of the butter and the 1 tbsp olive oil in a small pan over medium heat for about 5 minutes.

STEP 3. Stir the remaining 2 tbsp butter into the quinoa and fluff with a fork. Spoon into shallow bowls, and arrange the avocado, walnuts, grapefruit, and cabbage around the outer rim of the bowls. Drizzle with olive oil, sprinkle with a few grains of smoked sea salt, and season with pepper. Serve warm.

CAULIFLOWER CURRY

This is the kind of dish that will remind you why vegetables are so deserving of the center stage on your plate. It is healthful and rich, with just the right amount of fat and flavor to satisfy your every need. Cauliflower has any number of consummate companions, but walnuts ground almost to a butter gives this curry a rich, roasted depth.

———————————————— SERVES 4 ————————————————

2½ cups/600 ml water

1½ cups/315 g jasmine rice

1 cup/115 g toasted walnuts (see page 273)

¼ cup/60 ml extra-virgin olive oil

1 large head cauliflower, cut into florets

1 tsp turmeric

1 tbsp garam masala

½ to ¾ tsp cayenne pepper (see Cook's Note)

1½ cups/360 ml vegetable stock (see page 270) or purchased vegetable stock

3 tbsp Asian or Hungarian hot-pepper paste (see page 26) or tomato paste

Sea salt

STEP 1. Bring the water to a boil in a medium pot over high heat. Add the rice, reduce the heat to medium, and cover tightly. Simmer until the rice is tender, about 20 minutes.

STEP 2. Grind ¾ cup/85 g of the walnuts to a fine meal in a food processor or coffee grinder, stopping just before they turn into a paste, about 2 minutes. Coarsely chop the remaining walnuts with a knife.

STEP 3. Heat the olive oil in your largest skillet over medium-high heat. Cook the cauliflower until lightly brown, stirring frequently, about 15 minutes. Scoot the cauliflower to the side of the pan. Add the turmeric, garam masala, and cayenne and toast until fragrant, about 30 seconds. Add the stock and the hot-pepper paste and whisk together. Bring to a simmer and stir to lightly coat the cauliflower in the spices. Continue to simmer until the sauce thickens slightly, about 2 minutes. Season with salt and add half of the ground walnuts and stir until combined.

STEP 4. Divide the cooked rice among bowls and top with the cauliflower curry. Sprinkle the chopped walnuts and the remaining ground walnuts on top. Serve warm.

COOK'S NOTE. To make your curry hot, add extra cayenne.

RED LENTILS WITH YOGURT

Red lentils, often found in Indian cuisine, are a nutritionally mighty legume. I like to think of them as beginner lentils since they cook fast, break down easily, and are easy to digest. The heat in this recipe comes from a jalapeño or serrano chile. Both will complement the other flavors beautifully and are easier to find than the traditional chiles this dish might otherwise call for. Top the finished lentils with yogurt, cilantro, avocado, and plenty of juicy lime wedges for a meal utterly brimming with color and nourishment.

_____ SERVES 6 _____

2 tbsp extra-virgin olive oil

1 large yellow onion, finely chopped

1 tsp minced garlic

2 tbsp grated peeled fresh ginger

2 tsp turmeric

1 tsp coriander seeds, crushed

1 small jalapeño or serrano chile, seeded and minced

2 cups/240 g red lentils, rinsed

6 cups/1.4 L vegetable stock (see page 270) or water

One 28-oz/800-g can crushed tomatoes in juice

1 tsp sea salt

Pita bread, naan, or flatbread for serving

1 avocado, peeled, pitted, and chopped (optional)

Small handful fresh cilantro leaves, coarsely chopped

¾ cup/180 ml plain or Greek yogurt

2 limes, cut into wedges

STEP 1. Heat the olive oil in a large saucepan over medium heat. Add the onion and cook, stirring occasionally, until soft and just golden brown, 7 to 10 minutes.

STEP 2. Add the garlic, ginger, turmeric, and coriander seeds and cook until fragrant, about 30 seconds. Stir in the jalapeño, lentils, stock, tomatoes and their juices, and salt. Raise the heat to medium-high, cover loosely, and bring to a boil. Reduce the heat to medium and simmer, stirring occasionally, until the lentils are tender, 18 to 25 minutes, depending on how much bite you like in your lentils.

STEP 3. Just before serving, lay the pita over a low flame on a gas stove top or toast on a griddle. Flip and rotate until just lightly browned.

STEP 4. Spoon the lentils into bowls and top with the avocado (if using). Sprinkle with cilantro, dollop with yogurt, and add a squeeze of fresh lime juice over the top. Serve warm with the pita bread.

MUSHROOM GULYÁS

Hungarian *gulyás*, or goulash as it's known in English-speaking countries, gets its rich red color from all the paprika, and that's likely to be the first thing you taste. As you spoon though the bowl, you'll get the flavors of mushrooms, zucchini, and tomato, but it's the paprika you'll be left with again at the end.

The first time I made this dish for my Hungarian husband, outside of his mother's watch, it was good, but not delicious. He asked me how much paprika I used. When I said a heaping two tablespoons, thinking that was generous, his response was "That's a good start." Hungarians love their paprika. But that's the point; it is the warm, round flavors you both see and taste that make traditional gulyás worthy of being a national dish.

Since mushrooms are the meat of this gulyás, the more flavorful the mushroom you use, the more exciting the results. I've made this with everything from button to oyster and hen of the woods to the tiny foraged gems of the Bakony forest in Hungary.

In Hungary, we cook gulyás over a live fire in a giant *bogracs*, or kettle. When everyone goes to bed, the leftover gulyás sits over the embers as the fire dies down. Since gulyás gets better the longer it cooks or sits, like any good stew, the fire is started up again the next day and gulyás ladled out into eager bowls until it all is gone. Make yours ahead if you have the foresight.

——————————————— SERVES 6 TO 8 ———————————————

¼ cup/60 ml extra-virgin olive oil

2 yellow onions, chopped

4 long Hungarian, banana, or Italian frying peppers, seeded and chopped

1½ lb/680 g assorted wild mushrooms such as oyster and hen of the woods, cleaned, trimmed, and cut into bite-size pieces

1½ lb/680 g cremini or button mushrooms, cleaned, trimmed, and cut into bite-size pieces

Coarse sea salt and freshly ground pepper

4 garlic cloves, smashed and peeled

1 tsp caraway seeds

Heaping 3 tbsp sweet paprika

3 to 4 tbsp Hungarian sweet or hot paprika paste (see page 26), or 1 tbsp hot paprika

4 large firm, ripe tomatoes, chopped

2 carrots, peeled and coarsely chopped

2 large Yukon gold or 2 medium russet potatoes, peeled and chopped

2 zucchini, peeled and coarsely chopped

1 bay leaf

6 cups/1.4 L vegetable stock (see page 270) or water

2 tbsp fresh bread crumbs

Sour cream, crème fraîche, or plain yogurt for dolloping

Whole-grain bread, dumplings, or cooked noodles for serving

STEP 1. Heat the olive oil in a large pot over medium heat. Add the onions and Hungarian peppers and cook, stirring occasionally, until soft and just golden brown, 5 to 6 minutes. Add the mushrooms and cook, stirring occasionally, until softened, about 8 minutes, seasoning lightly with salt and black pepper as you go. Taste a mushroom; it should be full flavored and well seasoned—all your other flavors will build on this. Season with more salt and black pepper as needed.

STEP 2. Meanwhile, finely chop the smashed garlic with a chef's knife. Add the caraway seeds and a pinch of salt, and chop and scrape against the cutting board with the flat side of your knife, repeating each motion over and over to make a garlic paste. Add the garlic paste, sweet paprika, and paprika paste to the pot and stir quickly with a wooden spoon to coat the onions, Hungarian peppers, and mushrooms.

STEP 3. Add the tomatoes, carrots, potatoes, zucchini, and bay leaf. Pour the stock over all and stir until combined. Cover loosely, raise the heat to high, and bring to a boil. Reduce the heat to low and simmer until the vegetables are tender and the broth is deeply flavored, about 45 minutes. Stir in the bread crumbs and cook until they disappear and thicken the soup, about 10 minutes.

STEP 4. Ladle the gulyás into bowls and dollop with sour cream. Serve warm with bread. Store any leftovers in an airtight container in the fridge for up to 4 days; reheat on the stove top over low heat.

COOK'S NOTE. The quality of your paprika, like a good wine, does matter. If you can get your hands on it, paprika paste gives great depth, heat (if you use the hot or csípős paprika paste), and aroma to gulyás.

SOMEN NOODLE BOWL
WITH BROCCOLINI AND BOK CHOY

When the mood for a brothy bowl of vegetables strikes, this soup is the answer. And like any great broth-based soup, it's the dashi, a broth made with kombu, dried shiitake mushroom, and bonito flakes (optional here), that's the crux of the flavor. In Japan, the noodle of choice for this dish is saimin or somen, which can be found in many Asian grocery stores, but ramen, udon, or soba will work if they're all you can find.

Like many of the Asian-inspired dishes in my kitchen, this may not be authentic, but it ranks high in satisfaction. The broth is traditionally made with dried shiitakes, for example, but while you're buying fresh mushrooms for the garnish, you can make a good broth with the stems and a few additional fresh shiitakes. Use filtered water to make the dashi. Though this is traditionally served with Japanese mustard, I like it with the gochujang paste I make for bibimbap, though neither are essentials. If your broth is flavorful, the noodles and vegetables are all you need.

———————————————— SERVES 4 ————————————————

DASHI

1 small piece of kombu or dried seaweed

8 dried or 4 fresh whole shiitake mushrooms

One 2-in/5-cm piece peeled fresh ginger, thinly sliced in coins

2 qt/2 L water

Sea salt

¾ cup/10 g bonito flakes (optional)

3 tbsp tamari or soy sauce, plus more as needed

1 bunch broccolini, trimmed

2 baby bok choy or 3 leaves Chinese or napa cabbage, thinly sliced

8 oz/225 g somen, ramen, udon, or soba noodles

4 shiitake mushroom caps, very thinly sliced

3 or 4 green onions, thinly sliced

Gochujang paste (see page 175) for topping

STEP 1. *To make the Dashi:* Combine the kombu, whole shiitakes, ginger, and water in a medium pot and bring to a boil over high heat. Reduce the heat to medium-low and simmer until the dried shiitakes are rehydrated or the fresh shitakes have given the broth a rich flavor, 8 to 10 minutes. Remove from the heat; add 1 tsp salt, the bonito flakes (if using), and the tamari; and let steep until the flavors come together, about 30 minutes.

STEP 2. Bring a large pot three-fourths full of salted water to a boil over high heat. Add the broccolini and cook until bright green, about 2 minutes. Remove with a slotted spoon and set aside on a plate. Add the bok choy and cook until bright green, about 1 minute. Remove and place next to the broccolini. Add the noodles and cook until soft, 3 to 5 minutes, according to the package directions. Drain the noodles.

STEP 3. When the vegetables and noodles are cooked, taste the broth. It should be rich and gingery, with a nice sea flavor. When it tastes good to you, strain the broth into a large bowl and discard the solids. (You can make the dashi up to 3 days in advance; just be sure to cool completely and store in an airtight container in the fridge.) If you'd like a deeper flavor, steep another 20 minutes before straining.

STEP 4. Return the strained broth to the medium pot and heat over medium heat until simmering, about 2 minutes. Ladle the noodles into deep bowls and arrange the broccolini, bok choy, and sliced shiitake over the top. Scatter with the green onions and top with gochujang paste. Serve hot with more gochujang paste and tamari.

COOK'S NOTE. Dashi broth is sometimes made with shrimp shells, which impart a deeper sea flavor to the broth. Without them, the broth sings with mushroom and ginger tones. If you eat seafood and wish for a rich sea taste, add about two handfuls of shrimp shells to the water with the kombu and proceed.

NOODLE KNOW-HOW

Often, a package of udon, soba, or somen includes several bundles of noodles. Generally, one bundle makes enough for one or two servings of soup. Make the broth ahead and keep it on hand in the fridge for up to three days. For a fast weeknight meal, add the cooked vegetables and cook the noodles of your choice.

STROZZAPRETI
WITH VEGETABLE RAGU

There's no beating around the bush here—chopping all the vegetables for this delicious vegetable ragu is a bit of work. But you'll be rewarded with a heaping bowlful of flavor and oodles of leftovers that get better every day they spend in the fridge. Strozzapreti is just a plain fun pasta shape to eat, but this sauce is amazing on orecchiette, gnocchi, or polenta (see page 155), too.

What makes a bowl of ragu so delicious in the hands of an Italian chef or nonna is the generous layers of flavorful garnishes on top. Don't skimp on adding both a creamy and an aged cheese for a truly memorable finish.

--- SERVES 4 TO 6 ---

VEGETABLE RAGU

5 tbsp/75 ml extra-virgin olive oil

1 lb/455 g wild or button mushrooms, cleaned, trimmed, and chopped

1 large yellow onion, chopped

1 bulb fennel, halved, cored, and chopped

2 large carrots, shredded

Sea salt and freshly ground pepper

1 lb/445 g kabocha or butternut squash, peeled, seeded, and chopped

3 large garlic cloves, smashed

2 tbsp tomato paste

Pinch of red pepper flakes

½ tsp sweet or smoked paprika (see page 25)

½ tsp fennel seeds (optional)

1 cup/240 ml dry white or red wine such as sauvignon blanc, pinot grigio, or Chianti

1 bay leaf

1 tbsp finely chopped fresh thyme

3 cups/720 ml vegetable stock (see page 270) or water

One 28-oz/800-g can San Marzano or plum tomatoes in juice

1 lb/455 g strozzapreti pasta

Soft creamy cheese like fresh sheep's milk ricotta or mascarpone cheese for dolloping

Aged sheep's milk cheese such as pecorino or brebis for grating

A few small fresh mint leaves

STEP 1. *To make the Vegetable Ragu:* Heat the olive oil in a large soup pot or wide heavy-bottomed saucepan over medium-high heat. Add the mushrooms and cook until they begin to brown and release their liquid, 6 to 8 minutes. Add the onion, fennel, and carrots and cook until soft and just golden brown, 5 to 7 minutes. Season with ¾ tsp salt and ¼ tsp black pepper.

STEP 2. Add the squash, garlic, tomato paste, red pepper flakes, paprika, and fennel seeds (if using) and cook until the paste browns and the liquid has almost evaporated, about 1 minute. Add the wine and stir, scraping the bottom of the pan to get all the good brown bits. Reduce the heat to medium and cook until the sauce thickens slightly, about 5 minutes.

STEP 3. Add the bay leaf, thyme, and 2 cups/480 ml of the stock. Add the tomatoes and their juices, passing them through clean hands on the way to the pot to crush and swish them. Cook to reduce the sauce slightly, about 15 minutes.

STEP 4. Add the remaining 1 cup/240 ml stock and reduce the heat to medium-low. Cook, uncovered, at a slow, steady simmer with small bubbles popping up all over the surface of the sauce, for about 1 hour or more (the longer it cooks, the better the flavor), to create a thick sauce studded with vegetables. Season with ¾ tsp salt and 1 tsp pepper. Taste and season with more salt and pepper as needed.

STEP 5. Bring a large pot three-fourths full of salted water to a boil over high heat. Add the strozzapreti to the boiling water and cook until al dente, about 9 minutes. Drain, reserving ⅓ cup/75 ml of the pasta cooking liquid for the sauce.

STEP 6. Add the cooked pasta to the sauce and toss gently to coat, adding the pasta cooking liquid as needed, 1 tbsp at a time, to your desired consistency. Scoop the dressed pasta into shallow bowls and dollop with ricotta. Grate the pecorino over the top, season with pepper, and sprinkle with mint. Serve warm.

CHEESE FOR TOPPING PASTA

A rich, hearty pasta sauce, like a ragu, is deserving of a decadent finish. One could certainly grate aged Parmigiano-Reggiano cheese over this sauce, but watch this dish (and plenty of other pasta dishes) come to life when you top with a subtly sweet, creamy cheese, such as fresh, locally made ricotta or mascarpone, followed by the nutty, salty smooth flavors of aged pecorino or a small sheep's milk brebis cheese. It's these two cheeses in combination that take a dish from merely delicious to truly memorable.

WHOLE-WHEAT PENNE WITH PUMPKIN, ROSEMARY, AND PINE NUTS

The clean-out-the-fridge-and-pantry meal that comes together by sheer accident is gratifying on so many levels. This could be one of those, or it could just as easily be something you plan for, a welcome meal for when pumpkin season arrives at last. You'd never know either way, because it feels so thoughtful. It could star your very own marinara sauce and be served as a fall feast for friends, or it could be just the thing for dressing up your favorite jarred sauce when you need a fast little cheat to elevate the obvious.

———————————————— SERVES 4 TO 6 ————————————————

2 to 3 tbsp extra-virgin olive oil

3 or 4 garlic cloves, smashed

1 small pumpkin or butternut squash, peeled, seeded, and chopped

Pinch of red pepper flakes

2 small sprigs fresh rosemary

Sea salt and freshly ground black pepper

1 lb/455 g whole-wheat penne

4 cups/960 ml marinara sauce (see page 206)

Parmigiano-Reggiano or pecorino cheese for grating

¼ cup/15 g toasted pine nuts (see page 273)

STEP 1. Bring a large pot three-fourths full of salted water to a boil over high heat.

STEP 2. Meanwhile, heat 2 tbsp of the olive oil in a large skillet over medium heat. Add the garlic, pumpkin, red pepper flakes, and rosemary and cook until the pumpkin is tender, 7 to 10 minutes, adding the remaining 1 tbsp of oil if needed. After the pumpkin absorbs all the oil, add 2 tbsp boiling water and continue cooking. Season with salt and black pepper. If you like, chop up a few of the crispy rosemary sprigs for garnish, or remove and discard them.

STEP 3. Add the penne to the boiling water and cook until al dente, about 9 minutes. Drain, reserving ¼ cup/60 ml of the pasta cooking liquid for the sauce.

STEP 4. Warm the marinara sauce in a large pot over low heat. Add the cooked pasta to the sauce and toss gently to coat, adding the pasta cooking liquid as needed, 1 tbsp at a time, to your desired consistency.

STEP 5. Scoop the dressed pasta into shallow bowls and spoon the pumpkin mixture over the top. Grate or shave Parmigiano-Reggiano over the top with a vegetable peeler and sprinkle with the pine nuts. Serve warm.

BLANK-SLATE BAKED RISOTTO

In Italy, risotto is considered fast food. Can you imagine? But the truth is, it *is* fast. Fast, easy, and delicious. And knowing that, aren't you inspired to whip up a pot of it tonight? If it's the standing over the stove stirring every few minutes that has deterred you from making risotto a regular item at home, try baked risotto. Baked risotto, especially white risotto (made with white wine and finished simply with butter and cheese), has become my fast food, the ideal blank canvas for any, and I mean *any*, seasonal flavors I love.

While you let the oven do the work, you're free to devise any number of delicious combinations to stir in or serve on top, from roasted pumpkin and sage to shaved corn and dill. Or if you like yours straight-up with cheese, use the extra time while it bakes to learn this recipe by heart. I promise it will come in handy.

―――――――――――――――――――――― SERVES 2 TO 4 ――――――――――――――――――――――

1 tbsp extra-virgin olive oil

½ yellow onion, finely chopped

¾ cup/150 g Arborio rice

¼ cup/60 ml dry white wine such as sauvignon blanc or pinot grigio

2½ cups/600ml hot vegetable stock (see page 270 and Cook's Note) or water

Sea salt and freshly ground pepper

2 tbsp unsalted butter

¼ cup/30 g freshly grated Parmigiano-Reggiano cheese, plus more for topping

1 Risotto Topper (see facing page)

STEP 1. Preheat the oven to 400°F/200°C/gas 6.

STEP 2. Heat the olive oil in an ovenproof saucepan or Dutch oven with a lid over medium-high heat. Add the onion and cook, stirring occasionally, until soft and translucent, about 3 minutes. Add the rice and stir to coat with the oil. Add the wine, stir into the rice, and cook until the wine has evaporated, about 1 minute. Add 2 cups/480 ml of the hot stock, ¾ tsp salt, and a pinch of pepper and bring to a boil. Cover and transfer to the oven.

STEP 3. After 25 minutes, check the risotto. Most of the liquid should be absorbed and the rice just cooked.

STEP 4. Remove the risotto from the oven and stir in the remaining ½ cup/120 ml hot stock, the butter, and Parmigiano-Reggiano.

STEP 5. Serve warm, topped with more Parmigiano-Reggiano and your topper of choice.

COOK'S NOTE. When you make risotto, use a vegetable stock flavored with the same vegetables you plan to stir in your risotto. For example, add asparagus stalks in your vegetable stock and reserve the tips for stirring in at the end; make a broth of dried porcini for risotto topped with mushrooms; or add a few peelings of butternut squash to your stock for risotto topped with roasted squash.

RISOTTO TOPPERS

There is no wrong way to top a risotto. Here are a few pairings to get you started.

- spinach, mushrooms, and Parmesan cheese
- scallops and Parmesan cheese
- sweet potato and roasted apple
- asparagus and poached egg
- butternut squash and goat cheese
- mushrooms and thyme
- aged grating cheese and wild mushrooms
- peas, goat cheese, and cherry tomatoes

- smoked salmon, corn, dill
- blue crab and truffle
- saffron, lemon zest, peas, and shrimp
- grilled asparagus, lemon zest, butter, and pecorino
- wild mushroom, sage, and goat cheese
- Dungeness crab

BARLEY RISOTTO WITH RADISHES, SWISS CHARD, AND PRESERVED LEMON

This modern, vegetable-lover's risotto is made with barley, a homey whole grain that is easy to love, and one that will love you back with extra iron and minerals. Bright radishes and tart preserved lemon, both bold in texture and flavor, soften into the creamy texture of barley that's been cooked like risotto. When the season changes from spring to late summer, make this again with multicolored young carrots instead of radishes.

───────────────────── SERVES 4 ─────────────────────

4½ cups/1 L vegetable stock (see page 270) or water

2 tbsp unsalted butter or extra-virgin olive oil

1 cup/200 g pearl barley, rinsed

8 to 10 small radishes

1 bunch Swiss chard, stemmed and torn into large pieces

1 preserved lemon, seeded and thinly sliced

Sea salt

Small handful fresh dill, coarsely chopped

8 large fresh mint leaves, coarsely chopped or torn

STEP 1. Bring the stock to a simmer in a small saucepan over medium heat. Reduce the heat to medium-low to keep warm. Heat the butter in another medium saucepan over low heat. Add the barley and stir to coat, toasting it lightly in the butter. Add 2 cups/480 ml of the stock and bring to a boil over medium heat. Reduce the heat to medium-low, and simmer until the stock is mostly absorbed, stirring frequently, about 5 minutes.

STEP 2. Add the radishes and remaining stock, ½ cup/120 ml at a time, stirring frequently, until the barley is tender, about 45 minutes. Add the chard and stir until wilted, about 5 minutes. Stir in the preserved lemon and add up to ¾ tsp salt, depending on how salty your broth or lemons are.

STEP 3. Remove from the heat. Stir in the dill and mint. Serve warm or at room temperature.

BOTTOMLESS POT OF BIBIMBAP

If you've lived in New York as long as I have, you learn to love a steaming stone pot of Korean bibimbap as much as a comforting bowl of mashed potatoes. Bibimbap, which means "mixed rice" in Korean, is so much more than that. The steamy soft white rice is a comforting cushion for sautéed carrots, spinach, and kimchi, and for the grand finale, a fried egg, often tossed tableside with spicy red-pepper gochujang paste. This filling, flavorful meal is surprisingly easy to execute at home. With all the vegetables, there's no reason not to make it a habit. Consider yourself armed with the best of both worlds—flavor and health. Bibimbap is vitality in a bowl, from your very own kitchen.

SERVES 4

GOCHUJANG PASTE

4 tbsp Asian hot-pepper paste, such as sambal oelek

2 tbsp toasted sesame oil

1 tbsp toasted sesame seeds (see page 274)

2 green onions, finely chopped

1 tsp unbleached raw sugar

BIBIMBAP

6 cups/1.2 kg short-grain white rice such as sushi rice

3 large carrots, peeled

1 medium zucchini

3 cups/720 ml water

1 tbsp toasted sesame oil

2 to 3 tbsp peanut oil

3 to 4 handfuls spinach leaves

Sea salt

4 eggs, fried sunny-side up (see page 272)

Kimchi (page 250) or purchased kimchi for topping

Sesame seeds for sprinkling

STEP 1. *To make the Gochujang Paste:* Whisk together the hot-pepper paste, sesame oil, toasted sesame seeds, green onions, and sugar. Set aside.

STEP 2. *To make the Bibimbap:* Rinse and soak the rice in enough water to cover while you prepare the vegetables. Cut the carrots and zucchini into matchsticks and set aside. Drain the rice and combine with the 3 cups/720 ml water in a pot with a tight-fitting lid. Bring to a boil over medium heat, reduce the heat to medium-low, cover tightly, and simmer until the rice is tender, about 20 minutes.

STEP 3. Heat your largest large cast-iron skillet over medium heat. Add the sesame oil and 1 tbsp of the peanut oil and heat until shimmering. Cook the carrots, zucchini, and spinach, one at a time, until wilted and toothsome but tender enough to pierce with a fork, 3 to 5 minutes per vegetable. Transfer the vegetables to a platter as you cook them and cover loosely to keep warm. Season with ½ tsp salt.

CONTINUED

STEP 4. Drizzle the remaining 1 or 2 tbsp peanut oil over the bottom of the cast-iron skillet or a clay pot, if you have one, and add the cooked rice. Heat the skillet over medium heat until the prized crispy layer of rice along the bottom forms, 6 to 8 minutes. (If you have them, you can do this in four smaller cast-iron skillets or ramekins, which are fun.)

STEP 5. Lay the fried eggs on top of the rice, followed by the cooked vegetables and the kimchi. Sprinkle sesame seeds over the top and dollop with gochujang paste. Serve warm with more gochujang paste. Each diner should toss the bibimbap all together with chopsticks before eating.

INDONESIAN RICE BOWL

In the first draft of this book, I included an authentic Indonesian fried rice, a dish I learned to make when I visited my friend's family in Bali many years ago. Via e-mail and Skype chats and several trips to the Indonesian market in New York City's Chinatown, I worked hard to duplicate the taste I'd grown to love.

The very weekend the book was due, I was in Mill Valley outside of San Francisco, where I ordered the Indo Rice Bowl at Boo Koo, a little shop celebrating Asian street food. What I got—a bowl of steamy rice topped with vegetables and salmon—was anything but authentic, but it was utterly delicious. So good, in fact, that I went back to get it again the next day. What I love is that it was absolutely accessible, easy for anyone to make out of the gleanings of your pantry and garden, no special trips to the store required. In the end, this dish, my version of the Indo Rice Bowl, is the one that belongs in this book, one to be made weekly, without great effort but with tremendous reward.

SERVES 4

1 bunch Swiss chard

2 baby bok choy

Peanut oil for frying

Sea salt

1 small zucchini, cut into matchsticks

2 carrots, peeled and cut into matchsticks

½ tsp grated peeled fresh ginger

4 green onions, thinly sliced

Handful bean sprouts (optional)

1 tbsp rice vinegar

1 seedless cucumber, cut into matchsticks

6 cups/1.2 kg cooked long-grain or jasmine rice

Teriyaki Salmon (facing page; optional)

STEP 1. Separate the chard stems from the leaves and cut both into bite-size pieces. Separate the bok choy stems from the leaves and cut both into bite-size pieces.

STEP 2. In a large, deep skillet or wok over medium heat, heat ½ in/12 mm peanut oil until shimmering. Reduce the heat to medium-low, add the chard and bok choy stems, and cook until soft, about 3 minutes. Add the chard and bok choy leaves and cook until wilted, about 5 minutes. Season with salt and turn off the heat. Add the zucchini, carrots, ginger, and green onions to the pan and toss to wilt slightly. Season with salt. Toss together with the bean sprouts (if using).

STEP 3. In a small bowl, combine the vinegar and cucumber.

STEP 4. Spoon the rice into bowls and top with the vegetable mixture, cucumber, and pieces of salmon (if using). Serve warm with chopsticks.

TERIYAKI SALMON

Just like at Boo Koo, I like the optional teriyaki salmon add-on. For those who do eat fish, the tangy-sweet teriyaki pairs well with the other flavors at play, and this technique is a go-to for any fish you might find.

———————————————— SERVES 4 ————————————————

1 cup/240 ml soy sauce

¼ cup/60 ml honey

2 tbsp rice vinegar

One 1-in/2.5-cm piece peeled fresh ginger, finely chopped

1 clove garlic, smashed

2 lb/910 g wild salmon fillet, pinbones removed

Extra-virgin olive oil for brushing

STEP 1. Whisk together the soy sauce, honey, rice vinegar, ginger, and garlic in a wide, shallow dish. Add the salmon, turning to coat, and marinate for 10 minutes. Preheat the broiler to high. Line a baking sheet with aluminum foil and brush with olive oil.

STEP 2. Remove the salmon from the marinade, letting any excess marinade drip back into the dish, and place on the prepared baking sheet. Broil the salmon until slightly firm but still slightly pink inside, about 12 minutes, brushing with the marinade once or twice during cooking. Break into portions with a knife before adding to the recipe.

CHICKPEAS, FARRO, AND SAUSAGE
IN SOFRITO BRODO

Starting with the same ingredients used to make a sweet smoky sofrito (onions, tomatoes, and paprika; see page 256), any number of heady Spanish-style soups could be on
your horizon. Chickpeas, farro, and a soy or grain-based sausage make this steamy, richly
flavored soup hearty and nutritionally complete, and a soothing winter staple. Opt for a
firm sausage with good spice, like chorizo or chipotle, for the fullest flavor.

———————————————— SERVES 4 ————————————————

¼ cup/60 ml olive oil, plus more for the bread

2 large yellow onions, finely chopped

Sea salt

4 large or 6 medium ripe plum tomatoes

Heaping 1 tsp pimenton or smoked paprika

Freshly ground pepper

½ cup/120 ml dry white wine

1 bay leaf

1 cup/170 g quick semi-pearled or pearled farro

1½ cups/240 g cooked or canned chickpeas,
    drained and rinsed

2 links spicy grain or soy sausage, cut into
    1-in/2.5-cm pieces

1 baguette or another crusty bread, sliced on
    the bias

¼ cup/7 g finely chopped fresh parsley

STEP 1. Heat 2 tbsp of the olive oil in a medium skillet over medium heat. Add the onions
and season with about ½ tsp salt. Cook until golden, stirring occasionally, about 30 minutes. Taste; the onions should taste subtly sweet.

STEP 2. While the onions cook, cut the tomatoes in half lengthwise. Grate the tomato on
the course side of a box grater into a bowl all the way down to the skins. Discard the skins,
and add the pulp and juices to the onions along with the pimenton. Cook until thick, about
5 minutes. Taste and season with salt and pepper as needed.

STEP 3. Add the wine and bay leaf and bring to a simmer. Cook until the wine is almost
cooked off. Add 6 cups/1.4 L water and the farro and bring to a simmer. Simmer until the
farro is tender, 20 to 22 minutes. Stir in the chickpeas.

STEP 4. Meanwhile, heat 2 tbsp oil in a cast-iron or nonstick skillet. Add the sausage and cook
until crispy and warmed through, 3 to 5 minutes. Turn off the heat and reserve.

STEP 5. Preheat the broiler or toaster oven to medium. Just before serving, brush your bread
generously with olive oil and broil or toast until golden and crispy.

STEP 6. Stir the sausage into the soup. Spoon the soup into four bowls. Sprinkle each with
parsley and serve with generous stacks of toasted bread.

SWEET POTATO AND KALE TORTILLA SOUP

Tortilla soup is the chicken noodle soup of Mexican cuisine, but with the flavors of chile and tomato, even traditionalists won't miss the chicken or chicken broth in this vegetarian version. Made with sweet hunks of sweet potato and just-wilted kale, it is both hearty and nutritious. Tortilla soup's charm is in its strong finish, with buttery avocado, snappy radishes, and, of course, a handful of crackling-hot tortilla strips. This is truly a vegetable meal in a bowl but fiery and brothy enough to evict any winter blues that have overstayed their welcome. It's also a great crowd-pleaser and a perfect soup to serve for Super Bowl Sunday or a casual weekend supper.

SERVES 4 TO 6

2 tbsp extra-virgin olive oil, plus more for frying

1 yellow onion, thinly sliced

2 garlic cloves, minced

1 or 2 jalapeño chiles, seeded and minced

1 tsp chili powder

¾ tsp ground cumin

1 large sweet potato or garnet yam, cut into bite-size cubes

5 to 6 cups/1.2 to 1.4 L vegetable stock (see page 270) or water

One 14½-oz/415-g can diced tomatoes

Sea salt

1 bunch kale, stemmed and chopped

4 fresh small Corn Tortillas (page 140) or purchased corn tortillas, thinly sliced

Full-fat plain or Greek yogurt for dolloping

Queso fresco for sprinkling

Fresh cilantro leaves for sprinkling

1 avocado, peeled, pitted, and chopped (optional)

4 radishes, thinly sliced (optional)

4 to 6 limes, cut into wedges

STEP 1. Heat the olive oil in a medium saucepan over medium heat. Add the onion, and cook, stirring occasionally, until soft and just golden brown, 5 to 8 minutes. Add the garlic, jalapeños, chili powder, and cumin and cook until fragrant, about 1 minute. Add the sweet potato, stock, and tomatoes with their juices and bring to a boil. Add ¼ tsp salt, cover loosely, and reduce the heat to medium-low. Simmer until the sweet potatoes are completely tender, 30 to 35 minutes. Uncover the pot, add the kale, and cook until just wilted, about 3 minutes.

STEP 2. Meanwhile, line a plate with paper towels and set near the stove. In a small, shallow skillet, heat 1 in/2.5 cm olive oil over medium heat. To test the temperature of the oil, drop a tortilla strip into the skillet; the oil should sizzle and the tortilla cook to a pale golden brown. If it turns dark brown quickly or the oil is smoking, reduce the heat. Working in batches, fry the tortilla strips until golden brown, 1 to 2 minutes. Transfer the tortilla strips with a slotted spoon to the paper towel–lined plate and immediately season with salt.

STEP 3. Ladle the soup into bowls and garnish with fried tortilla strips, yogurt, queso fresco, and cilantro, plus additional toppings such as avocado and radishes at your whim. Serve warm with the lime wedges.

BLACK PEPPER TOFU POT

I fell in love with the black pepper in my grandma's gravy, usually on Sunday-morning biscuits. Big flecks of coarsely ground black pepper didn't reappear in my repertoire until culinary school, and I'm not sure how I lived so many years without it. When Jean-Georges Vongerichten's restaurant Perry St in New York City opened smack in the middle of my culinary training, I treated myself to the tasting menu and had something (could have been duck, crab, or tofu—it didn't matter) in a bowl bombed with black pepper that knocked my socks off. It's the kind of heat that's familiar—not like chiles or Tabasco—warming through and through and deeply gratifying. It can turn tofu into something as earthy and indulgent as a steak, utterly memorable when slathered in a silky, shallot-y butter sauce.

SERVES 4

1 bunch green onions

Wondra or all-purpose flour for coating

Vegetable oil for the pan

1 tsp toasted sesame oil

Two 14-oz/400-g packages firm tofu, drained and patted dry, cut into 1¼-in/3.25-cm cubes

½ cup/115 g unsalted butter

2 shallots, thinly sliced

1 Fresno or red jalapeño chile, seeded and thinly sliced

1 head garlic, cloves smashed

One 1-in/2.5-cm piece peeled fresh ginger, sliced into thin matchsticks

2 tbsp dark or regular soy sauce

1 to 2 tbsp unbleached raw sugar

2 tbsp coarsely cracked pepper

4 to 6 cups/530 to 790 g steamed brown or sushi rice

STEP 1. Cut the green onions into 2-in/5-cm lengths and then slice lengthwise into matchsticks. Set the white and green parts aside separately.

STEP 2. Pour the flour into a shallow bowl. Line a plate with paper towels and set near the stove. Heat a thin layer of vegetable oil in your largest skillet over medium heat. Just before frying, add the sesame oil to the pan.

STEP 3. Working in batches, lightly dust the tofu cubes in the flour, tossing to coat and shaking off any excess. Add the tofu to the hot oil with a slotted spoon, making sure that none of the pieces touch. Fry until the tofu cubes are golden with a thin crust on most sides, turning as needed, about 8 minutes. Lift the tofu out of the oil with the slotted spoon, letting the oil drip back into the pan, and transfer to the paper towel–lined plate. Repeat until all the tofu cubes are fried, coating the tofu in the flour as you go and adding more oil to the pan as needed.

STEP 4. Wipe out the skillet. Melt the butter in the skillet over medium heat. Add the shallots, chile, garlic, and ginger and stir. Cook until fragrant and soft, about 8 minutes, adding the white parts of the green onions after a few minutes. Add the soy sauce, sugar, and pepper and stir to bring the sauce together.

STEP 5. Seconds before serving, return the tofu and the green parts of the green onions to the skillet and toss to coat completely. Divide the rice among deep bowls and spoon the tofu and sauce over the rice. If you like your tofu crispier, spoon the tofu and the green parts of the green onions over the rice (without returning them to the pan) and drizzle the sauce over the top. Serve hot.

COOK'S NOTE. You can use a wok if you have one, which is traditional for this style of dish, but because the bottom is more narrow than a skillet, you may have to fry the tofu in smaller batches.

CHAPTER 6

platefuls

Some days or nights you need fill-your-belly food—sticky or saucy, rich in flavor but not in fat. Sit-down-with-knife-and-fork kind of meals. Platefuls. These are comfort foods, though some of them are sophisticated. There are pastas, but not like you've seen before; they are filling piles of vegetable-centric delights.

There may be no greater lesson in vegetarian versatility than that found in Pasta for Four Seasons (PAGE 189). There you'll see just how quick (25 minutes quick) and easy it is to create fresh and amazing sauces with seasonal produce, like Orecchiette with Ricotta and Chard. Use these recipes as templates to expand and explore each and every vegetable in your top-twenty list and embrace how every texture and taste can shine when twirled and swirled with your favorite noodles.

And then there's messy filling food. Artichoke Enchiladas (PAGE 196), a reinvented classic (made with your own homemade tomatillo sauce), are a crowd-pleaser so surprisingly good you'll serve them without explanation, then watch carnivores fight over the last bite. For those with a Southern soul, the Back 40 Slab Pie (PAGE 198) is stuffed to the gills with vegetables.

Each and every one of these meals makes good on the promise that a mostly vegetarian diet is lush, full, and filling.

ANGEL HAIR WITH LENTILS AND OYSTER MUSHROOMS

One of the singular most spectacular taste moments of my life was at the restaurant Le Bernardin, in New York City. At the time, I was working in another of the city's top restaurants, Café Boulud, and was more than willing to spend what must have been an entire day's pay on any dish at the hands of Eric Ripert. The dish was a plate of wispy angel hair pasta spun in a cream sauce topped with uni (sea urchin) and caviar. I can still recall the shocking simplicity, pure flavor, and awe of every bite.

One doesn't need a taste for seafood or splurging to really treat themselves. In the dish that follows, I replaced the caviar with lentils and the uni with oyster mushrooms, which I consider two great delicacies of the earth. You can add the taste of the sea with flecks of sel gris and tiny slivers of nori swirled into the sauce. This is a dish to impress, a pasta designed entirely for pleasure.

SERVES 4

1 lemon

One 1-in/2.5-cm piece of nori (optional)

6 tbsp/85 g unsalted butter

2 shallots, very thinly sliced

Pinch of fresh thyme leaves, chopped

2 tbsp warm water

Sel gris and freshly ground pepper

½ cup/105 g green or brown lentils, rinsed

1 garlic clove, minced

8 oz/225 g oyster mushrooms, cleaned, trimmed, and sliced

½ cup/120 ml heavy cream

12 oz/340 g angel hair pasta

STEP 1. Zest the lemon, then cut it in half and remove the seeds. Thinly slice the nori (if using) into paper-thin strips with a sharp knife.

STEP 2. Melt 4 tbsp/55 g of the butter in a heavy-bottomed saucepan over medium heat until the butter forms brown bits on the bottom of the pan and smells nutty and toasty, about 6 minutes. Add the shallots and thyme and swirl together, cooking until the shallots are soft but not browned, about 4 minutes. Add the warm water and whisk together until you have an emulsified sauce, like a vinaigrette. Season with sel gris and pepper and transfer to a small bowl.

STEP 3. Bring a large pot three-fourths full of salted water to a boil over high heat. Add the lentils, cover, reduce the heat to medium-low, and simmer until the lentils are tender but still hold their shape, about 15 minutes.

STEP 4. Wipe out the pan used for the shallots and melt the remaining 2 tbsp butter over medium heat. Add the garlic and cook until fragrant, about 5 minutes. Add the mushrooms and cook until they begin to brown and release their liquid, about 5 minutes. Raise the heat to medium-high and cook, stirring occasionally, until the mushrooms are just crispy but still juicy, seasoning with sel gris and pepper toward the end of cooking. Add the cream, reduce the heat to medium, and simmer until the cream reduces slightly and just naps the mushrooms, about 2 minutes. Whisk in the shallot-butter mixture a spoonful at a time to create a uniform sauce.

STEP 5. When the lentils are almost done cooking, add the pasta to the pot with the lentils and cook until al dente, about 5 minutes. Drain the pasta and lentils, reserving about ¼ cup/60 ml of the cooking liquid. Add the pasta and lentils to the mushroom cream sauce, along with the lemon zest and nori (if using). Squeeze half the lemon over the top and toss together with tongs. Loosen the sauce with the reserved cooking liquid if needed. Taste, and squeeze the remaining lemon half over the top.

STEP 6. Spoon the dressed pasta into shallow bowls and sprinkle with sel gris. Serve warm.

SOUTHERN-STYLE BARBECUE SPAGHETTI WITH TEMPEH

One day I found myself sitting across from my dear friend's toddler, Andrew, and his plate of pasta. Andrew is an Indonesian American boy being raised in the South, and his pasta was unlike anything I'd ever seen before—big fat linguine noodles swirled up with chunks of pulled pork, all coated in barbecue sauce. He made it look so good. Leave it to a Southerner to put barbecue sauce on pasta, but something about it made perfect sense. If his mother, Anjee, were raising the little guy as a vegetarian (and she decidedly is not), this version is what I'd make him. And since tempeh hails from her Indonesian ancestry, I'm pretty sure she'd approve.

In sharp contrast to the nuanced Angel Hair with Lentils and Oyster Mushrooms (page 186), this dish is bold with a big hit of barbecue flavor. You can make your own amazing barbecue sauce, and sometimes I recommend you do. But this is down-and-dirty fast cooking with a jar of your favorite smoky-sweet mesquite sauce. Stir in a big handful of kale at the end to give yourself good reason to pile your plate high.

--------------------------------- SERVES 4 ---------------------------------

12 oz/340 g whole-wheat linguine

2 tbsp extra-virgin olive oil

8 oz/225 g plain tempeh, cut into 1-in/2.5-cm cubes

Sea salt and freshly ground pepper

1 cup/240 ml purchased smoky-sweet mesquite barbecue sauce

1 large bunch kale, stemmed and chopped

STEP 1. Bring a large pot three-fourths full of salted water to a boil over high heat. Add the linguine to the boiling water and cook until al dente, about 8 minutes.

STEP 2. While the pasta cooks, heat the olive oil in a large skillet over medium-high heat until shimmering. Pat the tempeh cubes dry and add them to the olive oil. Cook until the tempeh cubes are golden brown on most sides, turning as needed with a spatula, about 8 minutes. Season lightly with salt and pepper.

STEP 3. Drain the pasta, reserving about ¼ cup/60 ml of pasta cooking liquid for the sauce. Add the barbecue sauce and cooked pasta to the tempeh and toss gently to coat, adding the pasta cooking liquid as needed, 1 tbsp at a time, to your desired consistency. Add the kale and toss together with tongs. Cover loosely, reduce the heat to low, and cook, tossing once or twice, until the kale is just wilted but still bright green. Scoop the dressed pasta onto plates and serve hot.

PASTA FOR
FOUR SEASONS

Pasta lovers already know there are few things quite as satisfying as a bowl of starchy, sub-stantive noodles. Whether you eat pasta weekly or more often, learning how to make a quick pan sauce with seasonal vegetables will serve you year-round. Many of these recipes are as simple as they come—little "ears" of pasta (orecchiette), napped with a simple sauce made from Swiss chard, grated cheese, butter, and the pasta cooking liquid, for example—and taste darn good.

Use these four recipes as a guide for adding anything from leafy greens to juicy tomatoes to your pasta tonight. Take a spin around the market or your garden for inspira-tion—anything you love is welcome here. Switch up the pasta shapes, too. There are dozens of tucks and twists out there just waiting to soak up every bit of unctuous sauce.

SPRING

ORECCHIETTE WITH RICOTTA AND CHARD

——————————— SERVES 4 ———————————

1 large bunch Swiss chard

12 oz/340 g orecchiette

2 tbsp extra-virgin olive oil

2 tbsp unsalted butter

Pinch of red pepper flakes (optional)

2 oz/55 g freshly grated ricotta salata, Asiago, or pecorino cheese, plus more for serving

Freshly ground black pepper

Freshly ground nutmeg (optional) for sprinkling

Fresh ricotta cheese for dolloping

Fleur de sel or sel gris

STEP 1. Bring a large pot three-fourths full of salted water to a boil over high heat. Meanwhile, separate the chard stems from the leaves and cut both into bite-size pieces. Add the orecchiette to the boiling water and set the timer for 10 minutes.

STEP 2. Heat the olive oil in a large skillet over medium-high heat. Add the chard stems and cook until tender-crisp, 3 to 5 minutes. When the timer goes off, add the chard leaves to the boiling pasta water and cook for 2 minutes more. Drain, reserving ¼ cup/60 ml of the pasta cooking liquid for the sauce. Put the pasta and chard back in the pot over low heat. Add the chard stems and residual oil, along with the butter, red pepper flakes (if using), and the reserved pasta cooking liquid, 1 tbsp at a time, to bring it all together. Add the ricotta salata and toss it all together. Season with black pepper and sprinkle with nutmeg (if using).

CONTINUED

STEP 3. Scoop the dressed pasta into four shallow bowls, dollop with fresh ricotta, and season with fleur de sel. Garnish with more ricotta salata, if desired. Serve warm.

COOK'S NOTE. Since the chard leaves cook in the pasta cooking liquid, the same nutritious water flavors the sauce. Save any remaining cooking water as a fast, flavorful vegetable stock for puréed vegetable soups.

SUMMER

MUSHROOM AGNOLOTTI WITH SWEET CORN, HEIRLOOM TOMATOES, AND ARUGULA

SERVES 4

2 ears of corn

1 lb/455 g purchased wild mushroom agnolotti or ravioli

2 tbsp extra-virgin olive oil

1 small yellow onion, thinly sliced

1 garlic clove, thinly sliced

1 to 2 firm, ripe heirloom tomatoes, chopped

2 tbsp unsalted butter

Sea salt and freshly ground pepper

4 handfuls arugula or baby arugula

Freshly grated Parmigiano-Reggiano or pecorino for topping

STEP 1. Bring a large pot three-fourths full of salted water to a boil over high heat. Shave the kernels off of the ears of corn with a serrated knife (see page 265) and reserve; add the cobs to the water. Add the agnolotti and set the timer for 6 minutes.

STEP 2. Meanwhile, heat the olive oil in a large skillet over medium-high heat. Add the onion and garlic and cook until the garlic is fragrant, about 2 minutes.

STEP 3. Add the corn kernels to the skillet and cook over medium-high heat until tender-crisp, about 1 minute. Add the tomatoes and toss until they soften and release some juices, about 2 minutes more.

STEP 4. Drain the pasta, reserving $^{1}/_{4}$ cup/60 ml of the cooking liquid. Put the pasta back in the pot over low heat with the reserved cooking water, the corn, tomatoes, and butter. Toss together and season with salt and pepper. Stir in the arugula and toss until just wilted.

STEP 5. Scoop the dressed pasta into shallow bowls and top generously with Parmigiano-Reggiano. Serve warm.

BUCATINI WITH SPICY CHERRY TOMATOES, AGED FETA, AND SHRIMP

SERVES 4

12 oz/340 g bucatini or other fat spaghetti noodle

3 tbsp extra-virgin olive oil

2 garlic cloves, minced

2 pt/600 g cherry tomatoes, halved

½ tsp red wine vinegar (optional)

1 tbsp water (optional)

12 oz/340 g wild Patagonian or gulf shrimp, peeled and deveined (optional)

Generous pinch of red pepper flakes

Sea salt and freshly ground black pepper

6 oz/170 g aged feta cheese, crumbled

Handful fresh basil leaves, thinly sliced

STEP 1. Bring a large pot three-fourths full of salted water to a boil over high heat. Add the bucatini to the boiling water and cook until al dente, about 9 minutes. Drain, reserving ⅓ cup/75 ml of the pasta cooking liquid for the sauce.

STEP 2. Meanwhile, heat 2 tbsp of the olive oil in a large skillet over medium-high heat. Add the garlic and tomatoes and cook, stirring occasionally, until the tomatoes burst and the juices start to bubble, about 3 minutes. If your cherry tomatoes don't give out a lot of juice, add the red wine vinegar and water. Add the shrimp (if using) and red pepper flakes, season with salt and black pepper, and toss together until the shrimp is just cooked through, about 2 minutes.

STEP 3. Put the pasta back in the pot over low heat with the reserved pasta cooking liquid and sauce, and toss together with tongs over low heat. Remove from the heat, stir in the feta and basil, and toss together, adding the remaining 1 tbsp olive oil.

STEP 4. Scoop the dressed pasta into shallow bowls and serve warm.

WINTER
WHOLE-WHEAT LINGUINE WITH TREVISO AND GOAT CHEESE
FALL
BUCATINI WITH SPICY CHERRY TOMATOES, AGED FETA, AND SHRIMP

ORECCHIETTE WITH RICOTTA AND CHARD

SUMMER

MUSHROOM AGNOLOTTI WITH SWEET CORN, HEIRLOOM TOMATOES, AND ARUGULA

WHOLE-WHEAT LINGUINE
WITH TREVISO AND GOAT CHEESE

SERVES 4

12 oz/340 g whole-wheat linguine or spaghetti

2 tbsp extra-virgin olive oil, plus more for drizzling

1 medium yellow onion, thinly sliced

2 garlic cloves, thinly sliced

1 anchovy, preferably salt-packed, finely chopped (optional)

1 small head Treviso or radicchio, chopped (see Cook's Note)

Pinch of red pepper flakes

Splash of aged balsamic or white balsamic vinegar

1 tsp lemon zest

Sea salt and freshly ground black pepper

3 oz/85 g goat cheese

⅓ cup/40 g toasted walnuts (see page 273), finely chopped

STEP 1. Bring a large pot three-fourths full of salted water to a boil over high heat. Add the linguine to the boiling water and cook until al dente, about 9 minutes. Drain, reserving ⅓ cup/75 ml of the pasta cooking liquid for the sauce.

STEP 2. Meanwhile, heat the olive oil in a large skillet over medium-high heat. Add the onion and cook until soft. Add the garlic and anchovy (if using) and cook, stirring until the garlic is fragrant. Stir in the Treviso and red pepper flakes and toss together until wilted, about 2 minutes. Stir in the balsamic vinegar and lemon zest.

STEP 3. Add the pasta back to the pot with the reserved pasta cooking liquid, the Treviso mixture, and a drizzle of olive oil. Season with salt and black pepper and toss together with tongs over low heat. Add the goat cheese and give the pasta another two tosses to coat, leaving visible clumps of goat cheese.

STEP 4. Scoop the dressed pasta into shallow bowls, top with the walnuts, and serve warm.

COOK'S NOTE. Treviso, radicchio's longer, leaner cousin, has the same bitter profile and vibrant color as radicchio. Use whichever is more accessible to you for this pasta. Both soften into the sauce and contrast with the burst of lemon zest and creamy goat cheese beautifully.

SUNNY-SIDE UP YAM AND
BLACK BEAN TOSTADAS WITH AVOCADO

When you really want a full plate, and one that's hard to forget, make tostadas, loaded up with yams and black beans and topped with a fried egg. If you didn't know any better, this dish would come across as an over-the-top, diner-style indulgence—and it is. But examined for its parts, you'll also find loads of good-for-you stuff, like protein (in the eggs and black beans), potassium, iron, fiber, vitamin A (there's seven times your daily vitamin A needs in half a yam!), and omega-3s and -6s (from the avocado and egg).

———————————————————— SERVES 2 TO 4 ————————————————————

2 lb/910 g garnet yams or sweet potatoes

2 cups/340 g cooked black beans (see page 273)

Extra-virgin olive oil for frying

4 fresh small Corn Tortillas (page 140) or
   purchased corn tortillas

1 or 2 large eggs

Fine sea salt and freshly ground pepper

2 tbsp unsalted butter or extra-virgin olive oil

Zest and juice of 1 lime (optional)

1 bunch watercress, washed and stemmed

Finishing oil for drizzling

1 large, ripe avocado, peeled, pitted, and sliced

STEP 1. Preheat the oven to 375°F/190°C/gas 5. Prick the yams with a fork and roast until they can easily be pierced with a fork or butter knife, 35 to 45 minutes.

STEP 2. Warm the beans with 2 to 3 tbsp water—just enough to make them saucy and enticing—in a small skillet over low heat. Keep warm.

STEP 3. Meanwhile, line a plate with paper towels and set near the stove. In a medium, shallow skillet, heat 1 in/2.5 cm olive oil over medium-high heat. To test the temperature of the oil, drop a piece of tortilla into the skillet; the oil should sizzle and the tortilla cook to a pale golden brown. If it turns dark brown quickly or the oil is smoking, reduce the heat. Working in batches, fry the tortillas, pressing down with tongs to submerge them under the oil from time to time, until crispy and golden, 2 to 3 minutes. Transfer the tortillas to the paper towel–lined plate to crisp and cool.

STEP 4. Drain off most of the oil, leaving just enough to fry an egg or two sunny-side up (see page 272). Season the egg with salt and pepper. Set aside.

STEP 5. Remove the yams from the oven, split open, and scoop out the flesh into a medium bowl. Discard the skins. Mash in the butter and lime zest and juice (if using) with a fork until smooth. Season with salt.

STEP 6. Layer the yam mash on plates or a large platter and top with the tortillas. Drizzle the watercress with finishing oil and season the egg and avocado with pepper. Layer the beans on the tortillas and top with the fried egg, watercress, and avocado. Serve warm.

ARTICHOKE ENCHILADAS

Despite its indulgent reputation, Mexican food, at its origin, is packed with grains and vegetables. Though we most often equate Mexican food with white rice, quinoa—the protein-packed ancient Incan grain—is a winning substitute. In these enchiladas, quinoa is combined with artichokes and cheese, rolled inside corn tortillas, and smothered in a homemade enchilada verde sauce that's made with fresh tomatillos. Therein lies the true luxury of this dish, a sauce so pleasingly tangy you'll want every bite drowned in it.

The secret to a good enchilada sauce is balance. Control the heat to your liking with whole or seeded serrano chiles (seeds in for hot, seeded for mild), and finish with the warming heat of cayenne pepper and cooling freshness of lime.

SERVES 4

QUINOA

1¼ cups/300 ml water

¾ cup/145 g quinoa

¼ tsp sea salt

2 tbsp extra-virgin olive oil, plus more for the baking dish

1 red onion

1½ lb/680 g tomatillos, husked

2 serrano chiles, seeded for a milder sauce

½ cup/120 ml vegetable stock (see page 270) or water

Sea salt

1 tsp unbleached raw sugar

¾ cup/130 g fresh, frozen, or unmarinated jarred artichoke hearts (see Cook's Note)

10 fresh small Corn Tortillas (page 140) or purchased corn tortillas

2½ cups/290 g grated Monterey Jack cheese

Handful fresh cilantro leaves, plus more for topping

1 cup/115 g Cotija, queso añejo, queso fresco, or feta cheese, crumbled

Cayenne pepper for sprinkling

1 lime, cut into wedges

STEP 1. *To make the Quinoa:* Bring the water, quinoa, and salt to boil in a medium saucepan over medium-high heat. Reduce to medium heat, cover, and simmer about 25 minutes. Set aside. (You can prepare the quinoa up to 2 days in advance; just be sure to cool completely and store in an airtight container.)

STEP 2. Lightly brush a 9-by-13-in/23-by-33-cm baking dish or casserole with olive oil. Preheat the broiler to high.

STEP 3. Halve the onion. Slice one half into thin rings and cut the other half into wedges. Arrange the onion wedges, tomatillos, and serranos on a baking sheet and broil until the tomatillos are soft and browned, 15 to 20 minutes, turning with tongs halfway through cooking. Transfer the onion, tomatillos, and serranos with any of their liquid to a blender or food processor, add the stock, and purée until smooth, about 3 minutes. Add ½ tsp salt and the sugar and pulse a few times to combine.

STEP 4. Meanwhile, toss the artichokes with the 2 tbsp olive oil in a bowl and season lightly with salt.

STEP 5. Steam or warm the tortillas in the microwave (see page 144); keep them wrapped. Toss the artichokes and quinoa with two-thirds of the Monterey Jack in a bowl. Place a tortilla on the work surface. Spoon 2 to 3 tbsp of the artichoke mixture down the middle of the tortilla, add some cilantro leaves, and roll up the tortilla, leaving the ends open. Tuck the enchilada, seam-side down, into the prepared baking dish. Repeat with the remaining tortillas and artichoke filling, lining up the enchiladas side by side in the baking dish. Broil until the tortillas are crisp and golden around the edges, 3 to 4 minutes.

STEP 6. Pour most of the tomatillo sauce over and around the sides of the enchiladas and sprinkle the remaining Monterey Jack on top. Broil until the cheese is golden brown, 1 to 2 minutes more. Remove from the oven and top with the sliced onion, Cotija, and remaining cilantro.

STEP 7. Divide the enchiladas among plates and sprinkle them lightly with cayenne. Serve warm with lime wedges.

COOK'S NOTE. The beauty of the artichoke filling is that it will truly work with whatever artichokes you can find, from fresh to frozen or even canned. If all you can find is marinated artichokes, drain your artichokes and pat dry, and skip the step of seasoning the artichokes before filling your enchiladas.

BACK 40 SLAB PIE

Slab pie is a thing of wonder. It couldn't be simpler, by some standards, though it's a work of delicious architectural achievement to others. Generally a square or rectangular pie made with a flaky all-butter (or, if you're new to pie baking, part butter and part shortening) crust, slab pies are usually stuffed with a sweet fruit filling. It was created by heartland farmwives, from whom I hail, and built to serve crowds of hungry folks, usually fresh from hard work in the fields.

In that spirit, my savory slab pie celebrates the kind of veggies that might be growing in that farm family's own garden, easy enough for any of us to grow in raised beds or containers in our patch of soil, no matter how humble, or gather locally from our nearby farmers. Some people need an extra nudge to eat their cruciferous vegetables—like broccoli and cauliflower. Layered with cheese inside savory, crumbly dough and wrapped like a package, this is it. A generous green salad and a glass of rosé are welcome companions.

SERVES 6 TO 8

CRUST

3½ cups/440 g all-purpose or whole-wheat white flour

Pinch of unbleached raw sugar

1 tsp fine sea salt

½ cup/115 g vegetable shortening

1 cup/225 g cold unsalted butter, cubed

1 tbsp apple cider vinegar

⅓ cup/75 ml ice water

VEGETABLE FILLING

½ large head cauliflower, stem trimmed

1 small head broccoli, stem trimmed

2 medium carrots, peeled and thinly sliced on the diagonal

4 tsp extra-virgin olive oil

1 small zucchini, thinly sliced lengthwise

Fine sea salt and freshly ground pepper

3 tbsp whole-wheat or fresh bread crumbs, or panko (see page 261)

2 oz/55 g fontina cheese, grated

8 oz/225 g cheddar, Colby, or Muenster cheese, thinly sliced

1 tsp finely chopped fresh thyme leaves

1 large egg, lightly beaten

1 firm, ripe tomato, thinly sliced

STEP 1. *To make the Crust:* To make the dough by hand, whisk together the flour, sugar, and salt in a medium bowl. Using your fingers or a pastry cutter, blend the shortening into the flour mixture until it resembles couscous with some pea-size pieces remaining. Add the butter and continue to work together until the mixture resembles a coarse meal. Add the vinegar and give the dough a few strokes with a fork, then add the ice water, stirring with a fork with a light touch until you have a rough, shaggy dough.

To make the dough in a food processor, pulse together the flour, sugar, and salt to combine. Add the shortening, followed by the butter, and pulse until the mixture resembles coarse meal, 10 to 15 pulses. Add the vinegar, then gradually add ice water and pulse a few times to combine.

CONTINUED

STEP 2. Divide the dough in half on a lightly floured work surface. Flatten both halves into squares about 1 in/2.5 cm thick. Wrap in plastic wrap and refrigerate at least 1 hour and up to overnight.

STEP 3. *To make the Vegetable Filling:* Bring a large pot three-fourths full of salted water to a boil over high heat. Cut the cauliflower crosswise to make thin cauliflower steaks (see page 264). Cut the broccoli thinly through the stems as well. It won't fall into steaks like the cauliflower (it lacks the unifying central vein), but aim for thin slices that you can layer and stack.

STEP 4. Add the cauliflower to the boiling water and cook until just tender-crisp, 4 to 5 minutes. Remove with a wire strainer. Add the broccoli to the boiling water and cook until bright green and just tender-crisp, 2 to 3 minutes. Repeat with the carrots, cooking about 3 minutes. Keeping the vegetables separated, pat each vegetable dry as you remove it from the water, and toss each with about 1 tsp olive oil in a bowl. Toss the uncooked zucchini in 1 tsp olive oil. Season all the vegetables with salt and pepper. Set aside in separate bowls.

STEP 5. Preheat the oven to 425°F/220°C/gas 7. Generously butter an 8-by-8-in/20-cm-by-20-cm oven-to-table baking dish.

STEP 6. Roll out the dough on a lightly floured work surface, one portion at a time, to a 12-in/30.5-cm square that's about ⅛ in/3 mm thick. Transfer one portion of the dough to the baking dish with your hands. Tuck the dough into the corners and let the excess hang over the sides by about ½ in/12 mm, trimming off any dough beyond that. Sprinkle the bread crumbs over the dough in the pan bottom and then top with fontina. Place the cauliflower and then the broccoli over the fontina in flat layers. Top with one even layer of the cheddar, followed by the zucchini, thyme, and carrots. Top with another even layer of the cheddar, reserving a bit of cheddar for the very top.

STEP 7. Place the remaining square of dough on top of the filling. Press the crusts together along the edges with your fingers, trimming any long portions (so the crust doesn't get too thick) and pinching it together to make a scalloped edge. Cut slits in the top of the crust with a paring knife in any pattern you wish, stars or simple slits are both welcome, to allow steam to escape as the pie cooks.

STEP 8. Brush the top of the pie with the beaten egg. Bake until the top is evenly golden brown, about 30 minutes.

STEP 9. Meanwhile, season the tomato with salt and let drain on a paper towel for about 15 minutes.

STEP 10. Reduce the oven temperature to 400°F/200°C/gas 6. Lay the tomato over the top of the pie crust and top with the remaining cheddar. Continue baking until the pie is cooked through, the crust is golden around the edges, and the cheese is bubbly, about 30 minutes. Transfer to a cooling rack and let cool for about 20 minutes. Cut into large squares or rectangles. Serve warm.

BAKED SQUASH WITH SHALLOTS, OYSTER MUSHROOMS, AND HERB GREMOLATA

Roasted squash in their skin are a worthy centerpiece for your plate. That they require a knife and fork to eat is just the beginning of why this meal is so satisfying. It is earthy, sweet, filling, and loaded with flavor. But the best thing about this delicious dish is that it all bakes in the oven (save a simple green garnish), leaving you with so little work it's like sitting down to a meal that seems to have almost made itself.

The gremolata topping is an absolute must, adding a punchy burst of flavor and a beautiful flourish to the finished dish. When it's in my garden, I use equal parts parsley and sorrel for a lemony zing. Improvise with whatever greens or herbs you have at the ready.

--- SERVES 4 ---

1 butternut squash, seeds remove and cut into quarters lengthwise

4 small shallots, peeled and halved

⅓ cup/75 ml extra-virgin olive oil

Sea salt and freshly ground pepper

1 acorn or delicate squash, seeds removed and cut in wedges

8 oz/225 g oyster or shiitake mushrooms

4 garlic cloves, peeled

½ cup/15 g sorrel or arugula, chopped

½ cup/15 g parsley leaves, chopped

⅓ cup/45 g toasted pine nuts (see page 274)

Juice and zest of 1 lemon

STEP 1. Preheat the oven to 400°F/ 200°C /gas 6.

STEP 2. Coat the butternut squash and shallots with 2 tbsp of the olive oil, season with salt and pepper, and lay cut-side down on a rimmed baking sheet, without touching. Place on the top rack of the oven to bake, 10 minutes. Meanwhile, toss together 2 tbsp olive oil with the acorn squash, mushrooms, and garlic. Season with salt and pepper and spread out on a second rimmed baking sheet. Add to the oven and bake until both squash are fork-tender, the shallots are soft and golden brown, and the mushrooms are mostly roasted, with some golden and crispy parts, about 35 minutes more.

STEP 3. Meanwhile, stir together the sorrel, parsley, pine nuts, and lemon zest and juice with the remaining olive oil. Season with salt and pepper.

STEP 4. Transfer the roasted butternut squash to a platter, arrange the remaining vegetables around it, and top with the gremolata, or toss all together in your favorite big, shallow bowl and scatter the gremolata wildly over the top. Serve warm.

meals
to share

It's easy to romanticize a time when life revolved around the field and the table, when whole communities would gather for a harvest feast. Often these feasts centered on a large Sunday roast. But the true inspiration of a harvest feast is gratitude that the land itself has provided a huge bounty, all at once. This is an opportunity to make the true centerpiece of the meal the vegetables themselves.

With this chapter, I challenge us all to commit to gathering, to sitting with the ones you love around a table of plenty. It matters very little if you share the food philosophies of your friends. Show off your own with a big, vegetable fantasia. Gather around a giant pan of Spring Vegetable Paella (PAGE 204) rich with mushrooms and spring peas. In the summertime, set the table outdoors and set the stage around a luscious Eggplant Parmesan Summer Supper (PAGE 206) made with your own homegrown summer gem. For any time of year and every appetite, there's pizza (see PAGE 213)—glorious, crackling-crust artisan pies, handmade by you with absolutely any vegetable you love.

SPRING VEGETABLE PAELLA

My Spanish friends tell me that at home, paella is cooked on an open fire over orange tree branches in the backyard. Friends and family gather around a crackly fire, fragrant with the occasional snap of orange oil, blistering off fallen orange leaves. I hope to sit around that fire one day. But even without it, paella is the perfect dish for gathering folks, served outside on the first warm evenings of spring, when peas and artichokes have just hit the market.

The base of this recipe can be made with any number of stunning spring stars. Give fiddlehead ferns their moment, or make it just with mushrooms and artichokes. Stir in peas or top with pea shoots. Whichever vegetables you choose, be generous.

SERVES 6

2 tbsp extra-virgin olive oil

8 oz/225 g assorted mushrooms such as shiitake, oyster, and button mushrooms, cleaned, trimmed, and sliced (see page 266)

Sea salt and freshly ground pepper

2 cups/410 g Sofrito (page 256)

Small pinch of saffron threads

1 cup/200 g short-grain brown rice such as Arborio

2 cups/330 g cooked chickpeas (see page 273) or one 15-oz/430-g can chickpeas, rinsed and drained

2½ to 3 cups/600 to 720 ml homemade vegetable stock (see page 270) or purchased vegetable stock

1 head garlic, unpeeled

4 fresh artichokes, cleaned and quartered (see page 263)

Handful fiddlehead ferns, blanched (see page 263; optional, see Cook's Note)

1 or 2 handfuls fresh shelled peas or sugar snap peas, sliced on the diagonal

Small handful pea shoots (optional)

2 lemons, cut into wedges

STEP 1. Heat the olive oil in a paella pan or your largest shallow skillet on medium-high heat. Add the mushrooms and cook, stirring occasionally, until they are crispy but still juicy, 6 to 8 minutes, seasoning with salt and pepper toward the end of cooking. Transfer to a plate and set aside.

STEP 2. Add the sofrito and saffron to the pan and stir together. Add the rice and cook over medium-heat, stirring into the sofrito, to absorb the flavors and toast the rice a little, about 5 minutes.

STEP 3. Stir in the chickpeas, stock, and 1 tsp salt and bring to a simmer. Meanwhile, slice off the top one-fourth of the head of garlic so the cloves are exposed. Nestle it down into the rice. Place the artichoke hearts and mushrooms around the pan.

STEP 4. If you're cooking on an electric range, preheat the oven to 350°F/180°C/gas 4. Bring the liquid to a boil over medium-high heat. Reduce the heat to medium-low, stir in fiddlehead fern (if using), cover, and transfer to the oven. Bake until the rice is fully cooked, 45 minutes to 1 hour.

If you're cooking on a gas range, bring the liquid to a boil over medium-high heat. Reduce the heat to medium-low, stir in the fiddlehead ferns (if using), cover, and cook until the rice is fully cooked, 45 minutes to 1 hour.

STEP 5. Do not peek, and do not stir! An authentic paella should have a layer of crusty rice (called *socarrat*) on the bottom of the paella pan. Add the peas to the pan in the last 2 minutes of cooking. When the paella is cooked, cover with a newspaper (Spanish-style) and set aside for a few minutes before eating.

STEP 6. Garnish the paella with pea shoots (if using) and lemon wedges. Serve straight from the pan with spoons. Squeeze fresh lemon juice over the paella as you eat it.

COOK'S NOTE. Fiddlehead ferns are the furled fronds of young ferns that have not yet opened, an uncultivated seasonal specialty found only in the early spring. These omega-3- and omega-6-rich vegetables should be washed well and cooked thoroughly by steaming, boiling, sautéing, or pickling.

EGGPLANT PARMESAN
SUMMER SUPPER

At first instinct, eggplant Parmesan is a winter meal, hearty and filling. But assuredly, if you've ever grown your own eggplant or bought them from the hands of the farmer who has, you will want to show them off at their peak. In-season summer eggplant almost entirely lacks the bitterness that older, off-season eggplants can have. Put them front and center in one of the most satisfying of all meals.

When you fry eggplant on the stove top, each piece soaks up a tremendous amount of oil. Eggplant roasted in the oven while the sauce simmers is lighter and faster, and there's less mess to clean up when guests arrive. Serve your feast outside under a tree, with a big pile of angel hair pasta, sparkling Lambrusco, and green salad—an instant portal to Italian villa life.

Like most dishes with red sauce, eggplant Parm gets better the second night, and more so on the third. If you're lucky enough to have any leftovers, pile them on rosemary focaccia rolls for a decadent, if messy, sandwich.

SERVES 6

3 balls fresh mozzarella cheese

2 large eggplants (about 3 lb/1.4 kg), cut into ½-in/12-mm slices (see Cook's Note, page 208)

Extra-virgin olive oil for brushing

Sea salt and freshly ground black pepper

MARINARA SAUCE

1 tbsp extra-virgin olive oil

2 garlic cloves, smashed or minced

Generous pinch of red pepper flakes

Two 28-oz/800-g cans San Marzano or plum tomatoes in juice

Sea salt

1 sprig fresh basil (optional)

1 bay leaf

Freshly ground black pepper

1 tbsp unsalted butter, plus more as needed

¾ cup/90 g freshly grated Parmigiano-Reggiano cheese

1 lb/455 g capellini or angel hair pasta

STEP 1. Thinly slice the mozzarella and lay on a paper towel–lined baking sheet to drain while you prepare the rest of the ingredients. Preheat the oven to 375°/190°C/gas 5.

STEP 2. Lightly brush both sides of the eggplant slices with olive oil, season with salt and black pepper, and spread out on two baking sheets. Roast until soft and golden brown, about 35 minutes, flipping with tongs halfway through cooking.

CONTINUED

STEP 3. *To make the Marinara Sauce:* Heat the olive oil in a large pot over medium heat. Add the garlic and red pepper flakes and cook until fragrant, 1 to 2 minutes. Add the tomatoes and their juices, passing them through clean hands on the way to the pot to crush and swish them. Add 1/2 tsp salt (use a light hand if your tomatoes are presalted), basil (if using), and bay leaf and reduce the heat to medium-low. Gently simmer until the sauce thickens, about 30 minutes, crushing the tomatoes further with a wooden spoon to help them break down. Taste and add another 1/4 salt and pepper if needed and stir to combine. Remove and discard the basil and bay leaf.

STEP 4. Purée the whole thing together with an immersion blender until smooth. Stir in the butter to soften the acidity of the tomatoes. Taste and add more butter as needed. You should have about 5 cups/1.2 L of sauce.

STEP 5. When the eggplant is finished roasting, raise the oven temperature to 400°F/200°C/ gas 6.

STEP 6. Spoon about 1 1/4 cups/300 ml of the tomato sauce into a 9-by-13-in/23-by-33-cm baking dish and spread it to cover the bottom. Layer in about half the eggplant and sprinkle with one-third of the Parmigiano-Reggiano, eyeballing the ingredients to create even layers—exact amounts aren't so important. Top with half of the mozzarella slices. Spoon over a generous 1 cup/240 ml or so of sauce, followed by a second layer of eggplant, another third of the Parmigiano-Reggiano, and the remaining mozzarella. Sprinkle on the remaining third of the Parmigiano-Reggiano cheese. Bake until golden and bubbly, about 35 minutes.

STEP 7. Remove from the oven and let cool about 15 minutes. Meanwhile, bring a large pot three-fourths full of salted water to a boil over high heat. Add the pasta to the boiling water and cook until al dente, about 2 minutes. Warm the remaining marinara sauce over low heat. Drain the pasta and toss with the marinara sauce.

STEP 8. Serve the eggplant Parmesan warm with the angel hair pasta.

COOK'S NOTE. How an eggplant tastes to you is entirely dependent on if you're eating it in season, how many days it's been off the plant, and whether or not bitter is a pleasing flavor to you. I neither peel nor salt my eggplant, particularly when it's very fresh. But when in doubt, peel and generously salt the slices and set them aside in a colander or on paper towels to drain, about 15 minutes. Rinse and pat dry before roasting.

ROASTED TOMATO–SQUASH TAGINE FALL FEAST

Tagines are a North African tradition that are slowly making their way into mainstream Western food culture. Though it is an alluring centerpiece served in a traditional terra-cotta tagine dish, you hardly need one to make this. With so many jewel-toned vegetables and dates, plumped in saffron- and harissa-spiked broth, any simple serving bowl will make stunning art out of this meal.

———————————————— SERVES 4 ————————————————

12 plum tomatoes, halved

4 tbsp/60 ml extra-virgin olive oil

1 yellow onion, chopped

2 garlic cloves, minced

Generous pinch of saffron threads

2 tbsp Harissa (page 253) or purchased harissa

1 cinnamon stick

2 cups/480 ml water

1 medium butternut squash, peeled, seeded, and cut into bite-size pieces

4 large carrots, peeled and cut into bite-size pieces

Sea salt and freshly ground pepper

6 pitted Medjool dates

2 cups/330 g cooked chickpeas (see page 273) or one 15-oz/430-g can chickpeas, drained and rinsed

Juice of ½ lemon or 1 tsp cider vinegar, plus more as needed

COUSCOUS

2 cups/345 g instant couscous

1½ cups/360 ml vegetable stock (see page 270) or water

2 tbsp unsalted butter

Sea salt

½ cup/70 g sliced or chopped almonds, toasted almonds (see page 273), or Marcona almonds (optional)

Handful fresh cilantro leaves (optional)

STEP 1. Preheat the oven to 375°F/190°C/gas 5. Toss the tomatoes with 2 tbsp of the olive oil in a large bowl. Spread out on a baking sheet, cut-sides down, and roast until soft and slightly reduced and concentrated (the skins will shrivel), about 45 minutes.

STEP 2. Meanwhile, heat the remaining 2 tbsp olive oil in a large skillet over medium-high heat. Add the onion and cook until soft, 4 to 6 minutes. Add the garlic, saffron, and harissa to the skillet and stir to coat the onion and cook until fragrant, about 2 minutes. Add the cinnamon stick and water and bring to a boil. Stir in the butternut squash and carrots, and season with salt and pepper. Cover, lower the heat to medium-low, and simmer until the squash and carrots are tender, about 30 minutes, adding the dates in the last 6 minutes of cooking. Stir in the chickpeas. Taste and season with salt and pepper. Stir in the lemon juice. Cover and keep warm over very low heat.

STEP 3. *To make the Couscous:* Put the couscous in a medium bowl. Bring the stock to a boil in a medium pan over medium heat. Pour over the couscous. Add the butter, cover with a plate, and let the couscous absorb the stock for about 3 minutes. Remove the plate and fluff the couscous with a fork. Taste and season with salt if needed.

STEP 4. To serve, divide the couscous among large shallow bowls. Spoon the tagine over the couscous and top with the roasted tomatoes. Garnish with the almonds and cilantro, if desired.

GLAZED WINTER VEGETABLE MEDLEY
WITH CHESTNUTS AND CAPER BERRIES

A bowl of earthy, parsley butter–glazed root vegetables with chestnuts, caper berries, and deeply cured black olives is a vegetable lover's dream. This is the French countryside in a bowl—humble vegetables in their most exalted form. It earns a place in your entertaining files because of all the care you'll put into each and every vegetable—prepared in the way that highlights each texture and flavor best, some roasted in olive oil, while the others are simmered and glazed in butter. You wouldn't demand this precision of yourself on any night, but when guests are coming and vegetables are the absolute pièce de résistance, they are deserving of attention to every detail.

This is a great example of the magical duo of olive oil and butter—the former for roasting, the latter for glazing—resulting in the most luxurious vegetable coating imaginable. Serve these bowls of gilded vegetables warm with a crusty baguette or your other favorite French bread.

SERVES 4

12 fingerling potatoes, halved lengthwise

4 tbsp/60 ml extra-virgin olive oil

Sea salt and freshly ground pepper

½ head cauliflower, cut into large florets

4 large shallots, quartered

6 tbsp/85 g unsalted butter

1 bunch golden beets, peeled and cut into bite-size pieces

1 bunch baby turnips, scrubbed and trimmed

1 bunch carrots, peeled and cut into bite-size pieces on the diagonal

2 parsnips, peeled, cored, and cut into bite-size pieces on the diagonal

3 sprigs fresh thyme

1 to 1½ cups/240 to 360 ml vegetable stock (see page 270) or water

½ tsp unbleached raw sugar

5 oz/140 g roasted peeled chestnuts (see Roasting Chestnuts, page 212)

Handful fresh parsley, finely chopped

Finishing oil for drizzling

Fleur de sel or sel gris

Handful caper berries

Oil-cured black olives or kalamata olives for topping

STEP 1. Preheat the oven to 400°F/200°C/gas 6. Toss the potatoes with 2 tbsp of the olive oil in a large bowl. Season with salt and pepper and spread out on a baking sheet. Toss the cauliflower and shallots in the same bowl with the remaining 2 tbsp olive oil, and spread out on a second baking sheet. Cover both baking sheets loosely with aluminum foil and roast until the vegetables are tender but with just a little browning, about 40 minutes, stirring with a wooden spoon as needed.

CONTINUED

STEP 2. Meanwhile, in a large, shallow straight-sided skillet, melt 2 tbsp of the butter. Add the beets, turnips, carrots, and parsnips and toss to coat. Season with salt and pepper, add the thyme and enough stock to come about halfway up the vegetables (you want them to steam, not completely boil). Cover loosely with foil, bring to a simmer, and cook until the vegetables are tender and the stock reduced to 2 to 3 tbsp of liquid, 10 to 12 minutes. Remove the foil and reduce the stock further, if needed. Set aside until the roasted vegetables are cooked.

STEP 3. When the roasted vegetables are cooked, add 2 tbsp butter and the sugar to the beets, turnips, carrots, and parsnips. Season with salt and pepper. Cook until heated through and glazed, about 4 minutes. Add the chestnuts and toss to glaze. And the roasted vegetables to the skillet and toss together with 2 tbsp butter and parsley. Drizzle with finishing oil and season with fleur de sel and pepper.

STEP 4. Divide among bowls, making sure each one has an even mix of vegetables and chestnuts. Top with caper berries and olives. Serve warm.

COOK'S NOTE. Seasoning throughout this dish is vital to make sure each individual vegetable arrives at the table at its very best. On that note—if you decide to use red instead of golden beets, braise them separately and toss in with the finishing oil at the very end to avoid serving a bowl of uniformly pink vegetables.

ROASTING CHESTNUTS

To roast fresh chestnuts (and you really should, at least once in your life), make a crisscross slit on the domed side of the chestnut with a thin, sharp knife. Roast at 425°F/220°C/gas 7 until the shells look as if they are about to peel off at the incision, about 20 minutes. Cool slightly and peel while warm. Eat, or add to a recipe as directed.

PIZZA FOR
FOUR SEASONS

Pizza is an always-appropriate meal for guests, especially when you're hand-selecting the toppings from the season's best. Few foods are more universally chic than artisan personal pies.

Whether you're entertaining at home or just treating yourself to a homemade pizza, making dough from scratch is an easy 30-minute start-to-finish affair (see page 260). If you make the dough a day or two in advance and let it set in the fridge overnight, not only do you have it at the ready, but also it can help the dough mature, improve in flavor, and make it significantly easier to stretch.

These four pizza combinations are here to serve as inspiration, as well as a guide to how to top each style of pie. Each smallish pizza and its corresponding toppings is enough to serve two. Scale up to serve crowds of four, six, or eight and let each pair of eaters add their own toppings to their tastes.

COOK'S NOTE. Move frozen pizza dough from the freezer to the fridge the night before baking. Remove the pizza dough from the fridge and bring to room temperature at least 1 hour before preparing the pizza.

SHAPING PIZZA DOUGH

Before you begin, make sure your dough is well rested and has come to room temperature (if previously refrigerated). Lightly dust a pizza peel or baking sheet with cornmeal and set nearby. On a well-floured work surface, sprinkle the dough and your hands with flour. Stretch the dough with your hands, beginning at the edges, moving the pizza in a circle, pulling rather than flattening the dough. Continue to stretch and rotate the dough until it is about 8 in/20 cm wide, with plenty of bubbles all over the surface (which makes for a crispier crust).

Once you have the basic shape, stretch the dough by draping it over the back of your hands and wrists, letting it hang down so gravity does the work until you have roughly a 12-in/30.5-cm circle or oblong shape, considering the final baking vessel: oblong if you're baking on a rectangular baking sheet, and round or any other desired shape if you're transferring from a pizza peel to a pizza stone. Don't lose heart if your pizza turns out more like an amoeba (plenty of mine have). Assuredly, it's the taste that counts. Transfer to the prepared pizza peel or baking sheet and top your pizza before the dough becomes warm.

WHITE PIZZA WITH ARUGULA AND RICOTTA SALATA

———————— SERVES 2 ————————

Fine cornmeal for dusting

Flour for dusting

One 14- to 16-oz/400- to 455-g ball homemade
    pizza dough (see page 260) or purchased pizza
    dough, at room temperature

½ cup/115 g fresh ricotta cheese

2 tbsp extra-virgin olive oil

Heaping handful arugula

Maldon sea salt and freshly ground pepper

½ lemon

2 oz/55g ricotta salata cheese

Finishing oil for drizzling

STEP 1. Preheat the oven to 475°F/240°C/gas 9 and place a rack in the bottom third of the oven. If using a pizza stone, sprinkle a pizza paddle or peel lightly with cornmeal. If using a baking sheet, preheat it in the oven until it is very hot and then dust it with cornmeal.

STEP 2. On a well-floured work surface, sprinkle the dough and your hands with flour. Stretch the dough with your hands to make any shape of pizza you please (see page 213), roughly 12-in/30.5-cm round or oblong, stretching the edges lightly to form a circle, oval, or rectangle that is evenly thin throughout the middle. Carefully transfer the dough to the prepared pizza paddle or baking sheet with both hands.

STEP 3. Dollop the fresh ricotta all around the dough with a spoon, reserving 2 to 3 tbsp for the finishing touches. Spread the fresh ricotta around the pizza with an offset spatula or the back of a spoon and drizzle with 1 tbsp of the olive oil.

STEP 4. If using a pizza stone, slide the pizza onto the stone and place it in the oven. If using a baking sheet, place the hot baking sheet in the oven. Bake until the crust is crispy and brown, about 15 minutes.

STEP 5. Meanwhile, toss the arugula in the remaining 1 tbsp olive oil, season with salt and pepper, and add a squeeze of fresh lemon juice.

STEP 6. Remove the pizza from the oven and scatter the dressed arugula on top. Dollop with the remaining fresh ricotta and shave the ricotta salata over the top with a vegetable peeler. Drizzle lightly with finishing oil. Serve warm.

HEIRLOOM TOMATO PIE

SERVES 2

2 large firm, ripe heirloom tomatoes, thinly
 sliced

Sea salt

Fine cornmeal for dusting

Flour for dusting

One 14- to 16-oz/400- to 455-g ball homemade
 pizza dough (see page 260) or purchased pizza
 dough, at room temperature

4 to 6 oz/115 to 170 g fresh mozzarella or burrata,
 torn into small pieces, or ricotta cheese

2 garlic cloves, very thinly sliced

Handful fresh herbs such as basil or opal basil

Parmigiano-Reggiano cheese for grating

Finishing oil for drizzling

Freshly ground pepper

STEP 1. Season the tomatoes with salt and let drain on a paper towel for a few minutes.

STEP 2. Preheat the oven to 475°F/240°C/gas 9 and place a rack in the bottom third of the oven. If using a pizza stone, sprinkle a pizza paddle or peel lightly with cornmeal. If using a baking sheet, preheat it in the oven until it is very hot and then dust it with cornmeal.

STEP 3. On a well-floured work surface, sprinkle the dough and your hands with flour. Stretch the dough with your hands to make any shape of pizza you please (see page 213), roughly 12-in/30.5-cm round or oblong, stretching the edges lightly to form a circle, oval, or rectangle that is evenly thin throughout the middle. Carefully transfer the dough to the prepared pizza paddle or hot baking sheet with both hands.

STEP 4. Top the pizza with the mozzarella cheese, garlic, and a few tomato slices, reserving a few tomato slices for the finishing touches. Use a light hand, since pizzas tend to turn soggy if there are too many toppings.

STEP 5. If using a pizza stone, slide the pizza onto the stone and place it in the oven. If using a baking sheet, place the hot baking sheet in the oven. Bake until the pizza is puffed, crisp on the bottom, and evenly baked through, 8 to 12 minutes.

STEP 6. Remove the pizza from the oven and top with additional fresh sliced tomatoes and fresh herbs. Grate or shave Parmigiano-Reggiano over the top with a vegetable peeler, drizzle with finishing oil, and season with salt and pepper. Serve warm.

SWEET POTATO, BROWN BUTTER, AND SAGE PIE

¼ cup/60 ml full-fat plain yogurt

1 small sweet potato

Fine cornmeal for dusting

Flour for dusting

One 14- to 16-oz/400- to 455-g ball homemade pizza dough (see page 260) or purchased pizza dough, at room temperature

1 oz/30 g freshly grated Parmigiano-Reggiano cheese

1 tbsp extra-virgin olive oil

Sea salt and freshly ground pepper

1 tbsp unsalted butter

4 to 6 small fresh sage leaves

1 lime, cut into wedges

STEP 1. Set the yogurt in a small strainer or cheesecloth over a bowl for a few minutes to drain off excess liquid. Slice the sweet potato crosswise as thinly as possible with a mandoline or a very sharp knife—it's important that the slices be very thin so they cook completely in the oven.

STEP 2. Preheat the oven to 475°F/240°C/gas 9 and place a rack in the bottom third of the oven. If using a pizza stone, sprinkle a pizza paddle or peel lightly with cornmeal. If using a baking sheet, preheat it in the oven until it is very hot and then dust it with cornmeal.

STEP 3. On a well-floured work surface, sprinkle the dough and your hands with flour. Stretch the dough with your hands to make any shape of pizza you please (see page 213), roughly 12-in/30.5-cm round or oblong, stretching the edges lightly to form a circle, oval, or rectangle that is evenly thin throughout the middle. Carefully transfer the dough to the prepared pizza paddle or hot baking sheet with both hands.

STEP 4. Cover the pizza dough with a very thin scattering of Parmigiano-Reggiano to help the sweet potatoes stick, then cover completely with gently overlapping layers of sweet potato. Drizzle with the olive oil and season with salt and pepper.

STEP 5. If using a pizza stone, slide the pizza onto the stone and place it in the oven. If using a baking sheet, place the hot baking sheet in the oven. Bake until the pizza is puffed, crisp on the bottom, and evenly baked through, 8 to 12 minutes.

STEP 6. Meanwhile, melt the butter in a small pan over low heat; add the sage and continue cooking until the butter forms brown bits on the bottom of the pan and it smells nutty and toasty, about 6 minutes. Remove the sage leaves and discard or, if you really like sage, finely chop and set aside.

STEP 7. Remove the pizza from the oven and dollop with the strained yogurt and drizzle with the browned butter. If you like, add the chopped sage leaves. Serve warm with lime wedges.

ROBIOLA, SHAVED BRUSSELS SPROUTS, AND WALNUT PIZZA

SERVES 2

Fine cornmeal for dusting

Flour for dusting

One 14- to 16-oz/400- to 455-g ball homemade
pizza dough (see page 260) or purchased pizza
dough, at room temperature

2 to 3 oz/55 to 85 g Robiola cheese, thinly sliced

2 tbsp extra-virgin olive oil

Sea salt and freshly ground pepper

4 to 6 oz/115 to 170 g Brussels sprouts

1 tsp fresh lemon juice

Ricotta salata cheese for shaving

¼ cup/25 g toasted walnuts (see page 273),
coarsely chopped (optional)

2 tsp honey or truffle honey

STEP 1. Preheat the oven to 475°F/240°C/gas 9 and place a rack in the bottom third of the oven. If using a pizza stone, sprinkle a pizza paddle or peel lightly with cornmeal. If using a baking sheet, preheat it in the oven until it is very hot and then dust it with cornmeal.

STEP 2. On a well-floured work surface, sprinkle the dough and your hands with flour. Stretch the dough with your hands to make any shape of pizza you please (see page 213), roughly 12-in/30.5-cm round or oblong, stretching the edges lightly to form a circle, oval, or rectangle that is evenly thin throughout the middle. Carefully transfer the dough to the prepared pizza paddle or hot baking sheet with your hands.

STEP 3. Top the pizza dough with a few thin slices of Robiola cheese. Drizzle with 1 tbsp of the olive oil and season with salt and pepper.

STEP 4. If using a pizza stone, slide the pizza onto the stone and place it in the oven. If using a baking sheet, place the hot baking sheet in the oven. Bake until the pizza is puffed, crisp on the bottom, and evenly baked through, 8 to 10 minutes.

STEP 5. Meanwhile, shave or thinly slice the Brussels sprouts with a sharp knife. Toss together with the remaining 1 tbsp olive oil and the lemon juice. Sprinkle over the par-baked pizza and return to the oven. Bake until the Brussels sprouts are lightly charred and tender-crisp, about 4 minutes. Shave ricotta salata over the top with a vegetable peeler, scatter with the walnuts, and drizzle with the honey. Serve warm.

VARIATIONS ON A PIE

Try these six stunning combinations to keep your pizza stone in service.

- tomato sauce and caramelized onions
- crushed tomatoes, fresh mozzarella, red pepper flakes, and stracciatella di bufala cheese
- wild roasted mushrooms and fontina cheese
- cauliflower, shaved potato, and Gruyère cheese
- ricotta cheese, olive oil, and rosemary
- ramps and pecorino cheese

WHITE PIZZA WITH ARUGULA AND RICOTTA SALATA

HEIRLOOM TOMATO PIE

SWEET POTATO, BROWN BUTTER, AND SAGE PIE

ROBIOLA, SHAVED BRUSSELS SPROUTS, AND WALNUT PIZZA

sweets

For many months, nature is ripe with an opus of honeyed melons, tiny but potent strawberries, peaches nearly bursting from their skins. On those days, there's no greater pleasure than a ripe fig or a bowlful of berries. If you're craving decadence, you might even top them with folds of freshly whipped cream. One hardly needs a recipe for such things. But there are other days—warm-cookies-oozing-with-chocolate kind of days. For those, here's one more chapter of delights for you.

These aren't particularly vegetarian desserts—they are desserts for anyone who loves a sweet ending to a meal, because this book is not just about good eating, but good living. I always aim to go light on sugar—with just enough to boost the flavors at hand.

There is a philosophy here, of course, and that is one of pleasure. But like the other recipes in this book, every one of these desserts, indulgent hot fudge included, celebrates a flavor from the earth, from the bitter, alluring depth of cocoa to the peculiar sweetness of Meyer lemons. Each and every sweet in this chapter aims to delight and surprise.

BAKED APPLES

A dessert this simple is hard to resist. Like poached peaches (see page 226), it relies on the exceptional taste of the apple itself, freshly picked and still dense with tart, sweet juice that concentrates to baste itself (with a little help from cinnamon sugar) in the oven. I bake mine in a very hot oven because it's the crispy, almost–crème brûlée crackle on the top of the apple that makes this easy dessert one of my absolute favorites.

Many cooks don't core their apples all the way through, though I do, because I love the buttery, cinnamon-laced sauce that pools in the pan while baking, irresistible for spooning over each apple and a scoop of premium vanilla ice cream.

SERVES 6

3 tbsp unsalted butter, plus more room-temperature butter for the pan

6 crisp, sweet-tart apples such as Jonagold, unpeeled and cored

1 tsp ground cinnamon

3 to 4 tbsp unbleached raw sugar, depending on the sweetness of the apples

Vanilla ice cream (optional) for serving

STEP 1. Preheat the oven to 400°F/200°C/gas 6. Lightly brush a medium baking dish with room-temperature butter and place the apples, touching if necessary, in the dish, stem-sides up. Stir together the cinnamon and sugar in a small bowl. Put 1/2 tbsp butter inside each apple and sprinkle the tops with cinnamon sugar.

STEP 2. Bake until the apples are sitting in their own juices and starting to sink just a touch and the tops are crispy and caramelizing, 25 to 30 minutes. Cool just slightly in the baking dish on the countertop, about 5 minutes. Transfer the apples to small plates or shallow bowls and spoon the juices over the top. Serve warm, with or without ice cream.

BLACKBERRY FOOL

If you love fresh berries, there's almost no better summer sweet than a fool—a freshly whipped cream dessert with crushed or macerated berries folded in. And it couldn't be easier. The year we planted two blackberry bushes was the year the fool reentered my repertoire—for good. Make it with blackberries, raspberries, or blueberries, as plump and fresh and juicy as you can find them, stirred together with freshly whipped cream and crushed meringue. Take a peek in your herb garden for inspiration for adding flavor and garnish to this simple stunner.

_____ SERVES 4 _____

Heaping 2 handfuls fresh, ripe blackberries

1 to 3 tsp unbleached raw sugar

1 sprig flowering fresh lemon verbena or thyme, plus more for garnishing

1 cup/240 ml freshly whipped cream (see below) or plain yogurt

Handful of plain meringues, broken in pieces

STEP 1. Heat a handful of the blackberries with 1 tsp of the sugar and the lemon verbena in a small saucepan over medium heat until the berries just begin to burst, 2 to 3 minutes. Add the remaining 2 tsp sugar, as needed, to help the berries release their juice. Remove from the heat and stir in the remaining handful of berries.

STEP 2. Layer whipped cream, berries and their juices, and meringue pieces in small bowls or cups. Garnish with more lemon verbena before serving.

PERFECTLY WHIPPED CREAM

If you love a fresh fruit dessert, it pays to learn how to make whipped cream just right. Whip with a balloon whisk or electric mixer until very soft peaks form, adding just a dash of superfine or powdered sugar—or leave it out, depending on the sweetness of the dessert. Flavor with pure vanilla extract or the seeds of one vanilla bean and finish the cream by hand, whisking just until the cream holds a medium peak.

POACHED PEACHES

A perfectly tree-ripened peach is a treasure. And it seems more rare all the time. If you've ever had one from a roadside stand just minutes from where it grew, it's almost sacrilege to eat them any way but fresh. But for the others, the almost but not quite perfect gems, exalt them in their own peach-infused syrup; they keep well overnight in the fridge for weekend company. Don't be tempted to use the rock-hard off-season peaches you'll often find in the store for this simple yet stunning preparation. It depends on the luscious flavor of the ripe peach itself.

SERVES 6

4 lbs/2 kg firm, ripe yellow or white peaches

6 cups/1.4 L water

5 cups/1 kg unbleached raw sugar

1 vanilla bean

Full-fat plain yogurt, freshly whipped cream (see page 225), or vanilla ice cream for dolloping

Raw shelled pistachios or your favorite nut for scattering

STEP 1. Bring a large pot three-fourths full of water to a boil over high heat. Make a criss-cross slit in the bottom of each peach. Gently drop the peaches in the boiling water for 30 seconds. Remove one and test that the skin easily slides away from the flesh (the riper the fruit, the easier it is to peel). If not, leave the peaches in 30 seconds more. Remove the peaches carefully with a spoon, run under cold water, and peel with your hands or a paring knife. Save the peach skins for flavoring simple syrups or teas.

STEP 2. Combine the 6 cups/1.4 L water and the sugar in a large saucepan over medium-high heat. Split the vanilla bean and scrape the seeds into the pot. Bring to a simmer and stir occasionally until the sugar is completely dissolved, about 5 minutes. Add the peeled peaches. Reduce the heat to low, and simmer until the peaches are soft to the touch or until they can easily be pierced with butter knife, about 15 minutes. Turn off the heat. Gently transfer the peaches with a slotted spoon to a plate to cool. Let the syrup cool in the saucepan.

STEP 3. Spoon the peaches into shallow bowls and dollop yogurt on top. Drizzle with peach syrup and scatter pistachios over the top. If you have leftover peaches, pour any leftover syrup over them and store them in an airtight container in the fridge for up to 3 days.

COOK'S NOTE. I adore raw Sicilian pistachios because they are a gorgeous emerald green and pink, tender, and often sold shelled but any pistachiso will dress these up.

MUSKMELON FLOAT

You want to buy melon when it's ripe, and you can usually gauge a good melon by its smell. It should be floral and sweet, especially near the root end. Sometimes, if you don't eat it fast enough in the heat of summer, it can turn almost too ripe in just a day. When your melon is just right, or even a day after, make a batch of melon floats. This is a melon lover's egg cream.

SERVES 2

½ very ripe muskmelon or cantaloupe
Pinch of sea salt
1 tsp agave nectar (optional)

1 to 2 tsp orange-flower water or elderflower syrup
½ pt/235 ml vanilla ice cream or frozen yogurt
2 splashes of selzer water

Put the melon and salt in a blender and purée on high until completely smooth, 1 to 2 minutes. Taste and add the agave nectar, if needed, to sweeten the melon, and pulse until combined. Add 1 tsp orange-flower water. Taste and add up to 1 tsp more orange-flower water as needed. Scoop the ice cream into chilled glasses. Pour the melon purée over the ice cream and top each glass with a splash of seltzer water. Serve cold with straws.

CHOCOLATE SORBET

In the world of desserts, there could be nothing simpler than melting chocolate and water together in a pot, yet the simple act yields something so stunningly good—rich chocolate flavor that quite truly melts on your tongue, with a subtle, lingering hint of toasted cinnamon.

—————————————————— SERVES 6 TO 8 ——————————————————

1 lb/455 g high-quality milk chocolate, coarsely chopped

2 oz/55 g high-quality unsweetened chocolate, coarsely chopped

2½ cups/600 ml boiling water

Pinch of toasted Saigon or regular cinnamon

STEP 1. Place both chocolates in a food processor or blender. Pour the boiling water over the chocolate to melt, and process until smooth and silky, about 2 minutes. Add the cinnamon.

STEP 2. Transfer to the chilled bowl of an ice-cream maker and churn until frozen, according to the manufacturer's directions. Transfer to a freezer-safe container and freeze until firm enough to scoop, about 2 hours. Store in the freezer for up to 2 weeks.

DEEP DARK CHOCOLATE
HOT FUDGE

Homemade hot fudge is addictively good. And even if you only eat one banana split in your life, or especially if that's the case, it should be topped with your own homemade fudge. Once you have it in your home, you'll find many wonderful uses for it, like dressing up a plain yellow cake (as my grandmother did), making a fast egg cream, or turning ice cream and milk into a decadent shake. In a jar, this is a gift you'll be proud to give. And chances are you'll make friends of all ages.

In my first cookbook, *The Newlywed Cookbook*, I created a recipe for Deep-Dark-Secret Chocolate Cookies made with four kinds of chocolate, including cacao nibs, which lends a deep raw cacao edge. It's one of my favorite (and it turns out, most popular) recipes, and I couldn't resist trying cacao nibs in here, too. And I am glad I did. It is as intense as chocolate comes, for those of us who can't get enough. If you like your chocolate with a bitter edge, replace the bittersweet portion with a 70 percent dark chocolate studded with cacao nibs, like Valrhona Guanaja Grue Dark Chocolate Grand Cru. You won't regret the splurge.

--- MAKES ABOUT 3 CUPS / 720 ML ---

1 cup/200 g unbleached raw sugar

3 cups/720 ml heavy cream

¼ cup/60 ml agave nectar

4 oz/115 g high-quality unsweetened chocolate, coarsely chopped

2 oz/55 g high-quality bittersweet dark chocolate, coarsely chopped

⅓ cup/75 g unsalted butter, cut into cubes

1 tbsp pure vanilla extract

Your favorite ice cream for serving

STEP 1. Combine the sugar, cream, agave nectar, both chocolates, and butter in a heavy-bottomed medium pot and bring to a simmer over medium-high heat. Quickly reduce to medium-low heat, stir, and simmer until the chocolate and butter melt. Continue cooking on medium-low without stirring until it thickens to a thick, creamy sauce, about 5 minutes, but make sure the chocolate does not scorch. Remove from the heat, stir in the vanilla, and stir vigorously with a wooden spoon until a smooth sauce forms.

STEP 2. Serve warm over ice cream, or cool completely in the pot before adding to a clean glass jar with a tight-fitting lid. Store in the fridge for up to 2 weeks.

DIY PEANUT BUTTER AND PRETZEL CUPS

When you're craving the duo of peanut butter and chocolate, truly nothing else will do. A DIY peanut butter cup with dark chocolate and real nutty, chunky peanut butter (versus peanut butter sweetened with corn syrup) is an instant fix. The added surprise of jelly and pretzel evoke the best of American childhoods in one luxe little cup.

When you make these treats, don't cover the tops completely with chocolate. Part of the homemade charm is seeing a little peanut butter and jelly peeking out. And believe it or not, too much chocolate can wreak havoc on the judicious balance of sweet and salty.

——————————————— MAKES 6 PEANUT BUTTER CUPS ———————————————

6 oz/170 g bittersweet chocolate, coarsely chopped

9 or so thick sourdough pretzel sticks, halved

2 tsp raspberry or strawberry jelly

¼ cup/60 g chunky peanut butter (see Cook's Note)

Flaked sea salt such as Maldon

STEP 1. Line a six-cup muffin tin with paper liners, and clear a space just big enough in the freezer for the tin to fit flat. Place the chocolate in a heat-proof bowl and set the bowl over a pot of simmering water (be sure that the bowl doesn't touch the water). With the heat on low, stir once or twice until melted, about 2 minutes. Remove from the heat and set aside. Be sure not to let any water droplets get inside the bowl with the chocolate.

STEP 2. Spoon 1 tbsp of the melted chocolate into the bottom of each of the six cups. Press about three pretzel-stick halves about halfway into the chocolate and freeze for 5 minutes. Divide the jelly between the centers of each chocolate base, using the gaps between the pretzels to allow the jelly to pool. (Skip this step if you're making these in advance—the jelly turns the pretzels soggy if they sit overnight.) Divide the peanut butter between the six cups (about 2 tsp peanut butter each), scooping and dolloping onto the jelly in a slightly rounded heap. Lightly press down on the top of the mound to flatten slightly.

STEP 3. Spoon a scant 1 tbsp chocolate over the top of each cup, covering the top and most of the peanut butter so that it meets the chocolate base, but leaving just a few gaps for the peanut butter and jelly to peek through. Sprinkle the top with salt before the chocolate sets. Return the chocolate cups to the freezer to set, about 3 minutes. Remove and serve. If you're making ahead, skip the freezer and let the chocolate cups stand in a cool room to set overnight. Don't store in the fridge or freezer, which can cause the chocolate to bloom, or discolor. Store in an airtight container in a cool place for up to 2 days.

COOK'S NOTE. I'm normally a creamy peanut butter kind of gal, but don't use it here. The crunchy peanut butter gives both addictive texture and structure to the insides, so that the cups don't collapse at first bite. Opt for a peanut butter labeled "natural" (commercial or otherwise), made without added sugar, for that rich salty, peanut taste.

PEANUT BUTTER AND AMARANTH COOKIES

At first glance, these are cookies for the adventurous. But be assured, I've gotten good old-fashioned peanut butter–cookie people stuck on these. The fact that these cookies are gluten-free and vegan is just a perk for anyone who isn't trying to avoid wheat, dairy, and eggs, and a special treat for those who are. You don't need those ingredients here thanks to the fat and flavor of natural peanut butter. The amaranth flour makes these cookies seem rather daring, but don't let it scare you off. It's here for its sweet, nutty, and almost malty flavor. If its assertive flavor or aroma isn't for you, try barley flour, all-purpose flour, or a blend of the two. Toasted sesame oil gives these an added rich nutty tone and one more reason for it to earn its keep in your pantry.

MAKES 36 COOKIES

2 cups/200 g amaranth flour

1 tsp baking soda

¾ tsp fine sea salt

1 cup/260 g natural creamy peanut butter

½ cup/120 ml Grade B maple syrup

¼ cup/50 g unbleached raw sugar or turbinado sugar

¼ cup/60 ml canola oil

2 tbsp toasted sesame oil

STEP 1. Whisk together the flour, baking soda, and salt in a medium bowl. Beat together the peanut butter, maple syrup, sugar, canola oil, and sesame oil in the bowl of a stand mixer fitted with the paddle attachment until smooth. Add in the flour mixture and stir with a spatula until it just comes together. Form the dough into a ball, wrap in plastic wrap, and refrigerate for 20 minutes.

STEP 2. Preheat the oven to 350°F/180°C/gas 4, using the convection setting if available. Line a baking sheet with parchment paper. Scoop a heaping 1 tbsp of dough, roll into a ball, and place on the prepared baking sheet. Repeat with the remaining dough, leaving about 1 in/2.5 cm between balls. Gently press a fork into each ball to make a simple design with four lines on the top. Bake until puffed and set (they will still feel soft, but will stiffen as they cool), about 12 minutes.

STEP 3. Let the cookies cool slightly on the baking sheet. Serve warm for a tender and moist cookie, or transfer to a rack to cool completely for a crunchier texture. Wrap extras in an airtight container for up to 2 days, or freeze for up to 2 weeks.

PASTRY SHOP
ALMOND–CHOCOLATE CHIP COOKIES

These are a baker's pride—chubby, chunky, chocolate-laden chocolate chip cookies—given a subtle and inviting texture boost from ground almonds. They get their good looks from generous chocolate pistoles, round discs of chocolate used in the best pastry kitchens for melting, which are available online for home bakers (see page 280). You can certainly use chopped high-quality dark chocolate or bittersweet chocolate chips for these gorgeous cookies, but if you find pistoles, make a batch that's worthy of the finest pastry shop windows.

MAKES 24 COOKIES

⅓ cup/45 g skin-on almonds (see Cook's Note, page 235)

2¼ cups/280 g whole-wheat white flour

¾ tsp baking soda

¾ tsp fine sea salt

1 cup/225 g unsalted butter, at room temperature

¾ cup/155 g firmly packed dark brown sugar

¾ cup/155 g unbleached raw sugar

4 egg yolks, at room temperature, plus 1 large egg, lightly beaten

1 tsp pure vanilla extract

9 oz/255 g high-quality bittersweet chocolate pistoles, chopped bittersweet chocolate, or large chips

STEP 1. Preheat the oven to 375°F/190°C/gas 5. Line two baking sheets with parchment paper or silicone baking mats.

STEP 2. Pulse the almonds in a food processor, stopping when the almonds are still coarse, with some powdery bits.

STEP 3. Whisk together the flour, baking soda, and salt in a medium bowl. Beat together the butter and both sugars in a large bowl with an electric mixer on medium speed until light and fluffy, about 3 minutes. Beat in the egg yolks, two at a time, followed by the vanilla. Add the flour mixture and beat until it just comes together, scraping down the bowl as needed to make sure the butter is evenly incorporated. Give the dough a final mix with a mixer or by hand.

STEP 4. Divide the dough in half in the bowl (like splitting the Red Sea). Pour in half of the chocolate and half of the ground almonds and give the dough a few strokes with a wooden spoon to marble and streak the almonds and chocolate in. Add the remaining chocolate and all but 2 to 3 tbsp of the ground almonds. Fold in loosely, but don't mix in completely, so that visible streaks of ground almonds remain throughout the dough.

CONTINUED

STEP 5. Scoop a heaping 1 tbsp of dough and place on a prepared baking sheet. Repeat with the remaining dough, leaving about 3 in/7.5 cm between cookies, until both baking sheets are full. Brush each cookie with beaten egg, then sprinkle with ground almonds. Bake until the cookies are set and golden around the edges, but still soft in the center, about 10 minutes, switching the baking sheets between the top and bottom racks halfway through cooking.

STEP 6. Let the cookies cool slightly on the baking sheet, about 2 minutes. Transfer the cookies with a thin spatula to a wire rack to cool, or just slide the parchment paper with the cookies directly onto the wire rack. Let the baking sheets cool completely before using to bake the remaining dough, lining with more parchment paper if needed. Serve while the oozing chocolate layers are still warm. Store in an airtight container for up to 2 days.

COOK'S NOTE. You can buy almond meal or almond flour in specialty stores, but to add texture to this cookie, I like to make my own chunkier version from ground skin-on almonds.

ALMOND
CROISSANT

FALL
PEAR AND HAZELNUT TOAST

WINTER
ALMOND-TANGERINE TOASTS WITH ORANGE-FLOWER SYRUP

SUMMER
RHUBARB AND WALNUT TOAST

FRANGIPANE TOASTS
FOR FOUR SEASONS

As a young pastry cook in New York City, I was lucky enough to work for the pastry chef I most admired in the field. He was stern but joyful, and like a loving parent, he would pull out his favorite treats just for us on occasion when his mood struck—halves of croissant or even day-old brioche spread thick with frangipane and sliced almonds, baked, and practically doused with Grand Marnier syrup. In a new and often intimidating world of tough chefs and food folks, it was like the fleeting cozy afternoon bliss between school and homework, a glimpse of being spoiled and soothed by something delicious before the hard work set in.

It was almost ten years before I resurrected this treat from my memory to make at home, a bake-shop staple that belongs in your home, too. It starts with almond cream, or frangipane—which all good pastry chefs know as the best instant-dessert base, always at the ready in your fridge (where it keeps well for 2 weeks). From there you can build it into a frangipane toast or tartine of your dreams, using any seasonal fruit or nut you fancy for a little afternoon spoiling.

HOW TO MAKE (ALMOND CREAM) FRANGIPANE

Almond cream, or frangipane, is a sweetened ground-almond or almond flour base for desserts, pies, tarts, and more. Use this as a base for almond croissants and tarts, or swap in your favorite nuts. To make it, cream together 1 cup/225 g unsalted room-temperature butter and 1 cup/200g unbleached raw sugar until light and fluffy, about 2 minutes. Add 2 cups/230 g ground almonds or almond flour and beat together. Add in 2 large eggs and 2 egg yolks, one at a time, and then 2 tsp vanilla extract. Stir in $^1/_3$ cup/40 g oat, whole-wheat white, or all-purpose flour, and $^1/_2$ tsp fine sea salt, scraping the bottom for any dry or unmixed bits, until the mixture is evenly fluffy and smooth. Store in a container with an airtight lid in the fridge for up to 2 weeks. Makes enough for 12 croissants or almond toasts.

SPRING
ALMOND CROISSANT

SERVES 6

½ recipe almond cream (see above)
6 day-old croissants, halved lengthwise

Skin-on sliced almonds for sprinkling

Preheat the oven to 375°F/190°C/gas 5. Line a baking sheet with parchment paper. Divide all but ⅓ cup/75 ml of the almond cream over the bottom halves of the croissants. Cover with the top halves, using your hand to flatten the croissants just slightly. Spread more almond cream over the top of the croissants with an offset spatula, leaving some of the edges bare. Sprinkle with almonds. Bake on the prepared baking sheet until the cream is cooked through and the top is golden brown, about 20 minutes, covering the top with foil if needed to prevent overbrowning. Serve warm or at room temperature.

RHUBARB AND WALNUT TOAST

SERVES 6

½ recipe almond cream (see facing page), made with almonds or walnuts

6 slices day-old brioche

Unbleached raw sugar or turbinado sugar for sprinkling

1 cup/250 g poached rhubarb (see following), plus rhubarb syrup for dousing

Chopped toasted walnuts (see page 273; optional)

STEP 1. Preheat the oven to 375°F/190°C/gas 5. Line a baking sheet with parchment paper. Divide the almond cream among the brioche and spread to the edges. Bake on the prepared baking sheet until puffed and golden, about 20 minutes. Remove from the oven and sprinkle the tops with sugar. Turn off the oven and turn the broiler on high. Broil until golden on the edges, about 1 minute.

STEP 2. Meanwhile, heat the rhubarb and rhubarb syrup until just warm, 1 to 2 minutes. Spoon the poached rhubarb over the toasts and sprinkle with walnuts (if using). Douse the warm tarts with the rhubarb syrup. Serve warm.

PREPPING AND POACHING RHUBARB

Depending on the season and where you live, you might find slender, bright pink rhubarb with pale green leaves or deeper red rhubarb with fat stalks and deep green leaves. Look for firm, brightly colored stalks of rhubarb. Trim away any of the leaves, which are toxic and should not be consumed. Cut 2 lb/910 g of rhubarb into 2-in/5-cm lengths and combine with 2 cups/400 g unbleached raw sugar, 1 split and scraped vanilla bean, and just enough water to cover in a nonreactive pot (like stainless steel or enamel). Simmer or poach, shaking the pan occasionally, until just soft, about 3 minutes. Do not stir, which will break down the rhubarb. Remove the rhubarb with a slotted spoon, Continue cooking the liquid until syrupy, about 5 minutes. Cool and use as simple syrup. Store in an airtight container in the refrigerator for up to 1 week.

PEAR AND HAZELNUT TOAST

SERVES 6

½ recipe almond cream (see page 238), made
  with almonds or hazelnuts

6 slices raisin bread or 6 leftover halved Toasted
  Semolina Raisin Scones (page 50)

2 ripe, juicy pears, peeled and cut in wedges

Handful toasted hazelnuts (see page 273),
  coarsely chopped, for topping

1 tsp ground cinnamon

1 tsp unbleached raw sugar

Freshly whipped cream (see page 225) for
  serving (optional)

Preheat the oven to 375°F/190°C/gas 5. Line a baking sheet with parchment paper. Divide
the almond cream among the bread and spread to the edges. Bake on the prepared baking
sheet until puffed and golden, about 20 minutes. Remove from the oven and lay the pears
over the top and garnish with hazelnuts. Stir together the cinnamon and sugar in a small
bowl and sprinkle over the top. Serve warm, plain or with whipped cream.

WINTER

ALMOND-TANGERINE TOASTS WITH ORANGE-FLOWER SYRUP

SERVES 6

ORANGE-FLOWER SYRUP

½ cup/100 g unbleached raw sugar

½ cup/120 ml water

1 to 2 tbsp orange-flower water

½ recipe almond cream (see page 238)

6 slices day-old brioche

2 tangerines cut into segments (see page 264)

Unbleached raw sugar or turbinado sugar for
  sprinkling

Raw shelled pistachios, preferably Sicilian,
  for sprinkling

STEP 1. *To make the Orange-Flower Syrup:* Bring the sugar and water to a boil in a small
pan over medium-low heat and cook until the sugar is completely dissolved, about 5 minutes. Add the orange-flower water, to taste. Stir together, and keep warm over low heat.

STEP 2. Preheat the oven to 375°F/190°C/gas 5. Line a baking sheet with parchment paper.
Divide the almond cream among the brioche and spread to the edges. Bake on the prepared
baking sheet until puffed and golden, about 20 minutes. Remove from the oven and top
with the tangerine segments. Sprinkle with sugar. Turn off the oven and turn the broiler
on high. Broil until golden on the edges, about 1 minute. Sprinkle the tops with pistachios.
Douse the toasts with warm orange-flower syrup. Serve warm.

STRAWBERRY-RYE SQUARES

Thank goodness for the Apple-Rye Pancakes (page 47), which necessitated the creation of these addictive bars. I try not to ask you to buy a new ingredient, and only give you one way to use it. Pack these wholesome goodies into neat packages that are easy to put in a picnic basket or the side bag of a bicycle to fuel up for a long summer ride.

--- MAKES 12 TO 36 SQUARES ---

1¼ cups/130 g rye flour

1 cup/125 g all-purpose flour

2 cups/170 g old-fashioned rolled oats

1½ tsp baking powder

½ tsp fine sea salt

1 cup/225 g unsalted butter, at room temperature

1 cup/200 g firmly packed dark brown sugar

¾ cup/170 g unbleached raw sugar

1 large egg, plus 1 egg yolk

1 tsp pure vanilla extract

Scant 1 cup/240 ml strawberry preserves
    or your favorite jam

¾ cup/140 g lightly toasted walnuts
    (see page 273), coarsely chopped

STEP 1. Preheat the oven to 375°F/190°C/gas 5. Lightly butter a 9-by-13-in/23-by-33-cm baking pan and line with parchment paper so that there are overlapping flaps (see page 260). Butter and flour the parchment paper, and knock against the side of the counter to settle a thin dusting of all-purpose flour inside the pan; discard any extra flour in the pan.

STEP 2. Whisk together the rye flour, all-purpose flour, oats, baking powder, and salt in a medium bowl.

STEP 3. Beat together the butter and both sugars in a large bowl with an electric mixer at medium-high speed until light and fluffy, about 2 minutes. Beat in the egg, egg yolk, and vanilla. Add the flour mixture and stir slowly to mix completely.

STEP 4. Layer about two-thirds of the dough in the prepared baking pan, pressing the dough with your fingers to spread it completely over the bottom. It will look thin, but the dough will rise when baking. Spread the strawberry preserves on top of the dough. Drop the remaining dough in clumps to cover the jam, letting some jam peek through. Sprinkle with the walnuts.

STEP 5. Bake until the dough is set and just golden, 45 to 50 minutes. Transfer to the counter to cool slightly in the baking pan, about 15 minutes. Grab the flaps of parchment paper, lift out the whole batch, and transfer to a cutting board. Cut into 12 squares or 36 narrow bars. Serve warm or cool completely and serve at room temperature. Store in an airtight container for up to 3 days.

SPANISH SUGAR PIES

My grandmother was a locally famed cobbler baker, known for mixing lard and love into her dough without a recipe or measuring cup. Her cobblers were crisp and heavenly, with oodles of homegrown cherries or peaches oozing out the top; but I loved her sugar pies the best—the little scraps of dough from the cobbler trimmings that she'd sprinkle with sugar and bake off for those of us who just couldn't wait. You don't need lard or skill to make my modern version, a quick solution using store-bought puff pastry. My favorite Spanish olive oil biscuits, with a touch of anise, inspire the flavors I use here. These Southern favorites-turned–sophisticated sweets belong equally alongside an artisan cheese course and honeycomb on a holiday buffet as stacked and snacked on with a spoonful of Chocolate Sorbet (page 228).

SERVES 6 TO 8

Half of one 17.3-oz/490-g package puff pastry (1 sheet)

Superfine or unbleached raw sugar for dusting

Anise seeds, toasted and cracked, for sprinkling

STEP 1. Preheat the oven to 400°F/200°C/gas 6.

STEP 2. Roll the puff pastry sheet with a rolling pin on a lightly floured work surface to thin out and flatten slightly. Cut the dough into rounds with a small round biscuit cutter.

STEP 3. Line a baking sheet with a silicone baking mat or wax paper and dust lightly with sugar. Lay the raw pastry rounds on the sugar with about 2 in/5 cm between them. Cover with another silicone baking mat or sheet of wax paper and weigh down with another baking sheet. Place in the oven to cook for about 5 minutes.

STEP 4. Remove the top baking sheet and check to see that the puff pastry is glistening and wet looking, but not yet setting. Sprinkle the top with more sugar and anise. Replace the baking mats and baking sheets and return to the oven. Bake until golden and crisp, about 12 minutes.

STEP 5. Remove the top baking sheet and let the sugar pies set on the sheet on the countertop until crisp and completely cool. Serve at room temperature or store in an airtight container for up to 2 days.

RICOTTA FRITTERS
WITH MEYER LEMON GLAZE

Good news for vegetarians: Unless you overindulge in fatty cheeses and excessive dairy, your diet is likely to be low in saturated fat. If you're smart about it, that leaves a little wiggle room for the occasional fried treat like ricotta fritters.

This is the simplest little beignet, drizzled or dunked in a light glaze made of fresh squeezed Meyer lemon juice, which could just as easily be made with fresh cider in the fall. These fritters are absolutely worth serving to friends, or as a little something special just for you.

MAKES 12 FRITTERS

MEYER LEMON GLAZE
2 Meyer lemons
¾ cup/85 g confectioners' sugar

FRITTERS
Vegetable oil for frying
½ cup/60 g all-purpose flour
1½ tsp baking powder
Zest of 1 Meyer lemon
Fine sea salt
¾ cup/170 g fresh ricotta cheese
1 large egg, plus 1 egg yolk, lightly beaten
Generous 2 pinches of unbleached raw sugar
1 tsp pure vanilla extract

STEP 1. Before you begin, have everything you'll need handy so you can concentrate when you're working with the hot oil on the stove. Set up a wire rack over a baking sheet lined with paper towels, and set tongs, a slotted spoon, and a splatter guard (if you have one) near the stove.

STEP 2. *To make the Meyer Lemon Glaze:* Zest 1 lemon and set the zest aside for the fritter batter. Juice the lemons into a medium bowl. Whisk together the confectioner's sugar and about 2½ tbsp of the lemon juice in a small bowl. Cover with plastic wrap while you make the fritters.

STEP 3. *To make the Fritters:* In a large, deep frying pan or a heavy saucepan, heat 4 in/ 10 cm vegetable oil over medium-high heat until it reaches 350°F/180°C on a deep-fry thermometer. Keep hot over a steady low flame, letting it reach about 365°F/185°C but no higher (the temperature will drop when you add the batter).

STEP 4. Whisk together the flour, baking powder, lemon zest, and a pinch of salt in a medium bowl. Whisk together the ricotta, egg, egg yolk, sugar, and vanilla in another medium bowl or liquid measuring cup. Add to the flour mixture and whisk to combine.

STEP 5. To test the temperature of the oil, spoon a drop or two of the batter into the pan; the oil should sizzle and the batter should brown slowly and evenly and rise to the top.

STEP 6. Working in batches of three to four fritters, gently drop 1 tbsp of the batter into the hot oil at a time, giving each one space to set its shape before adding more. Fry until the batter puffs and is crisp and golden on one side, about 2 minutes. Flip the fritters in the oil with a slotted spoon until golden brown on both sides, about 2 minutes more. Transfer the fritters to the rack over the baking sheet with a slotted spoon. Repeat until all the fritters are fried.

STEP 7. Drizzle the warm fritters with the glaze. Stack the fritters high and serve warm.

pickles, sauces & such

In some countries, pickles and sauces are practically mandatory. In Korea, parts of Eastern Europe, and some Southern American states, pickles appear before the meal even starts. Similarly, sauces and spreads, like Harissa (PAGE 253) and Pico de Gallo (PAGE 252), are anything but optional in their native lands. They are a key component to certain dishes and make every bite appeal.

Taste some of these and you'll understand why. Pickles and pickly things (like Kimchi, PAGE 250), spreads and sauces (like pico de gallo) are what make food explode with flavor. These pickles and such are just the beginning, a composite of addictively useful accompaniments to the meals in this book. Make them ahead, keep them in the fridge, and you'll make everyday meals and entertaining on the fly a flavorful affair.

SMOKED PAPRIKA PICKLED OKRA

Forget preconceived notions about okra. Pickled okra, like any pickle, is robust, tangy, and pert. It's at home alongside any of the sandwiches in this book—or any sandwich you love for that matter—and a welcome intro to a breezy dinner of cheese, crackers, flavored popcorn, and other savories.

―――――――――――――――――――― MAKES 2 PT/850 G ――――――――――――――――――――

1 lb/455 oz okra, trimmed

2 cups/480 ml white wine vinegar or
    cider vinegar

2 cups/480 ml water

Heaping 2 tbsp unbleached raw sugar

1 tbsp smoked paprika or pimentón

1 tbsp sweet paprika

1 tsp black peppercorns

Heaping 1 tsp sea salt

STEP 1. Pack the okra into two clean canning jars, about 1 pt/480 ml each.

STEP 2. Combine the vinegar, water, sugar, both paprikas, peppercorns, and salt in a medium saucepan and bring to a boil over high heat. Stir until the sugar dissolves, about 2 minutes. Pour or ladle the brine over the okra, leaving about ¼ in/6 mm of space at the top of both jars. Close the jars tightly with the lids and rings and store in the fridge for up to 2 weeks.

PICKLED ONIONS

Working in restaurants turned me into somewhat of a quick-pickle addict—pickles made and stored in the fridge to be eaten within days—as a restaurant walk-in is always filled with artisan-style condiments such as these that are at the ready for flavoring the plate. You can have your own stash at home, too, which makes the work of putting together exciting meals day after day a carefree pleasure. If you had to choose just one pickle to keep around, this is it, ready to top sandwiches, burgers (see page 138), stack on quesadillas (see page 150), or in Soft Tacos with Mushrooms, Greens, and Onions (page 145).

———————————————— MAKES ABOUT 2½ CUPS/260 G ————————————————

2 red onions, thinly sliced

1½ cups/360 ml cider vinegar or red wine vinegar

½ cups/100 g unbleached raw sugar

4 black peppercorns

1 bay leaf

Put the onions in a large bowl. Combine the vinegar, sugar, peppercorns, and bay leaf in a small saucepan and bring to a boil over high heat. Stir until the sugar dissolves, about 2 minutes. Pour over the onions and set aside for 5 minutes. Test one onion slice—it should taste pickled yet still be crisp. Remove the onions from the pickling liquid, reserving both, and transfer the onions to a clean jar. Let the onions and pickling liquid cool to room temperature separately. Pour the liquid over the onions and use immediately, or store in the fridge for up to 1 week.

KIMCHI

Kimchi, the staple sour of Korean cuisine, is both fermented and pickled. And by some standards, it's one of the world's most healthful foods. It's also incredibly easy to make at home, requiring only patience and a few empty jars. For the price you pay for buying good kimchi in some markets, or for doing without when you can't find a jar at a nearby store, it's far easier just to go DIY, and really gratifying, too. No pickling project has ever made me more proud.

MAKES ABOUT 3 CUPS/465 G

1 large napa cabbage, washed

1 gl/4 L warm water

½ cup/100 g coarse salt

8 to 10 garlic cloves

One 2-in/5-cm piece peeled fresh ginger

⅓ cup/75 ml hot-pepper paste such as sambal oelek

¼ cup/60 ml fish sauce (optional)

1 tsp unbleached raw sugar

6 green onions, halved lengthwise and cut into 1-in/2.5-cm lengths

1 tbsp toasted sesame seeds (see page 274)

STEP 1. Slice the cabbage in half lengthwise. Trim out the tough root and cut the cabbage lengthwise into thirds or quarters, depending on how fat the cabbage is. Combine the water and salt in a very large bowl and stir to dissolve. Submerge the cabbage pieces in the water, cover with a plate to hold them down, and set aside for at least 2 hours on the countertop.

STEP 2. Meanwhile, finely chop the garlic and ginger by hand or in a food processor. Transfer to a large bowl and stir with the hot-pepper paste, fish sauce (if using), sugar, and green onions.

STEP 3. Drain and squeeze the cabbage leaves very dry, patting between the layers with a kitchen towel. Toss the cabbage in the hot-pepper mixture, covering each layer completely with the paste and rubbing in well. Pack the cabbage into a clean, sterilized tall glass jar and cover tightly. Leave the jar in a dark place overnight.

STEP 4. Check the kimchi after 1 day. When you see some bubbling, which signals fermentation, transfer the kimchi to the fridge. If the kimchi is not bubbling, let it sit in a dark place another half day to a day.

STEP 5. Store the fermented kimchi in the fridge for up to 3 weeks. Sprinkle toasted sesame seeds over the top before serving.

BUTTERMILK CHIVE DRESSING

Consider this the ranch dressing of your new repertoire. It is tangy (thanks to buttermilk), luscious (thanks to yogurt), and long on good flavor (due to chives, Sriracha, garlic, and black pepper) that begs you to drizzle it over greens of every kind. See it shine in the Buttermilk Fried Tofu Salad with Greens and Asparagus (page 102) and the Wild Mushroom and Little Gem Salad (page 112).

———————————————— MAKES 1½ CUPS/360 ML ————————————————

½ cup/120 ml full-fat plain yogurt or plain Greek yogurt

⅓ cup/80 g olive-oil mayonnaise

⅓ cup/75 ml buttermilk

1 garlic clove, minced

1 tbsp fresh lemon juice

Fine sea salt and freshly ground pepper

1 bunch chives, finely chopped

½ tsp Sriracha or other hot-pepper paste, plus more as needed

Whisk together the yogurt, mayonnaise, buttermilk, garlic, lemon juice, ¼ tsp salt, ⅛ tsp pepper, and chives in a medium bowl. Stir in the Sriracha. Taste and add more Sriracha, salt, and pepper as needed. Refrigerate until ready to serve. Store in an airtight container in the fridge for up 2 days.

PICO DE GALLO

Think of pico de gallo as a Mexican tomato relish, an über-fresh salsa, and the ideal topper for summer soy dogs or fish tacos, quesadillas (see page 150), or burritos (see page 151), among a zillion other foods that love the zing of tomatoes, lime, and chiles. This is an indispensible player in your taco lineup (see pages 145 to 148) and takes just a few minutes to make. For the best flavor, always use it the day it is made.

—————————————————— MAKES 1½ CUPS/240 G ——————————————————

2 jalapeño, serrano, Fresno, or other medium-hot chiles, seeded and minced

1 small red onion, minced

2 large firm, ripe heirloom or beefsteak tomatoes, chopped

1 garlic clove, minced

Juice of 1 lime

2 tbsp chopped fresh cilantro leaves

Sea salt

Finishing oil for drizzling

Toss together the jalapeños, onion, tomatoes, garlic, lime juice, and cilantro in a medium bowl. Season with salt and soften the bite and acidity of the onion and tomato with a drizzle of finishing oil. Serve at room temperature.

HARISSA

Harissa is a North African hot-pepper paste that's usually made with hot chile peppers, seasoned with spices and oil, and sometimes softened with carrots and roasted red peppers.

When I was thinking about all the crazy delicious things you can flavor with just a taste of purchased harissa, like Roasted Tomato–Squash Tagine Fall Feast (page 209), I had a lightbulb moment. You can make it! And when you do, it's usually better, and with far less salt and added preservatives. Make a batch and keep it in the fridge to have handy for whenever you need a spicy sweet addition to soups, sauces, and stews. You can even (don't tell my Hungarian husband) swap it out for paprika paste in Mushroom Gulyás (page 164) in a pinch.

MAKES 1¼ CUPS/325 G

6 assorted hot to mild dried chiles such as Anaheim, ancho, chile de arbol, and guajillo (see Cook's Note)

½ cup/120 ml boiling water

5 tbsp/75 ml neutral-flavored olive oil or grapeseed oil, plus more for storing

1 large garlic clove, minced

2 tsp sweet paprika

1½ tsp ground coriander

½ tsp cayenne pepper

½ tsp ground cumin

1 large carrot, peeled and finely grated

2 roasted red bell peppers (see page 269)

1 tbsp fresh lemon juice, plus more as needed

Sea salt

STEP 1. Place the chiles in a medium heat-proof bowl and pour the boiling water over them. Set the chiles aside to steep until soft, about 30 minutes. Strain and reserve the water, and clean the chiles by cutting off the top and scraping out the seeds (or keep the seeds if you like your harissa hot).

STEP 2. Heat the olive oil in a small skillet over medium heat. Add the garlic, paprika, coriander, cayenne, and cumin and cook until fragrant, about 1 minute. Add the carrot and cook to soften and bring out its sweetness, about 1 minute. Remove from the heat and set aside.

STEP 3. Add the chiles, 1 tbsp of their steeping liquid, and the roasted red peppers to a blender or food processor and purée to make a paste. While running, slowly pour in the garlic-carrot mixture to thicken the paste. Add the lemon juice and ½ tsp salt and pulse to combine. Taste and add up to ½ tsp more salt and lemon juice as needed.

STEP 4. Store in an airtight container, with a thin layer of oil on the top, in the fridge for up to 3 weeks.

COOK'S NOTE. When it comes to dried chiles, usually the smaller the chile, the hotter it is. For a deep, dark, roasty-colored, and not-too-hot harissa, use large dried Anaheim and ancho chiles, and just one or two tiny bright red-hot chiles de arbol. Though ancho, chile de arbol, and guajillo are all Mexican, and not North African, peppers, they are easiest to find and lend a great, intense flavor to homemade harissa.

CORN CREMA

In Mexico, boiled corn on the cob is served from street stands slathered with crema (like sour cream), grated Cotija cheese, and an ample dash of chile. This addictive blend of sweet and savory has found its way onto restaurant menus across the globe. Blended all together (without the cob, of course) with some cilantro, it becomes an impossibly simple way to dress up quesadillas, fish, or even a summer sandwich.

———————————————————————— SERVES 4 ————————————————————————

1 ear of corn, kernels removed and milked
    (see page 265)

2 cups/480 ml plain Greek yogurt

¼ cup/35 g Cotija cheese, broken into pieces

¼ to ½ tsp chili powder

Juice of 2 limes

1 small bunch fresh cilantro, coarsely chopped

2 tbsp extra-virgin olive oil

Sea salt

Put the corn kernels and corn milk, yogurt, cheese, chili powder, lime juice, cilantro, and olive oil in a blender or food processor. Season with salt and pulse until smooth. Serve at room temperature. Store in an airtight container in the fridge for up to 2 days.

GARLICKY GREEN SAUCE

There's a little Venezuelan restaurant in my neighborhood called Arepa Café, with fresh stuffed arepas and a sauce so hard to resist that I've heard the patrons refer to it as a drug. It's simple to make, potent with a heavy hand of garlic, cilantro, and lime. Use it on sandwiches, quesadillas, Lentil-Chickpea Burgers with Harissa Yogurt (page 138), Crispy Smashed Creamer Potatoes with Rosemary (page 126), and, of course, slather it liberally over your own homemade arepas (see page 43).

SERVES 4 TO 6

1 bunch fresh cilantro

2 garlic cloves, coarsely chopped

⅓ cup/80 g olive-oil mayonnaise or
   regular mayonnaise

¼ cup/60 ml fresh lime juice

4 green onions, green parts only,
   coarsely chopped

Sea salt and freshly ground pepper

Pick the leaves off the cilantro until you have a large handful. Swish the leaves in cold water and lift them out, leaving all the sand and dirt behind. Pat the leaves dry. Purée the garlic, mayonnaise, lime juice, green onions, and cilantro in a food processor or blender until smooth. Season with salt and pepper, transfer to a bowl, and serve at room temperature. Store in an airtight container in the fridge for up to 1 day.

SOFRITO

This flavor starter has origins in Spain. It's the holy trinity of aromatic flavoring that gives so many dishes, like paella, its signature taste. This version is not married to one culinary tradition, but I love the ease of the preparation and the heady dishes it begets. I learned this method from Katherine Alford, the vice president of the test kitchens at the Food Network, one day when we were tackling sofrito as the perfect accompaniment to a Spanish tortilla. I have since adopted her clever technique, just one of her many, for grating tomatoes down to their skins, half the work of peeling and chopping them. The first time I made sofrito with Spanish friends, I was surprised and thrilled to see them doing the same thing. Clever indeed. Use this as a starting point for Spring Vegetable Paella (page 204).

MAKES ABOUT 2 CUPS/410 G

⅓ cup/75 ml extra-virgin olive oil

2 large yellow onions, finely chopped

Generous pinch of unbleached raw sugar or turbinado sugar

Sea salt

4 beefsteak or 6 plum tomatoes

Heaping ½ tsp smoked paprika or pimentón

STEP 1. Heat the olive oil in a medium skillet over medium heat. Add the onions, sugar, and ½ tsp salt. Reduce the heat to medium-low and cook, stirring occasionally, until the onions are soft and pale golden, about 30 minutes. Taste the onions; they should be subtly sweet.

STEP 2. While the onions cook, cut the tomatoes in half lengthwise. Grate the tomatoes on the large holes of a box grater into a bowl all the way down to the skins. Discard the skins and add the pulp, juices, and paprika to the onions. Cook until the juices thicken, 12 to 15 minutes. Taste and season with more salt as needed. Store in an airtight container in the refrigerator for up to 1 week.

RASPBERRY SHRUB

A shrub is an old-fashioned summer drink, essentially a pickled fruit base that's the perfect thing to stir into cold sparkling water. You won't be surprised to hear me say this summer elixir is amazing with freshly picked berries, but it will give a longer life to any berries you have on hand. I made this for years with sugar, as is traditionally done, until one day in my test kitchen, I skipped the final step of adding sugar, and poured the raspberry-infused vinegar straight into sparkling water. Kombucha lovers, this drink is for you. The rest of you, add the sugar to taste (go easy), depending on the sweetness of the berries.

—————————————————— MAKES ABOUT 1¼ CUPS/300 ML ——————————————————

3 cups/375 g fresh raspberries

1 cup/240 ml apple cider vinegar

¼ to ⅓ cup/50 to 65 g unbleached raw sugar, depending on the sweetness of the berries

Seltzer water for serving

Lime wedges for serving

Tequila or gin (optional) for serving

Soak the raspberries with the vinegar in a large bowl overnight on the counter or in the fridge for up to 4 days. Add the sugar, stirring to dissolve. Strain, pressing the solids with a wooden spoon to get out as much liquid as possible. (Toss the pulp in the compost.) Cool the strained shrub and store in the fridge. To serve, mix 1 or 2 tbsp of the shrub with 1 cup/240 ml cold seltzer water and garnish with a wedge of lime, or a splash or tequila, if desired.

prep school

One of the fastest ways to make cooking more fun and rewarding is to learn the tricks of the trade. As you dig in to the recipes, study these pages for how-to's that will make you feel like a studied chef. These are tried-and-true tips, learned from grandmothers, gardeners, chefs, and good old-fashioned trial and error during my years in the kitchen. Read, explore, and find the ways that work best for you.

HOW TO MEASURE

To measure flours, ground nuts, cocoa, and other dry ingredients for the recipes in this book, spoon the ingredient lightly into a dry measuring cup until it is full. Sweep across the top of the cup with the edge of a spatula or knife to level off the ingredient without packing it down.

To measure stock, dairy products, oil, and other wet ingredients, pour into a liquid measuring cup. Set on a level surface and view the measuring line at eye level to ensure the liquid is at the desired mark.

OIL: WHEN AND HOW MUCH?

It's easy to learn to eyeball an appropriate amount of oil for cooking. A few swirls of oil around the pan or a thin sheen in the pan is a good start. For measured amounts in sauces, vinaigrettes, and spreads, use a liquid measure with a pour spout to gradually add oil in a thin stream, while whisking constantly.

TO PREP A GRILL

Prepping a grill or grill pan requires just three steps.

STEP 1. Use a grill grate brush or stone to remove buildup from the grill grates or grill pan.

STEP 2. Oil the grill grates well. Dip a thin, old towel or a paper towel folded up and dipped into a neutral, high-heat oil like safflower or peanut oil. Holding it with tongs, rub it along the grill grates. Set aside.

STEP 3. Preheat a gas grill or grill pan to medium-high heat and wait until the grill is evenly hot before cooking, or prepare a charcoal grill until the charcoal is evenly hot. If needed, give the grates a final rub with oil before cooking.

GOOD JUDGMENT

This part I can't teach you, but I assure you, you have it. Every time you're in the kitchen, you'll be making judgment calls about how to make things just right. Look for the visual cues in each recipe (cook until golden brown, for example) and use these as your guide. Temperature and time cues (like medium-high, and cook for 15 minutes) are there to help, too, but they are just cues, since they can be altered by the many variables that make my kitchen different from yours. Most important, use your nose, eyes, ears, and tasting spoon throughout every recipe to make sure things are turning out the way *you* like them.

BAKING

LINING A BAKING PAN

To help make removing and serving savory pies, bars, and sweets easier, line your baking dish with parchment paper or foil trimmed to fit so that there is a 1-in/2.5-cm overhang on two sides. Trim a second piece of parchment paper or foil and overlap facing the other way, so that the lined pan has 1-in/2.5-cm flaps on all sides. Brushing the pan with butter or oil first helps the parchment paper to stick. If the recipe calls for buttering *and* flouring the pan, butter the pan first, add the parchment paper, butter the parchment paper, and then dust the lined pan evenly with flour.

BLENDING BISCUITS AND PIE CRUSTS

Scones, shortbreads, pie crusts, and some cookies require a studied hand when blending to create the flaky, tender texture that makes them so good. Recipes may say to rub cold butter into the flour with your hands until the flour is coated in the butter and some pea-size pieces remain. Other recipes use the term *coarse meal*. The goal is to coat flour with fat, so that the glutens don't develop.

If it's warm or you tend to have warm hands, set a bowl of ice water and a towel for drying nearby. With cold hands, pinch the butter into the flour in a large bowl. Alternatively, pulse in a food processor to bring the butter and flower together more quickly. Be careful not to overwork the dough, which can make biscuits and pie crusts tough instead of flaky.

GET YEAST SMART

If you've never worked with yeast before, or if you don't have a thermometer to test the temperature of the water, try this technique when making homemade pizza dough (at right) or Homemade

Four-Grain English Muffins (page 52): Dip your finger in the warm water. It should be just a little warmer than your body temperature, like a very hot whirlpool bath. To test your judgment, sprinkle just a few grains of yeast over the water. If they soften and puff in the water, the temperature is likely just right. Add the remaining yeast and set aside until foamy (like shaving cream) and softened, about 5 minutes.

HOW TO FAKE BUTTERMILK

Real buttermilk was the slightly tangy liquid left over when cream separated from milk. Modern-day buttermilk is cultured milk. To make fake buttermilk at home, add 1 tsp lemon juice to 1 cup/240 ml whole milk. Set aside for 15 minutes until it looks curdled, then stir. Use in place of buttermilk, noting that it will be slightly thinner than real buttermilk. Start with slightly less "fake buttermilk" than called for in the recipe and add more as needed.

SCRATCH PIZZA DOUGH

Whisk a pinch of sugar into 1¼ cups/300 ml warm water in a small bowl. Sprinkle 2¼ tsp/7 g yeast over the top, which will feed on the sugar and come to life. Set aside until the yeast is foamy, 5 to 10 minutes. Stir in 2 tbsp olive oil. Stir 2 cups/255 g bread flour and 1 cup/175 g whole-wheat or whole-wheat white flour together with 1 tsp fine sea salt. Make a well in the center of the flour mixture and pour in the yeast mixture. Stir with a fork to make a shaggy dough. Knead with your hands or a wooden spoon for 3 to 5 minutes to make a cohesive ball. Turn onto a lightly floured work surface and knead until the dough is a smooth and elastic ball, about 5 minutes, adding up to ¼ cup/30 g more flour as needed to just keep it from sticking. Place each ball of dough in a lightly oiled plastic bag, seal, and refrigerate overnight or up to 3 days or freeze for up to 1 week. Defrost frozen dough in the refrigerator overnight and remove the dough from the refrigerator 2 hours before you plan to use it.

GRILLED OR TOASTED BREAD ———————

Crunchy and satisfying toasted bread makes a
restaurant-grade accompaniment to the simplest
vegetables, sauces, salads, and soups. It can be
topped (like bruschetta), floated (like a crouton),
or served alongside a composed salad. Slice or
tear open a baguette or other rustic breads in your
desired shape. Brush generously with olive oil or
melted butter on one side all the way to and over the
crusts. Grill on a preheated grill or grill pan set over
medium heat, or toast in a 425°F/220°C/gas 7 oven
until lightly golden and slightly darker around the
edges. Serve warm. You can also quickly toast bread
in butter and oil in a cast-iron skillet over medium
heat. Flip with tongs and toast until evenly golden
brown, adding butter or oil as needed.

MAKE BREAD CRUMBS ———————

Panko, coarse Japanese bread crumbs, are worth
keeping stocked in your pantry. All other bread
crumbs are easy to make out of scraps of stale
bread. Cut off the crusts and store stale baguettes,
sourdough, or ciabatta in the freezer in a plastic
bag. When you have a stash and extra time, defrost
and pulse bread scraps in a food processor to make
crumbs. Store in an airtight container in the pantry
for 2 weeks, or in the freezer, double bagged, for up
to 1 month.

FRUITS AND VEGETABLES

BLANCHING

To slightly soften the texture and flavor of fresh vegetables, or to accentuate their color, plunge them briefly in boiling, salted water. Remove and refresh them under cold water or in a bowl of ice water for a few seconds only. Drain well and pat dry before using. Be sure to season blanched vegetables well.

SCRUB OR PEEL?

Many vegetables are right at home peeled or unpeeled, like carrots, potatoes, summer and winter squash, turnips, and sometimes cucumbers. Consider the size and source of the veggie and its final destination before you decide whether to peel or not.

Homegrown and locally grown, young veggies (baby turnips or carrots, for example) often only need to be scrubbed, a bonus since many nutrients reside in the skin. Peel vegetables that aren't organic or have a waxy or filmy layer on the skin or outer layer, as well as anything you plan to purée. The skin on some winter squash, like butternut or delicata, is lovely roasted, for example, but those same squashes should be peeled before they are cooked and puréed for soup.

FILTERED WATER: A CLEAN START

When making broth, adding plain or salted water to a soup, or boiling vegetables, potatoes, or pasta, always start with clean filtered water, the same water you enjoy drinking, for the best results.

CLEAN AND PREP ARTICHOKES

Start by selecting artichokes with tightly packed leaves and bright coloring, all indicators of freshness. Avoid artichokes with a blackened stem near the cut, which indicates it has been stored too long. Prepare a bowl of acidulated water (see following). Slice off the stem with a stainless-steel chef's knife, leaving only about 1 in/2.5 cm. Slice off the top third of each artichoke leaf. Turn the artichoke upside down and place it on the work surface. Pull off all the dark green leaves, leaving only light, tender green leaves. Trim off the tough skin around the artichoke bottom with a paring knife. Scrape out the choke (the inedible, hairy, and prickly portion) with a melon baller or sturdy round teaspoon. Place the edible portion in the acidulated water until ready to use.

ACIDULATED WATER

When holding prepped apples, artichokes, and many other sliced fruits for longer than a few minutes, store them in a bowl of water with a squeeze of lemon juice or vinegar to prevent them from oxidizing and turning brown. Potato slices can be stored in plain water and patted dry before using.

HOW TO BUY, CLEAN, AND STORE ASPARAGUS

For both fat, meaty asparagus and its slender, snappy counterpart, look for firm stalks with pert, smooth skin and fresh tips, avoiding any with slimy or wet tips. Asparagus is full of water, so if you can't cook it immediately, store stalks upright in a glass with a little water, like flowers, and cover the tips with a damp paper towel in the fridge. To trim and clean them, snap off the woody stems where they break naturally and peel the bottom halves of any fat stalks. Reserve the ends for making vegetable stock (see page 270).

HOW TO PEEL, ROAST, AND SERVE BEETS

TO PEEL A RAW BEET Wear plastic or latex gloves and use a vegetable peeler to peel along the curve of the beet. Roast or cook as desired.

TO ROAST WHOLE AND PEEL AFTER Preheat the oven to 450°F/230°C/gas 8. Trim the beet tops to 1 in/2.5 cm and scrub the skins. Drizzle generously with olive oil and sprinkle with salt and pepper. Wrap each beet in aluminum foil individually. Roast until the beets are just fork-tender, 45 minutes to 1 hour, depending on the size.

Set aside until cool enough to handle; cut off the root and stem ends and scrape off the skins with a paring knife or your hands. Quarter a large beet or halve smaller ones and toss with additional olive oil, salt, and pepper, or slice into rounds. Store roasted whole beets well wrapped in the fridge for up to 1 week.

SHAVING BRUSSELS SPROUTS AND CABBAGE

Strong but highly nutritious brassicas like cabbage and Brussels sprouts are often enjoyed most in small doses. Shave Brussels sprouts with a sharp chef's knife or mandoline into thin, wispy shavings and eat raw as a cold salad or a pizza topping (see page 217). Shave savoy or napa cabbage the same way for soups and stuffing raw into fish tacos.

CAULIFLOWER STEAKS

Cauliflower can be broken or cut into florets, but cutting crosswise through its central vein produces meaty "steaks" that are perfect for roasting and treating as a main course. Remove the leaves and trim the stems, leaving the core intact. With the cauliflower core-side down on a cutting board, slice into ½-in/12-mm steaks with a sharp knife, reserving any loose florets.

CITRUS

CITRUS ZEST The zest of limes, lemons, tangerines, and oranges is full of essential citrus oils that are highly fragrant and flavorful. Scrub citrus with homemade fruit wash (equal parts water and cider vinegar) and rub off any wax with a kitchen towel. Zest clean fruit with a Microplane, zester, paring knife, or vegetable peeler.

CITRUS SEGMENTS Chefs call the citrus segments between the peel, pith, and the membrane *suprêmes*, a name deserved because it is a supreme skill to make them. With practice, it's easily mastered at home.

Place your citrus on the cutting board and cut off a little bit from both ends to create flat surfaces. Set the citrus on one of the flat ends. Using a large, sharp knife, shave off the skin, peel, and as much of the pith as possible along the curve of the fruit. Squeeze any juices from the skin into a small bowl and reserve.

Working over the bowl with the juices with a sharp paring knife, hold the fruit in your non-dominant hand and use your dominant hand to cut the segment along the membrane. Cut along the opposing membrane (in a V), releasing the segment and collecting any juices and the fruit itself in the bowl below. Repeat with all the segments, then squeeze any remaining juices from the membranes and discard.

SHAVING AND MILKING
AN EAR OF CORN

Set the corn cob inside a center of a Bundt pan or angel food cake pan, or position it at 45 degrees on your cutting board. Shave the corn from its cob with a sharp, serrated knife. Flip the knife over and rub the dull side along the empty cob to pull out all the milky juices and remaining corn pulp; adding to the shaved corn kernels.

ENDIVE, RADICCHIO, AND TREVISO

Peel away any browned or bruised outer leaves. Separate the leaves, wash, and spin-dry, or core with a paring knife and cut into wedges or quarters. For thin slices, keep the core intact, quarter, and cut thinly crosswise until you reach the stem end.

A FENNEL HOW-TO

Trim the feathery stalks of fennel into a V where the stalks meet the bulb end. Trim off the bottom end and pull away the first layer of the bulb, saving all the trimmings for stock. Slice to use as an aromatic, or quarter to roast, sauté, or braise. If you're prepping ahead, soak the fennel in acidulated water (see page 263) to prevent browning until you're ready to use it, and pat dry before cooking.

GARLIC, THREE WAYS

SMASHED Often a peeled clove of garlic, smashed with the flat side of your knife, is a quick trick for flavoring soups, stocks, sauces, and sautéed vegetables. Save yourself time by making this your go-to garlic technique.

PASTE For a richer garlic flavor, either raw in dressings or cooked, finely chop smashed garlic with a chef's knife. Season with a pinch of sea salt, and continue to chop and scrape against the cutting board with the flat side of your knife, repeating each motion over and over to make a garlic paste. Be sure to clean your cutting board well after.

ROASTED Slice the top off a head of garlic, leaving the cloves intact but exposed in their skins. Drizzle liberally with olive oil, wrap tightly in foil, and roast at 350°F/180°C/gas 4 until soft and fragrant, 45 to 55 minutes. Serve whole or squeeze the cloves and use in dressings, sauces, pastes, pastas, and purées.

WASHING AND STORING GREENS

Many a delicious meal has been ruined by gritty greens. All greens should be washed very well, whether you've grown or picked them yourself or purchased them in a supermarket in a container labeled "prewashed." Start with a big bowl of clean water. Separate tightly bound leaves. Give the greens several dunks in the clean water. Lift the greens out, drain the water, and wash them a second and sometimes third time, until the water is clean. Spin or pat dry. Store washed greens wrapped in damp paper towels in a plastic bag for up to 3 days. If the greens have stems, such as arugula, wrap the stems in damp towels as well.

STORING, SLICING, AND
CHOPPING HERBS

STORING PARSLEY AND BASIL Most leafy herbs like parsley and basil keep well for a short time trimmed in a glass on the countertop. Trim basil stalks clean (like flowers) and place in tepid water. Cover the leaves loosely with a plastic produce bag and tie around the glass to create a little greenhouse. Store out of the sun, and refresh the water often. Basil will keep fresh on the counter for 1 week or more at room temperature.

For longer storage of most herbs, wrap parsley, sage, rosemary, thyme, cilantro, chives, and some spring onions and green onions loosely in a damp paper towel and store in individual plastic bags. Be careful not to store heavy vegetables on top of herbs and let them breathe.

CLEAN AND CHOP Wash herbs just before you plan to use them. Spin-dry in a salad spinner or pat dry before slicing, chopping, or mincing with a very sharp knife. Dull knives can bruise herbs. If you use fresh herbs often, consider keeping a dedicated ceramic knife for chopping herbs.

NO WASTE SYSTEM Pick or buy herbs just before you plan to use them. Add clean stalks and stem trimmings to vegetable stocks. Add roots and wilted, past-prime herbs to compost.

CHIFFONADE (ANYTHING) *Chiffonade* is just a fancy French term for finely sliced. To chiffonade basil, arugula, or other herbs and leaves, stack the clean and well-spun or dried leaves. Roll them into a tight cylinder and slice thinly with a sharp knife.

CLEAN AND SLICE LEEKS

Leeks, homegrown or purchased, often have soil trapped in their inner layers. Trim the tough green layers back and peel away a few outside layers. Lay each leek on the cutting board and make a parallel cut into the pale green and white parts of the leek. Roll half way and repeat to make an X so you have leek quartered lengthwise, held together by its stem. Wash well in a bowl of clean water several times. Pat dry and slice crosswise until you reach the stem.

Alternatively, cut the leeks into rings and swish vigorously in a bowl of clean water. Lift out with your hands, replace the water, and repeat until water is clear.

CLEAN AND TRIM MUSHROOMS

Cook all mushrooms soon after getting them home, if possible, or store them in the fridge in a lunch-size paper bag—never in plastic—so that they can breathe, for up to three days, depending on how fresh they were when you brought them home.

Wild mushrooms, like delicate morels and chanterelles, can be quite dirty. Halve large ones lengthwise and brush clean; rinse in cold water only if they seem especially dirty or sandy and pat immediately dry afterward. Other mushrooms and all cultivated mushrooms can be brushed clean with a mushroom brush, dry paper towel, or kitchen towel. Trim any spongy, nubby, or extra-dirty bits.

Mushrooms are usually eaten whole, halved, or sliced—stem and cap—unless specified, such as shiitakes, whose woody stems should be removed and added to stock for extra flavor. Oyster mushrooms should be trimmed from their woody central stem. Portobello caps are best enjoyed when the gills are scraped off. Hold the cap in the palm of your hand, and scrape off the gills with a spoon and discard. Peel the cap when eating whole.

CARAMELIZE ONIONS

Heady caramelized or richly browned onions have the power to transform soups, stews, sauces, and dips and are a smart thing to keep on hand for topping pizzas and stuffing into crêpes and omelets. Cut onions into ¼-in/6-mm thick slices. For every 1 onion, heat 2 tbsp olive oil in a large skillet over medium heat. Add the onions and cook, stirring occasionally, until soft and just golden brown, about 15 minutes. Continue cooking, stirring more frequently, until the onions darken into a deep caramel color with a rich aroma and soft texture, 15 to 20 minutes more.

ROASTING PEPPERS

Roasting peppers gives them a richer and softer quality that makes a colorful and flavorful base for soups and sauces like romesco and harissa (see page 253).

OVER THE STOVE TOP Roast the peppers directly on a gas flame, turning with tongs and propping them on the burner grates until they are charred evenly on all sides. Transfer them to a metal or other heat-proof bowl, cover the bowl tightly with plastic wrap, and set aside to steam, 10 to 15 minutes. Pull away the charred skin with a paper towel and discard. Continue cleaning, discarding the charred skin and seeds, but preserving the flesh and juices until the peppers are mostly clean. Do not rinse.

IN THE OVEN Toss the peppers in olive oil and broil on a baking sheet with the broiler set to high, turning as needed with tongs, until the peppers are evenly charred. Continue with removing skin and cleaning as directed above.

HANDLING CHILES

The oil in hot chiles gives them their heat and also lingers for hours on your hands. Trim, halve, and scrape seeds from chiles with a sharp paring knife. Wash your hands and cutting board well with hot soapy water after handling, and be careful not to touch your eyes or lips.

TRIM AND CLEAN SQUASH

Cut a thin slice off the top and bottom so the squash can sit flat on your cutting board. For butternut squash, cut in half where the neck meets the round, bulbous portion. Cut in half lengthwise and scoop out the seeds with a soupspoon or, if peeling, peel with a swivel-bladed vegetable peeler, which can handle its curves. Butternut and delicata squash can be roasted in their skins.

OVEN-ROASTED TOMATOES

Roasted tomatoes make a quick garnish or side to anything from Blank-Slate Baked Risotto (page 172) to toasted bread. It's an easy way to treat summer tomatoes from the vine or the perfect thing for getting an occasional tomato fix from otherwise lifeless winter plum tomatoes. Preheat the oven to 400°F/200°C/gas 6. Toss 2 lbs/910 g halved plum tomatoes or small tomatoes from the vine with olive oil, salt, and pepper. Roast until they are just soft, about 30 minutes.

WASTE NOT, WANT NOT

Food waste in the Western world is as big a concern as commercialized farming. Vegetarians have an easy opportunity to eat a virtually no-waste diet, especially if you turn veggie scraps into stocks (see page 270) or compost. Grains, both dried or cooked and stored well, last quite a long time. But some of the most nutritious foods—namely fruits and vegetables—are also highly perishable. I'm the first person to go wild on a good farmers' market day and bring home more than we could ever eat. Keep your fridge and freezer clean and organized, and make a plan for how to use your veggies as soon as you buy them. Any overflow that you can't consume at its peak freshness makes great juices, smoothies, soups, and stocks.

MAKING A VEGETABLE STOCK

If your larder is well stocked with vegetables and aromatics, you'll rarely, if ever, need to shop for dedicated stock ingredients. It comes together quickly from the peelings, ends, and nubs of your everyday vegetable prep. Keep vegetable trimmings in a plastic bag in the fridge until you gather enough to make a stock. A classic veg stock usually includes carrot, onion, celery, celery leaves, bay leaf, peppercorns, parsley, dill or thyme, and Parmigiano-Reggiano or another hard-nutty cheese rind.

BASIC FORMULA FOR VEGETABLE STOCK

10 cups/2.4 L water

1 parsnip

2 yellow or white onions

1 garlic clove

2 carrots

3 stalks celery

Bundle of assorted fresh herbs

2 bay leaves

1 tbsp peppercorns

Combine all the ingredients in a stockpot or large saucepan. Bring to a boil over high heat, reduce to medium-low, and simmer for 2 hours, skimming any foam that bubbles on the top every so often. Strain and refrigerate for up to 4 days, or freeze for 8 months. Makes 8 cups/2 L.

OTHER STOCK FLAVORINGS

- organic potato peelings and scraps (including sweet potato)
- celery root nubs
- shallots, leeks, or green onions
- overripe tomatoes or 1 sun-dried tomato
- asparagus stems
- kale or chard stems and leaves
- dried mushrooms (like shiitake) or cleaned fresh mushroom trimmings and stems

MAKING MUSHROOM STOCK

Homemade mushroom stock is easy to make with dried mushrooms such as shiitake or porcini, or even the trimmings of fresh mushrooms. Dried mushrooms will yield a richer, more full-flavored mushroom stock. Fresh mushroom trimmings will yield a paler, more subtle mushroom broth. Place dried or fresh mushroom caps and stems in a large heat-proof bowl and pour boiling water over them (the more mushrooms-to-water, the richer your stock will be). Season with a hearty pinch of sea salt. Cover and let the mushrooms steep until the broth is rich brown and flavorful, 20 minutes to 2 hours, depending on the mushroom. Taste and continue to steep as needed. Remove the mushrooms from the broth with a slotted spoon and discard. Ladle the mushroom broth into another bowl, leaving behind any debris that remains. Cover and store in the fridge for up to 2 days.

QUICK STOCK

Sometimes, the water from blanching or cooking vegetables for another dish makes a good quick stock. See the stock made from cooking Orecchiette with Ricotta and Chard (page 189), which is a great, nutrient-rich broth for mushroom soup. Be creative and resourceful. One note of caution: Go easy on strong flavors, like asparagus stems, cauliflower, or cabbage, which can easily overpower vegetable stock.

TAILOR YOUR VEGETABLE STOCK

Once you get good at making vegetable stock, you can tailor it to the dish where it's destined. For example, I add extra spring onion trimmings to a stock that's headed for Pea Soup with Rye Croutons and Chive Blossoms (page 85); my impromptu spring onion stock would be equally appreciated as the base for a ramp-topped risotto.

EGGS

ALL ABOUT EGGS

"BOILED" EGGS Though they are called soft-boiled and hard-boiled, eggs should be cooked or simmered in hot water, rather than boiled. Truly boiled eggs can be tough and rubbery; simmered eggs are creamy and luscious. To make soft-boiled eggs, place the eggs in a large bowl of warm water. Meanwhile, bring a small pot of water to a boil over high heat. Lower to a simmer and gently lower the eggs into the water with a spoon. Set the timer for 6 minutes, and keep the water at a low simmer. When the timer goes off, immediately remove the eggs from the pan and rinse under cool water. Serve in an egg cup or peel and serve warm.

POACHED To poach an egg, bring 2 to 4 in/5 to 10 cm of water to a rapid simmer in a large non-stick saucepan or skillet with straight sides. Reduce the heat so that the water is barely simmering. Add 1 tbsp white vinegar and a pinch of salt. Crack each egg into a small teacup, and bring the edge of the cup level with the surface of the water. Slip each egg into the water gently. Simmer until the white is set, about 3 minutes. Remove with a slotted spoon and drain well on paper towels before serving.

FRIED To fry an egg sunny-side up, heat a thin layer of oil or butter in a cast-iron pan or a skillet over medium-high heat. When the oil is glistening or the butter is foamy, crack one egg and release the egg into the pan (the lower to the pan you hold it, the less likely the yolk is to break). Fry until set and almost crispy around the edges. Cover the pan and continue to cook until the yolk is soft but not too runny, about a minute. Remove the egg from the pan with a flexible spatula and serve warm.

To make the egg over easy, flip the egg gently in the pan after the first side is set and crispy around the edges, trying not to break the yolk. Count to ten slowly and then slide the egg out onto a plate.

SEPARATING EGGS

To separate the yolk from the white of the egg, crack it firmly once against the countertop and pull apart the two halves of the shell, holding them split-side up. Let the white drain into a bowl, and continue to pass the yolk back and forth between the two shells until the white is contained in the bowl below and the yolk is reserved in the shell. Use a clean shell to retrieve any pieces that have fallen into the bowl. Traces of white in the yolk do no harm to the final preparation, unlike a yolk in the white, which must be removed before whipping.

BEANS, GRAINS, AND NUTS

SOAKING BEANS AND GRAINS ———

Dried beans and legumes, like chickpeas, and grains, like steel-cut oats and farro, all cook about 25 percent faster when soaked overnight. Soaking can also help beans and grains cook more evenly. Some beans will sprout after two days, and others will ferment. Soaking 8 to 12 hours is a good rule of thumb. For a quick soak, place the beans or grains in a pot and cover with water by about 3 in/7.5 cm. Bring to a boil, reduce to a simmer for about 2 minutes, and remove from the heat. Cover and set aside for 1 hour. Drain and cook the beans in clean water. Lentils, which cook in 30 to 40 minutes, generally do not need to be soaked.

SOAKING AND COOKING CHICKPEAS Start with one 1-lb/455-g bag dried chickpeas and soak them in water overnight in a medium soup pan or saucepan. The next day, bring them to a boil and skim off the white foam after 5 minutes of cooking. Drain, rinse, and return them to the pot. Cover with 4 cups/960 ml fresh water and aromatics (carrot, celery, and onion) for extra flavor for preparations like Lentil-Chickpea Burgers with Harissa Yogurt (page 138). Bring to a boil over medium-high heat. Reduce to a simmer, add ³/₄ tsp salt, and cook until completely tender, about 45 minutes. Drain, reserving 1 cup/240 ml of the cooking liquid for preparations like Hummus (page 60). You should have about 6 cups/985 g of cooked chickpeas.

SOAKING AND COOKING BLACK BEANS Soak 8 oz/225 g dried black beans in water overnight. Drain the beans from their soaking water, transfer to a medium saucepan, cover with water and a hearty pinch of salt, and bring to a boil over medium-high heat. Cover, reduce the heat to medium-low, and simmer until the beans are tender, about 40 minutes. Drain off some of the cooking liquid, leaving only enough so the beans are saucy. Use warm or store covered in the fridge for up to 5 days.

MEASURING BEANS, BEFORE AND AFTER COOKING Most small dried beans will double in size when cooked. Larger dried beans, including many heirlooms, will triple in size. You can estimate that 1 lb/455 g of dried beans yields 6 cups/985 g of cooked beans.

FROZEN BEANS AND LENTILS You'll sometimes find frozen cooked beans, like black-eyed peas and lentils, in the supermarket. Like canned or jarred beans and lentils, they are great for convenience and quick meals. If you cook dried and fresh beans in large batches to have on hand, cool beans to room temperature and freeze in well-labeled resealable bags for up to 1 month.

COOKING RICE ———

You can create perfect rice fairly easily by following the instructions on the back of a package. Be diligent about measuring and covering as instructed. If you eat rice once a week or more, it's worth investing in a rice cooker, which does the work for you and keeps your rice steaming hot until you're ready to serve. To cook rice in a pot, combine 2 cups/ 450 g rice and 4 cups/960 ml water. Bring to a boil, cover, and reduce heat. Simmer until the rice is tender, 40 to 50 minutes.

NUTS AND SEEDS ———

TOASTING NUTS Toasting improves the texture and flavor of many nuts. To toast large nuts like walnuts, hazelnuts, or pecans, spread them out in a single layer on a baking sheet. Bake in a 350°F/180°C/ gas 4 oven until they have darkened in shade just slightly and are fragrant, 8 to 10 minutes, shaking the pan halfway through baking to roll the nuts around. Let cool completely.

For smaller nuts, like pine nuts, and some seeds, like sesame seeds, toast them in a skillet over low heat in a thin sheen of oil. Turn them frequently until they are evenly golden brown, 2 to 4 minutes, depending on size.

Nuts burn easily. Always set a timer and watch carefully with your eyes and your nose. It's usually best to toast nuts whole before chopping. Toaster ovens are a quick fix for toasting nuts without preheating a larger oven. Turn the toaster oven to 350°F/180°C on the bake setting and toast as instructed.

TOASTING AND PEELING HAZELNUTS When you can't find blanched hazelnuts (which are evenly pale blond with no dark brown skins), roast in a 400°F/200°C/gas 6 oven for 5 minutes. Wrap them in a kitchen towel and rub vigorously against each other to remove the skins.

DIY NUT FLOUR Make nut flour or nut meal out of almost any nut by finely grinding to a powder. Start with cold or even frozen nuts. (Using warm or just-toasted nuts will almost certainly result in nut butter.) Pulse in the bowl of a food processor to a fine grind. Approximately 1¼ cup/120 g whole nuts yields 1 cup/120 g nut flour. Ground nuts easily pick up freezer odors. Keep frozen for several weeks at most.

DIY NUT BUTTER Nut butters are flavorful, filling, full of protein and minerals, and easy to make at home without added sugars and sodium. At home, you also have control over whether your nut butter is chunky or smooth, made with raw or roasted nuts. Purée 2 cups/280 g nuts (almond, cashew, peanuts, pecans, or hazelnuts—raw or roasted) in a food processor until completely smooth. You can also stop when still a bit chunky, if you prefer, and stir in 1 or 2 tbsp peanut oil to help it become spreadable. Season with a pinch of sea salt. Refrigerate up to 8 weeks.

DIY NUT MILK Nut milk is easy to make at home and is often creamier and more delicious than those found in the store. Process 1 cup/140 g blanched almonds, hazelnuts, or raw cashews in a food processor until it resembles a nut meal. Add 1¼ cups/ 300 ml boiling water, a pinch of sea salt, and 1 tbsp or so unbleached raw sugar, if desired. Process for 1 minute and then let steep for 10 minutes more. Process again until smooth and frothy. Strain through a fine-mesh sieve or cheesecloth, pressing as much of the liquids out as possible with a flexible rubber spatula or wooden spoon. Refrigerate until ready to serve.

For cashew cream, a rich substitute for heavy cream, use 1 cup/120 g raw cashews and ¾ cup/ 180 ml boiling water. DIY nut milks and creams have no preservatives and thus a shorter shelf life, so drink within a few days.

essential tools

FOR THE VEGETARIAN KITCHEN

BASIC TOOLS

Your two hands are your very best kitchen tools. Beyond that, the following is the basic gear that delivers big in the vegetarian kitchen.

COMFORTABLE CHEF'S KNIFE, PARING KNIFE, AND SERRATED KNIFE to slice, chop, and prepare fruit, vegetables, cheese, and bread.

SHARP KITCHEN SHEARS to snip chives, trim greens from the garden, clean artichokes, and more.

MICROPLANE to grate citrus zest, chocolate, fine feathery wisps of cheese, and nutmeg.

REAMER to juice citrus.

JAPANESE MANDOLINE to cut paper-thin slices of radishes, potatoes, and other vegetables.

IMMERSION BLENDER to blend vegetable soups and sauces.

POWERFUL UPRIGHT BLENDER, more powerful than an immersion blender, to blend smoothies and some soups, as well as DIY fruit juices and nut milks.

SALAD SPINNER to properly dry those well-washed greens.

CAST-IRON PANS to impart extra iron and flavor to your food.

MORTAR AND PESTLE, OR SPICE GRINDER to grind spices and nuts.

ERGONOMIC VEGETABLE PEELER to prep vegetables and slice cheese into paper-thin slivers and shavings.

BOX GRATER to make light work of grating carrots and other firm vegetables, cheeses, and even tomatoes.

RIMMED PROFESSIONAL-STYLE BAKING SHEETS to bake, toast nuts, cook pizzas, and roast vegetables at high heat.

SILICONE BAKING MATS keep baking sheets clean for years on end.

FOOD PROCESSOR OR MINI FOOD PROCESSOR to make light work of shredding potatoes or cabbage, and to quickly chop nuts, onions, celery, or carrots.

A CAST-IRON INVESTMENT

Invest in and cook with cast-iron pots, skillets, and a griddle or grill pan, which have been shown to add iron (nutritional iron, not the kind that would break your teeth) to your food. Use them to sear and sauté vegetables and fish, toast bread, fry eggs, make pancakes, and more. You can now buy pre-seasoned cast iron, but not all pots or griddles come that way. To season cast iron (which gives it a naturally nonstick finish), coat it with cooking oil and bake it in a 350°F/180°C/gas 4 oven for 1 hour. Dry it with paper towels and begin to use it. Every time you heat oil in the skillet, you reinforce the seasoning, eventually yielding a shiny black patina. To keep cast-iron clean and well seasoned, wipe with a damp paper towel after cooking, dry completely after every use, and never use soap. Avoid cast iron when cooking with tomatoes and other highly acidic foods.

GRATING CHEESE

Hard cheeses like aged Parmigiano-Reggiano and pecorino add different flavors and textures to vegetable and grain dishes as a garnish, depending on which tool you use.

ON A MICROPLANE Use this for a feathery, melt-in-your-mouth garnish to pile on top of pizzas and pastas.

WITH A VEGETABLE PEELER Use a vegetable peeler to shave long, thin shards of hard cheese when you need cheese to be a salty and substantial player to top pizzas, roasted vegetables, shaved salads, green salads, bruschetta, and more.

ON A BOX GRATER Use the smallest side of a box grater to get crumbly, pencil tip–size portions of cheese, most akin to the grated Parmesan found in a container in the supermarket.

ODE TO THE JAPANESE MANDOLINE —

A Japanese mandoline is an inexpensive and sturdy tool for quickly cutting vegetables such as cucumbers, radishes, and potatoes into paper-thin slices. I find the Japanese mandoline to be more efficient and easier to clean up and keep sharp than the more expensive stainless-steel French mandoline.

To use, adjust the blade to slice at the thickness you prefer. Hold the mandoline at a 45-degree angle on a sturdy surface. Use the hand guard or a thick towel to protect your fingers as you move the vegetable slowly back and forth along the blade. Collect the thinly sliced vegetables in a bowl or on a cutting board below.

PARCHMENT FOR ALL PURPOSES ——

Parchment paper is a fast fix for lining pans before baking. It makes releasing baked goods, transferring finishing products, and cleaning up baking pans much easier. For a greener approach, use silicone baking pads, which can be washed and reused thousands of times. For roasting and other baked preparations where browning is the goal, skip parchment or silicone baking mats and opt for aluminum foil instead.

PAN SIZE ——————————

The size of pan can make a big difference in the result of your finished dish. Too many vegetables cooked together in too small a space—what chefs call "crowding the pan"—can result in limp, steamed vegetables rather than tender-crisp, golden brown sautéed vegetables. Pay attention to the pan sizes noted in recipes, and cook in batches if needed.

sources

ABOUT FOOD AND SUSTAINABILITY

Outside your own garden, the best source for produce is usually your local farmers' market. Here's where to find the market and CSAs that sell local organic harvest nearest your zip code. www.localharvest.org

For more help navigating the world of local food. www.locavores.com

Issues about sustainability change frequently. To stay informed, get to know the resources on the following sites.

Marine Stewardship Council www.msc.org

Monterey Bay Aquarium Seafood Watch www.montereybayaquarium.org/cr/seafoodwatch.aspx

Sustainable Table www.sustainabletable.org

GARDENING

RESOURCES

Burpee Home Gardens www.burpee.com

Easy from Seed www.ezfromseed.org

Rodale www.rodale.com

SUPPLIES

Agrarian by Williams-Sonoma 877-812-6355 www.williams-sonoma.com/shop/agrarian-garden

Clarington Forge English Garden Tools 800-356-2196 www.claringtonforge.com

Fire Escape Farms www.fireescapefarms.com

Terrain 877-583-7724 www.shopterrain.com

SEEDS

Botanical Interests 877-821-4340 www.botanicalinterests.com

The Cook's Garden 800-457-9703 www.cooksgarden.com

Hudson Valley Seed Library 845-204-8769 www.seedlibrary.org

Johnny's Selected Seeds 877-564-6697 www.johnnyseeds.com

Renee's Garden 888-880-7228 www.reneesgarden.com

Seeds of Change 888-762-7333 www.seedsofchange.com

Seed Savers Exchange 563-382-5990 www.seedsavers.org

INGREDIENTS

CHEESE, OILS, OLIVES, AND SPECIALTY FOODS

Artisanal Cheese 877-797-1200 www.artisanalcheese.com

Di Bruno Bros. 888-322-4337 www.dibruno.com

Formaggio Kitchen 888-212-3224 www.formaggiokitchen.com

Gourmet Sleuth 408-354-8281 www.gourmetsleuth.com

Murray's Cheese 888-692-4339 www.murrayscheese.com

Saxelby Cheesemongers 212-228-8204 www.saxelbycheese.com

Vermont Butter Cheese Creamery 800-884-6287 www.vermontcreamery.com

Whole Foods Market www.wholefoodsmarket.com

CHOCOLATE

Callebaut Chocolate
312-496-7300
www.callebaut.com

ChocolateSource.com
800-214-4926
www.chocolatesource.com

Scharffen Berger
866-608-6944
www.scharffenberger.com

Valrhona Chocolate
888-682-5746
www.valrhona-chocolate.com

BEANS, LENTILS, GRAINS, AND SPECIALTY FLOURS

Anson Mills
803-467-4122
www.ansonmills.com

Arrowhead Mills
800-434-4246
www.arrowheadmills.com

Bob's Red Mill
800-349-2173
www.bobsredmill.com

King Arthur Flour
800-827-6836
www.kingarthurflour.com

Rancho Gordo
707-259-1935
www.ranchogordo.com

INTERNATIONAL INGREDIENTS

Amazon.com
www.amazon.com

Asian Food Grocer
888-482-2742
www.asianfoodgrocer.com

Otto's European and Hungarian
Import Store & Deli
818-845-0433
www.hungariandeli.com

MUSHROOMS

Pacific Rim Mushrooms
604-568-6033
www.pacrimmushrooms.com

SALTS

The Meadow
888-388-4633
www.atthemeadow.com

SPICES AND VANILLA

Kalustyan's
800-352-3451
www.kalustyans.com

Penzeys Spices
800-741-7787
www.penzeys.com

The Spice House
847-328-3711
www.thespicehouse.com

DISHES, COOKWARE, AND BAKING TOOLS

Canvas
347-338-2849
shop.canvashomestore.com

Crate & Barrel
800-967-6696
www.crateandbarrel.com

JB Prince
800-473-0577
www.jbprince.com

Kitchen Aid Appliances
800-541-6390
www.kitchenaid.com

Scandinavian Grace
845-657-2759
www.scandinaviangrace.com

Sur la Table
800-243-0852
www.surlatable.com

Williams-Sonoma
877-812-6355
www.williams-sonoma.com

index

acknowledgments

Writing books is my life's dream; it's possible due to the many generous people who believe in me and share their resources wherever they can. To every hand that touched these pages in any big or small way, thank you. This is *our* book, and I hope it makes you proud.

First and foremost, to my little family—András and Greta—you fill my world with love and laughter. You make life new again every day; this book, and everything I do, is for you. I'm blessed to be shaped and supported by amazing parents and my beloved siblings, who believe in my every wild idea, even vegetarianism. Each of you lends more confidence and joy to my path than you will ever know. I'm so lucky to have been born into a family that loves food and each other both with abandon.

My most sincere and humble thanks to the team at Chronicle Books, who make writing books my dream job. Bill LeBlond, I'm forever indebted to you (again) for so beautifully matching me to the perfect project to pour my heart into. Sarah Billingsley, for your trust and for championing my ideas. To Alice Chau, for your splendid design. To Lorena Jones, Peter Perez, David Hawk, Steve Kim, Doug Ogan, Marie Oishi, and the rest of the team at Chronicle, thank you for all that you do. You each have a huge fan on the other coast.

Abundant thanks go to my agent, Katherine Cowles, for your honesty and good judgment. To Jane Turks, whose sharp eyes and thoughtful queries made this book only better; to Yunhee Kim, for these beautiful images; to Rebecca Miller Ffrench, whose tireless pursuit of my vision shows on every page; to Anna Hampton, for your speed, good spirit, and those amazing set trays; to my recipe testers—vegetarians, mostly vegetarians, and curious carnivores—Donna Copeland, Amy Cosler, Jenny Goddard, Tim Copeland, Karen Rader, Kelly and Devin Cara, Brooke Campbell, Kristen Ferwerda, Kamliah Duggins, Justin Holden, Tim Vidra, Lorena Martinez, Cherie DeNoia, Jenn Uthoff, Inid Deneau, Angelina Jastrzebski, Angelica Davis, and Carissa Finn, who all added thoughtful layers to these pages; to the delightful Lily O'Dare, Michele Chase, Maia Cheslow, and Jacquie Chamberlain for recipe testing, assisting, and lending general joyful support. You are smart cookies. Thank you for your diligence, honest opinions, and good company. All were tremendous contributions to this work.

A thousand thanks for the generosity of Nicole Beauchemin, Leslie Freeman Designs, Jan Fell, Yuki Yoshimoto of Ystudiopottery, Lee Wolfe Pottery, Marilyn Baldwin Stoneware, From the Grapevine Antiques, The Van Deusen House, Liza Weiner and Canvas home store, Dave Pillard at Tenderland Home, Rick Regan at Cheese Louise, Scandinavian Grace, Marcey Brownstein, Peter and Liz Appelson, Nancy Howell, Maxanne Resnick, Sarah Brainard, Robin Kornstein, Rob and Jane Brundage, and especially to Josh Farley and WRK Design.

For your camaraderie, warmth, and wisdom I thank Dorie Greenspan, Lucinda Scala Quinn, Diane Jacob, Mark Bitterman, Andrew Schloss, David Joachim, Catherine McCord, Katie Morford, Tara Desmond, Aida Mollenkamp, Gaby Dalkin and the Food Posse gals, Nancy McDermott, Jill O'Connor, and (to borrow a line from Elissa Altman) the fairy godmother of American food writers everywhere—Antonia Allegra—who all, at one point, answered an email or phone call at a stage when I needed a vote of confidence. To the generous many cooks (chefs, restaurateurs, and cookbook authors) from whom I have taken inspiration in my kitchen—I am so grateful. I hope this book honors what you've taught me.

Last but never least, thank you to all who make writing and creating a constant and delicious pursuit. The friendship, support, and enthusiasm of so many named and unnamed, and each person holding this book, means the world to me.